# Rewriting the Rules of the European Economy

# Also by Joseph E. Stiglitz

*People, Power, and Profits:*
*Progressive Capitalism for an Age of Discontent*

*The Euro:*
*How a Common Currency Threatens the Future of Europe*

*Rewriting the Rules of the American Economy:*
*An Agenda for Growth and Shared Prosperity*

*The Great Divide:*
*Unequal Societies and What We Can Do about Them*

*Creating a Learning Society:*
*A New Approach to Growth, Development, and Social Progress*
(with Bruce C. Greenwald)

*The Price of Inequality:*
*How Today's Divided Society Endangers Our Future*

*Freefall:*
*America, Free Markets, and the Sinking of the World Economy*

*The Three Trillion Dollar War:*
*The True Cost of the Iraq Conflict* (with Linda J. Bilmes)

*Making Globalization Work*

*Fair Trade for All:*
*How Trade Can Promote Development* (with Andrew Charlton)

*The Roaring Nineties:*
*A New History of the World's Most Prosperous Decade*

*Globalization and Its Discontents*

# Rewriting the Rules of the European Economy

## AN AGENDA FOR GROWTH AND SHARED PROSPERITY

JOSEPH E. STIGLITZ

*In Collaboration with Carter Dougherty*
*and the Foundation for European Progressive Studies*

FOUNDATION FOR EUROPEAN
PROGRESSIVE STUDIES
FONDATION EUROPÉENNE
D'ÉTUDES PROGRESSISTES

W. W. NORTON & COMPANY
*Independent Publishers Since 1923*

For information about permission to reproduce selections from this book, write to
Permissions, W. W. Norton & Company, Inc., 500 Fifth Avenue, New York, NY 10110

For information about special discounts for bulk purchases, please contact
W. W. Norton Special Sales at specialsales@wwnorton.com or 800-233-4830

Manufacturing by LSC Communications, Harrisonburg
Production manager: Lauren Abbate

ISBN 978-0-393-35563-5

W. W. Norton & Company, Inc., 500 Fifth Avenue, New York, N.Y. 10110
www.wwnorton.com
W. W. Norton & Company Ltd., 15 Carlisle Street, London W1D 3BS

1 2 3 4 5 6 7 8 9 0

*To the progressives of Europe,*
*who defend European values each and every day.*

# CONTENTS

## PART III: INEQUALITY AND A TWENTY-FIRST-CENTURY EUROPEAN SOCIAL MODEL

## PART IV: MANAGING GLOBALIZATION FOR EUROPE AND THE WORLD

# ACKNOWLEDGMENTS

This report was written by

**Joseph E. Stiglitz,**
Chief Economist and Senior Fellow,
Roosevelt Institute

With coauthors

**Ernst Stetter,** Secretary General, FEPS, Belgium
**Carter Dougherty,** Americans for Financial Reform, USA
**Stephany Griffith-Jones,** Professor, IPD Columbia University, USA
**Isabel Ortiz,** Director, Global Social Justice Program, IPD Columbia University, USA
**Jeronim Capaldo,** Research Fellow, Global Development and Environment Institute, Tufts University, USA
**Daniela Gabor,** Professor, University of the West of England, UK
**Margit Schratzenstaller-Altzinger,** Deputy Director, Austrian Institute of Economic Research (WIFO), Austria

We would also like to acknowledge the following individuals for their various contributions that helped inform this work:

**Nell Abernathy,** Vice-President, Strategy and Policy, Roosevelt Institute, USA

**Lars Andersen,** Managing Director, Economic Council of the Labour Movement, Denmark

**Bilian Balev,** Deputy Chairman and Executive Director, Bulgarian Development Bank

**Eva Belabed,** Economist, former Counsellor, Austrian Representation to the OECD, Austria

**Peter Bofinger,** Professor, University of Würzburg, former Member of the German Council of Economic Experts, Germany

**Tamás Boros,** Director, Policy Solutions, Hungary

**Elva Bova,** former Senior Economic Policy Advisor, FEPS, Belgium

**Udo Bullmann,** Member of the European Parliament, President of the S&D Group, Germany

**Massimo D'Alema,** President, Fondazione ItalianiEuropei, former Prime Minister of Italy

**Anna Diamantopoulou,** President, DIKTIO, former Minister of Education of Greece

**Catalin Dragomirescu-Gaina,** former Senior Economic Policy Advisor, FEPS, Belgium

**Karl Duffek,** former Director, Karl-Renner-Institut, former International Secretary of SPÖ (RIP), Austria

**Annabel Garnier,** Deputy Secretary General, S&D Group, European Parliament, France

**Debarati Ghosh,** Managing Director, Think Tank, Roosevelt Institute, USA

**Naman Garg,** Research Assistant, Office of Joseph E. Stiglitz, Columbia University, USA

**Paolo Guerrieri,** Professor, Sapienza University, College of Europe, former Member of Italian Senate

**Andrea Gurwitt,** Editor and Publications Manager, Office of Joseph E. Stiglitz, Columbia University, USA

**Anton Hemerijck,** Professor, European University Institute, Italy

**Gustav A. Horn,** former Research Director, Macroeconomic Policy Institute, Germany

**Peter Hunt,** Managing Partner, Mutuo, UK

**András Inotai,** Professor, College of Europe, Belgium

**Maria Jepsen,** Director, Research Department, European Trade Union Institute, Belgium

**Lisa Kastner,** former Policy Advisor, FEPS, Belgium

**Inge Kaul,** Professor, Hertie School of Governance, Germany

**Aleksander Kwaśniewski,** Chair, Amicus Europae Foundation, former President of Poland

**Gerhard Marchl,** Head, European Affairs, Karl-Renner-Institut, Austria

**Marcel Mersch,** Head of Unit, S&D Group, European Parliament, Belgium

**Vassilis Ntousas,** Senior International Relations Policy Advisor, FEPS, Belgium

**José Antonio Ocampo,** Professor, IPD Columbia University, USA

**Özlem Onaran,** Professor, Director, Greenwich Political Economy Research Centre, University of Greenwich, UK

**Paulo Trigo Pereira,** Member of Parliament, Professor, Lisbon School of Economics & Management, Portugal

**Poul Nyrup Rasmussen,** former Prime Minister of Denmark, former President of the Party of European Socialists

**David Rinaldi,** Senior Economic Policy Advisor, FEPS, Belgium

**Maria-João Rodrigues,** President, FEPS, Belgium

**Rocio Sampere,** Director, Felipe González Foundation, Spain

**Vivien Schmidt,** Jean-Monnet Professor, Boston University, USA

**Jan-Erik Støstad,** Secretary General, SAMA, Norway

**Ania Skrzypek,** Senior Research Fellow, FEPS, Belgium

**Dimitris Tsarouhas,** Jean-Monnet Chair, Assistant Professor, Bilkent University

**Matthieu Teachout,** Research Assistant, Office of Joseph E. Stiglitz, USA

**Frank Vandenbroucke,** Professor, Free University of Amsterdam, Netherlands

**Andrew Salomone Viteritti,** Managing Editor, The Economist Intelligence Unit, USA

**Kristian Weise,** Director, CEVEA, Denmark

**Stuart Wood,** Member of the House of Lords, UK

# FOREWORD

**Europe today is** in a state of crisis, having experienced stagnation and sluggish economic growth over the past decade. Some countries, like Greece, Spain, Portugal, and Italy, have grappled with depression or recession for years. Those countries hit hardest after the 2008 financial crisis still suffer from unacceptably high unemployment, especially among young people.

To be sure, what became the European Union has achieved enormous progress since its founding in 1957. The founders of the European Union intended to establish a prosperous and peaceful Europe built on a set of common fundamental values, in particular freedom, solidarity, democracy, equality, respect for human dignity, the rule of law, and human rights. *Peace* has been and remains to this day the main objective of the European Union.

But the European project will be successful only if it ensures the well-being of European citizens, and a place for Europe in a harmonious, globalized world. Every day, both seem to slip further out of reach. Economic underperformance brought political and social uncertainty, threatening the integrity of the European Union as a whole, causing frustration among citizens, and encouraging populist movements around Europe. The prosperity the EU promised was supposed to foster solidarity, enabling in turn further European integration; economic failures have undermined the willingness to work together. Momentum toward broader and deeper integration has stopped or even reversed, as the 2016 Brexit vote so vividly demonstrated.

Against this backdrop, the European Union's political leadership cannot continue with a business-as-usual approach. Europe cannot continue to be a continent of peace and broadly shared prosperity without a renewal of the vision the EU's founders had over 60 years ago. Europe needs new institutions and new rules, governing both economy and polity, based on new ideas.

This book outlines a new set of rules for economic, political, and social governance in Europe that would help to recast a prosperous and equitable European Union marked by peace and solidarity within the context of globalization. These ideas flow from a diagnosis of what has gone wrong, manifested in the slow growth, rising inequality, and rapidly increasing economic insecurity for large parts of our societies. This diagnosis contrasts sharply with what EU leaders promised decades ago as European integration proceeded apace. Our conclusions are clear: incremental policy change will not solve the problems. To improve economic performance and create shared prosperity, the rules of the European economy—broadly understood to include the fundamental policies governing the EU—must be rewritten.

The Foundation for European Progressive Studies (FEPS) is very grateful to Professor Joseph Stiglitz for his willingness to lead and coordinate the process for developing and refining these new rules, which has involved a large team of scholars and policymakers from throughout the EU.

This book fits well with his earlier work with the Roosevelt Institute, the New York–based think tank dedicated to carrying forward the legacy and values of Franklin and Eleanor Roosevelt to restore America's promise of opportunity for all. Scholars associated with Roosevelt, including Professor Stiglitz, offered a pointed assessment of what had gone wrong in the United States. Their book, *Rewriting the Rules of the American Economy*,[1] provides a detailed analysis of how rules, institutions, and policies had changed in the United States over the last few decades, and how, by rewriting those rules, one could restore growth and shared prosperity. The goal, as with this book about Europe, was not to return to an earlier era, but to reformulate the rules to address the challenges of a twenty-first-century, globalized economy.

The American book enjoyed enormous political resonance. It provided essential planks of the still-emerging progressive economic agenda. Unusual for a policy-heavy book from a think tank, it was even reviewed in the mainstream press, including *The New York Review of Books*. But it also drew enough attention abroad that South Korean scholars, for example, published their own version of *Rewriting the Rules*.[2]

The cooperation with Professor Stiglitz on this volume about Europe rests on the longstanding partnership of FEPS with him and the Initiative for Policy Dialogue, which he founded, at Columbia University in New York. As the only progressive political foundation at the European level, we are most grateful to the group of high-level scholars from all over Europe who took part in a long process of brainstorming, reflection, and debate with the aim of developing proposals for new rules after more than ten years of economic, social, and political crisis.

We greatly appreciate all the valuable advice, insightful feedback, and continuous support we received from all contributors in this group. In particular, we would like to express our gratitude to the coauthors, who so enthusiastically turned all these ideas into the final product.

Ernst Stetter

# PREFACE

**It has been** about 40 years since Ronald Reagan and Margaret Thatcher ushered in the age of neoliberalism and American-style supply-side economics. While most people focused on tax cuts (especially for top earners) and deregulation (especially for the financial sector), a much more fundamental change was taking place in economic and legal frameworks. Bankruptcy laws, corporate governance, labor regulations, and monetary policy all underwent a transformation. The results are now unambiguous. Growth slowed relative to the years after World War II, and what growth occurred went largely to upper-income individuals. It's time that we recognize these failures on both sides of the Atlantic and chart a new course.

This was the view taken by the Roosevelt Institute, a think tank that grew out of the Presidential Library of Franklin Delano Roosevelt that is dedicated to advancing the values of FDR and Eleanor Roosevelt. The goal of the institute remains to map out a new strategy, adapted to the United States in the twenty-first century. In 2015, I headed a team from the Roosevelt Institute (including Felicia Wong,

Nell Abernathy, Adam Hersh, Susan Holmberg, and Mike Konczal) that wrote a short volume describing how the time had come once again to *rewrite* the rules for the American economy in ways that would create faster growth. But this time, we would ensure that all Americans would share in the benefits of that growth.

In that book, we emphasized that creating a more equal society entailed more than crafting progressive tax and expenditure policies. It entailed creating greater equality in *market* incomes by addressing, for instance, abuses that undermined competition, warped corporate governance, and lessened worker bargaining power. While brief, it was comprehensive. We identified the underlying drivers of recent changes in our economy, technological change and globalization. And we showed how policy could shape what were, to many people, mysterious, impersonal forces.

Our book provided a framework for creating a progressive society in which the economy might better serve the interests of ordinary citizens. In that sense, it provided a programmatic platform for progressives everywhere. We were pleased by the favorable reception it received in the United States, Europe, and Asia, and especially by the invitation to work with the Foundation for European Progressive Studies to write a similar book for Europe.

The challenge was daunting: 28 countries of the European Union (we worked without knowing how the Brexit process would end), each with its own economic and legal framework, and with additional complexity brought by the overlay of EU laws and institutions. FEPS assembled a large team to work on the project (see Acknowledgments), and the group met on several occasions to share perspectives. The possible range of subjects to be covered was, of course, enormous, and we had to narrow our focus to only the most important. We hope, however, what we say on the subjects we do cover will provide insights into what we would have said on the subjects we could not address given the limitations in time and space.

Since the book was written in the immediate aftermath of the financial and euro crises, it is no surprise that macroeconomics, the Stability and Growth Pact, the policies of austerity, and those of the European Central Bank are front and center. Neoliberalism played a more conscious and more important role in the design of the economic framework for the Eurozone than it did in the earlier ideas of Reagan and Thatcher, and ordinary Europeans paid a heavy price. But as we note in what follows, fundamental changes to the underlying economic framework may be extremely difficult, and that is why much of our discussion here is about what can be done within existing strictures.

But while macroeconomics—and the evident macroeconomic failures of the past decade—have naturally absorbed so much of Europe's attention in the years after the crises, we cannot neglect the rules of Europe that affect other important aspects of the European economy. Its overall structure, including competition policy (of increasing importance as Europe has to deal with new global technology giants) affects outcomes for ordinary Europeans. European tax policy (of increasing importance as firms have learned to game national policies to avoid paying taxes) exerts a profound influence on society. Labor market policy (of increasing importance as globalization amplified its effects) weakened worker bargaining power.

A distinctive aspect of the European economy is the European social model, sometimes referred to as the welfare state. Austerity took a tremendous toll on the welfare states and did so at a time when Europe needed to revamp them to reflect twenty-first-century economic realities. This book outlines how Europe can achieve this transformation.

And finally, all countries have been affected by globalization. The rules of globalization have, in many ways, not been working for large parts of society, which has driven the political discontent we have seen in the United States and Europe. While some countries have been doing a reasonably good job in coping with globalization, many have not, and we describe what can be learned from the successes and the failures.

It was an ambitious undertaking, contemplating how the rules of the European economy might be rewritten to create shared prosperity. Colleagues at the Roosevelt Institute encouraged us to embark on this European journey. What success we have achieved is due in no small measure to Ernst Stetter, the founding secretary general of FEPS, who held that position from 2008 until he stepped down in June 2019. The team of scholars and policy analysts that he helped assemble worked tirelessly, uncovering hard-to-find data, weighing alternative proposals, and drafting and redrafting various portions of the book.

In my office, first Debarati Ghosh and then Andrea Gurwitt smoothly managed the entire process, editing and reediting, while Gabriela Plump has done a wonderful job strengthening the long-term relationship between FEPS and the Initiative for Policy Dialogue at Columbia University, which helped support the project. Most importantly, the book could not have been completed without the tireless work of Carter Dougherty, whose insights into the European economy proved invaluable, whose calm persistence was essential to a collaboration of this complexity, and who was a masterful coauthor.

Joseph E. Stiglitz

# Rewriting the Rules of the European Economy

*Introduction*

# Europe Today and the Path Forward

**If the founders** of the European Union surveyed their continent today, they would surely marvel at the breadth and depth of their undertaking. The EU can rightly claim a role in ensuring that the last 70 years were different from the first half of the twentieth century, which was marked by two hot wars and one cold one. During its early decades, European integration helped create an unprecedented level of material prosperity and welfare for ordinary citizens. Europeans lived more comfortable, healthy, and fulfilling lives than at any other time in European history. And for countries integrated into the EU from central and eastern Europe and the Baltics, the European Union underpinned their successful transition from Communism and dictatorship to market economy and democracy.

But since the 2008 financial cataclysm and the euro crisis, the European economy has not performed well by virtually any measure.

Even when economic output has increased, large swaths of society have still suffered. The opportunities for European citizens to achieve reasonable levels of employment, security, education, and retirement have dwindled, in some countries precipitously. Inequality, a dark force that Europeans kept in check for decades, is now a fundamental socioeconomic characteristic of most European countries.

That inequality, combined with economic insecurity, has become fodder for political grievances. In some places, openly nationalist and anti-EU parties have gained ground in electoral backlashes driven by economic troubles and open intolerance, and have conjured up troubling historical memories. Immigrants, even from other European countries, and purported intrusions from the EU, are viewed as a threat, not only to some citizens' sense of identity and control of their own destiny but also to their economic well-being. The vote for Brexit is the illustration par excellence, but we should by no means ignore similar political strains elsewhere in Europe.

The project of European integration demands a political commitment to a thorough renewal of economic and social policy if it is to live up to the aspirations of its founders. Fortunately, European values—the recognition of basic human dignity, respect for the rule of law and human rights, social solidarity, and a balanced perspective on the role of the market, the state, and civil society—provide the touchstones for a new vision. These values have become even more important today, as they are challenged by right-wing extremists on both sides of the Atlantic. Today's moral imperative is to allow Europe's founding tenets to inspire the changes needed to reverse the current slide.

In German, *die Wirtschaft*—"the economy"—connotes both the economy in an abstract, broad sense and "the private sector," a narrower concept that too often drove European policy, to the exclusion of other factors, over the past 20 years. This book addresses the former connotation, asking how we can construct an economic and social system that improves the well-being of ordinary citizens and assures a balance among all segments of society: public, private (including small and large businesses), and civil society. It also asks how we can ensure that prosperity is sustainable in all of its dimensions—economic, political, social, and environmental—so that future generations can share its benefits.

To achieve this goal, we must always remember that *the economy is not an end in itself but a means to an end*—to improving the living standards and well-being of the people within the country in ways that do not impose harm on people outside the country. We emphasize, over and over, that rising GDP does not necessarily indicate greater well-being, particularly when we examine different slices of the population. There is no plausible moral or economic argument for a market economy whose growth benefits only a small number of people while excluding the great majority from its fruits.

The sad truth is that Europe is not performing well in this century. The three charts in Figure I.1 show GDP growth from 1980 to 2015 for the Eurozone, the United States, and the European Union. There was no increase in growth rates in the Eurozone after the creation of the euro. In fact, even before the onset of the financial crisis, growth was lower than in prior decades. Moreover, Eurozone countries responded to the crisis less effectively than the non-Eurozone countries. The smooth gray line shows what growth after 2000 would have looked like if it had continued on the same trajectory that it had followed for the previous two decades; the black line shows the actual outcomes. Especially in the Eurozone, the gap between precrisis GDP predictions and actual performance is large, and years after the crisis was still increasing, even though the economies of the Eurozone

## Figure I.1a: Eurozone

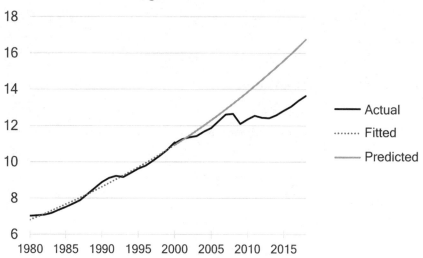

## Figure I.1b: United States

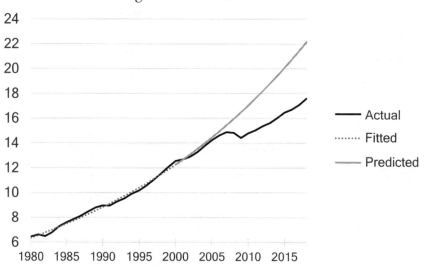

showed traditional signs of a recovery (such as reductions in unemployment rates). The crisis seems to have had a long-term effect.

By contrast, in the decade from 2008 to 2017, the United States grew an average of 1.55 percent annually, and 0.8 percent per capita,

## Figure I.1c: European Union

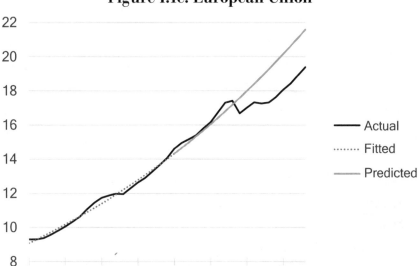

For each of the regions—Eurozone, United States, European Union—the figures show three lines. The black line is actual GDP (WEO, 2018). The gray dotted line is the fitted exponential trend on GDP data for 1980–2000. The solid gray line is an extrapolation of an exponential trend. The units for GDP are in trillion (constant 2009) dollars for the USA, and trillion (constant 2010) dollars for the EU and Eurozone.

*Source: World Economic Outlook, 2018.*

while the Eurozone grew only at 0.7 and 0.4, respectively. Why this difference? Part of the reason for the weak performance of the EU, we suggest, has to do with its macroeconomic framework. And a primary cause of the even more dismal performance of the Eurozone is its very structure. As we shall discuss at length, the euro eliminated key mechanisms for adjustment, which amplified the effects of crises such as the 2008 financial meltdown and brought on the sovereign debt disaster that followed.

While the overall growth performance of the EU was disappointing, an even more disconcerting dimension within the European economy emerged. The benefits of what little growth took place accrued mostly to the very top.

Inequality around Europe, not only in crisis countries, is growing: Figure I.2a highlights the unfortunate stagnation of average incomes of 90 percent of the population, even as the top 1 percent harvest more wealth, often in ways not available to less fortunate Europeans. Figure I.2b demonstrates how, in many European countries, a growing share of income flows to the highest earners. The increases over thirty years underscore how even Nordic countries started from much lower levels of inequality but were not immune from the trend, either. Increases before 2013 in Germany, France, Italy, and the United Kingdom stand out.

These data illustrate the instability and inequality of market economies. Thus, while markets can be powerful instruments for improving the well-being of individuals, they do not always work the way they should, and they do not always serve all of society. Since markets do not exist in a vacuum, they must be tempered, regulated, and structured by rules.

The rulebook for Europe is thick and complex. It includes strictures on deficits and debts; provisions governing labor, product, and financial markets; rules of corporate governance and bankruptcy, competition and intellectual property; and rules governing the central

### FIGURES I.2A AND I.2B: GROWING INEQUALITY FOR EUROPE

The data also show growing inequality for Europe as a whole: Figure I.2a shows the virtual stagnation of average incomes of the bottom 90 percent, in contrast to the soaring incomes of the top 1 percent. There is also a pattern of increasing inequality in most European economies. Figure I.2b illustrates that in many European countries, a growing share of income goes to the top 1 percent. The increases over the 30 years before 2013 were striking in Germany, France, Italy, and the United Kingdom. The Nordic countries started from much lower levels of inequality but were not immune to the trend, either.

Source: (I.2a) World Inequality Database (https://wid.world/); (I.2b) authors' calculations based on the World Inequality Database.

bank. These rules frame conduct in every aspect of the economy and in multiple aspects of our lives.

The rules are, of course, constantly changing. This book has a simple objective: to show how many of the changes in the rules in recent

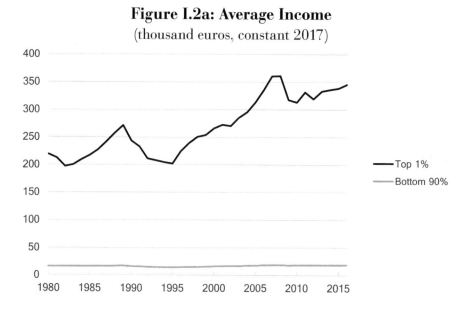

**Figure I.2a: Average Income**
(thousand euros, constant 2017)

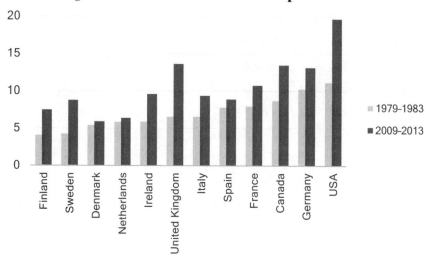

**Figure I.2b: Income Share of Top 1 Percent**

decades have weakened Europe's economy, led to slower growth and more inequality, and how a *rewriting of the rules of Europe's economy can bring a greater shared prosperity.*

Today there is a widespread belief that Europe's maladies are not temporary, a condition that will continue unless there are changes to the economic and social policies, rules, and structure. But the too-common view that Europe should simply accept the system's poor economic performance is wrong. It can do better. Some people also say that there is nothing wrong with Europe's rules, beyond perhaps some minor changes, and that the problem is a failure to enforce them.

In this book, we argue that the real problem is not with inadequate enforcement of Europe's rules, but with the rules, institutions, and structural reforms themselves. Indeed, one of the reasons that they have not been more strictly enforced is a realization of the disastrous consequences of doing so. If the EU had more rigorously enforced its own rules, Europe's economic performance would have been even worse.

We take a broad perspective on *rules.* In our usage, the word includes a panoply of institutions and regulations, both formal and explicit as well as informal and implicit. While markets are important, even the best-performing markets cannot solve many of society's key problems. There is an important societal role for the public sector (government) and for civil society. Government must provide what the private sector has not (or cannot) either efficiently or equitably provide. This group of tasks is large and critical: social protection, basic research, national defense, and education. We also ask about the right balance between the public sector, private sector, and civil society, and how the state must set the proper rules to govern each.

Of particular importance are the rules pertaining to the EU and the Eurozone as a whole. These rules were often introduced to prevent the actions of one country from having adverse effects on others; not infrequently, these turned out to be counterproductive.

Creating and maintaining the EU not only demanded new rules but new organizations that would institutionalize those rules and the values they reflected. At the same time, each country had to adapt its rules and institutions to mesh well with new EU rules and procedures. Today, anyone attempting to cast and recast the European Union, which is a tapestry of more than two dozen nations, is necessarily striving for originality and searching for ideas that have seldom, if ever, been tested and certainly not on such a scale. Substance and process are inseparable. How a policy is executed within and across national boundaries can be as important as the policy itself.

The challenge of designing rules that work for a diverse set of countries, each with its own history and rich culture, is far more difficult than the challenge the first 13 American states faced when they formed their own union almost 250 years ago. Finding European solutions exemplifies, to a far greater extent than in the United States, the description of politics by Max Weber: "Politics is a strong and slow boring of hard boards. It takes both passion and perspective. Certainly, all historical experience confirms the truth—that man would not have attained the possible unless time and again he had reached out for the impossible."

But the ideas for a new set of rules are out there. This book's diagnosis of Europe includes a mixture of praise and criticism. Europe has made great investments in physical and human capital, technology, and infrastructure. It is true that bold institutional innovations have to knit together a diverse group of countries and peoples within a democratic framework. However, the European economy is not effectively advancing the living standards of its people, at least to the extent that it can. And European leaders should be deeply troubled that parts of Europe are not doing well precisely because of the very rules the EU put in place to promote shared economic prosperity.

Leaders have not always responded well to the challenges posed by the creation of an ever-closer union, especially while that union created an integrated market and a common currency, the euro. And their failures in the face of ever-changing economic circumstances, especially following the financial crisis, have been stark.

So too, in many cases, and in many countries, Europe has failed to strike the right balance between markets, states, and civil societies. Many rules have contributed to the economic morass that Europe confronts today. Our goal with this book is to find those rules and institutions that have most poorly served Europe and propose alternatives.

European rules, regulations, and institutions are not products of natural law. These are all human creations, designed by mortals with good intentions. We should not have expected that the institutions, rules, and regulations that the EU's founders created would work decades later, or even succeed in their initial goal, especially given the unprecedented scale of political, economic, and social integration that Europe has sought. We have to constantly assess, as we do in this book, whether these rules, regulations, and institutions are serving the ends for which they were created—to create a more peaceful and prosperous Europe that fosters a stronger European identity.

In writing this book, we faced a particular challenge. The political rules of the EU make changing some of the economic rules—those embedded in the key treaties—extraordinarily difficult because they require a consensus among its members, and in many cases, unanimity. This political rule itself is flawed. It means, as recent events have demonstrated, that countries can flout even the basic premises of the EU—a commitment to human rights and democracy—without fear of punishment from Brussels or fellow EU members. If two countries lose their commitment to democracy (as this book goes to print, questions are being raised from both Hungary and Poland), any attempt by a large majority to discipline a single country will face a veto of another. Rules of unanimity should change. But this book is written in a more practical vein.

Instead, we take the approach of describing both what rules should be changed and what changes can come within existing rules. Policy is always an exercise in what economists invariably regard as second-best options, or options that arise when facing political or other constraints that would not exist in an ideal world. In this book, we are undertaking an exercise often in third- and fourth-best options, redesigning policy for a world in which Europe's current rules and institutions are far from ideal. Our analysis of what is wrong will often suggest obvious fixes: new rules or new institutions, either within particular countries or within the EU. We will also sometimes suggest changes based on a reinterpretation of existing rules or on institutions acting differently, within an existing mandate.

To a large extent, the flaws in the European economic framework are not random and haphazard but flow from a set of beliefs that were prevalent at the time of the EU's construction, especially those that dominated thinking in the early 1990s. Decisions were often guided by the belief that markets, on their own, would lead to economic efficiency so long as governments kept spending, deficits, debts, and inflation low. It is worth recalling how these decisions were attached to—indeed, contingent upon—a particular moment in history.

It was a moment of capitalist triumphalism. Those economic beliefs enjoyed a moment of popularity in the years after the fall of the Berlin Wall. However, to say the market economy accounted for the collapse of authoritarian regimes from Warsaw, to Bucharest, to Moscow is to misread history. Instead, it was the failure of a deeply flawed Communist system, pushed to the brink by the American devotion to a high-tech arms race, combined with a human yearning for freedom.

It was a moment between crises. Had the Eurozone been formed a few years later, when economic shocks rattled fast-growing East Asian economies, the perils of the formula would have been clearer. These Asian countries, which had obeyed all the strictures of the EU—the macroeconomic prescriptions of low deficits, debt, and inflation—were nonetheless unable to avoid a severe crisis. Their earlier successes, too, contravened the ultra-capitalist credo. For years they had enjoyed very high growth rates, in part thanks to substantial government intervention to an extent that EU rules do not allow. Evidently, what was thought of in Europe at the time as the necessary and sufficient conditions for growth and stability were neither necessary nor sufficient.

Further, America stood taller in the 1990s, and large parts of Europe fell hard for the apparent success of the American model. Many Europeans noticed the increase in American GDP but ignored the income stagnation, and outright declines in real income, experienced by large groups of American citizens. They also ignored the sense of income insecurity and the poor health, which was reflected in the United States having the lowest life expectancy among advanced countries. Europe looked at years of stable inflation in the United States and ignored the imbalances and excesses that would eventually lead to the greatest crisis in three-quarters of a century. In the aftermath of the 2008 crisis, it became apparent that the United States economy was neither stable, nor efficient, nor delivering for most of its citizens.

If the rules of Europe had been written in the aftermath of the crisis and recession, its framers would have been even more skeptical about the ability of markets, and especially financial markets, to work well on their own. That crisis made it abundantly clear that current rules, on both sides of the Atlantic, left a great deal to be desired. But for broader models of what makes for a successful economy, serving all or at least most citizens, Europe should not have looked across the Atlantic nor to distant countries in Asia. It should have looked within its own borders to find some of the most successful economies in the world. Within the varied experiences of the countries of the EU, there were and are good ideas for maintaining a prosperous and equitable European economy.

Economists dryly label the particular set of economic ideas about the efficiency and stability of unfettered markets that the European Union embraced in the early 1990s as "neoclassical economics." Others have categorized these ideas as neoliberalism or market fundamentalism. Whatever we call this belief system, it eventually hardened into a blind faith in markets in the following decades. The financial upheavals of 2008, the harrowing recession and hapless government response that followed, and the sovereign debt crisis that nearly tore the Eurozone apart originated, in large measure, with this set of ideas.

The markets-will-save-us mentality seeped into every subject this book addresses. The European Union abandoned government spending as a tool to cushion downturns and institutionalized a central bank that, out of an unfounded fear of even a slight increase in inflation, raised interest rates as Europe neared a deep downturn—the opposite of what was needed to stimulate the economy. The macro-allocation of state resources toward infrastructure, education, and other public goods often devolved into a debate over how, not whether, the private sector could do it better, despite ample evidence that governments are often best suited to carry out some of these definable tasks.

An unwarranted trust in private industry—and the belief that it could be relied on to be self-regulating and naturally competitive—became the political manifestation of Europe's confidence in markets. Companies were left to grow larger and larger. Measures that might have promoted competition rather than consolidation fell out of favor. Moreover, corporate governance was often judged on whether it maximized shareholder value and not whether it benefited society as a whole. Most destructively, as subsequent events would show, European governments, regulators, and thinkers greenlighted (even celebrated) a financial services industry that grew more reckless with every passing year. In a culture that celebrated the free market, the money that bankers raked in simply confirmed that they were smarter than the rest and able to regulate their own behavior. This windfall did not, as it should have, raise alarms that perhaps something was amiss.

An entirely predictable result of Europe's fealty to markets turned out to be rising inequality and increasing poverty. Redistribution of wealth became suspect, and institutions and laws that would have promoted more equitable allocation of wealth atrophied, including labor unions and minimum wage measures. The very notion of labor "markets," a disturbingly common term in Europe, embodied an assumption that people must resemble freely traded commodities. Social insurance programs, especially for older Europeans, faced pressure like never before, while private pensions became the new fad, with little regard to the risks and costs they imposed.

Meanwhile, a new international order took shape. By the late 1990s, thinking, writing, and preaching about globalization had grown into a cottage industry dominated by an international elite. Similarly fashioned around a near-worship of markets, globalization's most potent manifestation was a worldwide labor arbitrage that exposed European workers to new kinds of competition, some from within Europe, some from without, on a previously unimaginable scale. Trade policy, rather than trying to grapple with how this new reality would affect ordinary workers, amplified globalization with little thought to its economic, social, and political consequences.

At the same time that the world's political elites were designing policies on the premise that markets could do no wrong, central strands in economic theory were converging to demonstrate the limitations—in some cases, wrongheadedness might be a fairer term—of neoliberal doctrines. In the case of Europe, several broad insights merit mention:

■ The conditions under which markets work well—including when they are naturally competitive—are highly restrictive. Even small changes in the standard economic models, like the presence of small imperfections in information, undermine all the standard results. An economy in which many firms have even a small amount of market power behaves fundamentally differently from an economy in which no firm has any market power. Advances in game theory have given us tools to better analyze markets in which there are a limited number of firms and have demonstrated how different their behavior is from that depicted by the standard competitive model underlying neoliberalism.

■ When information is imperfect and asymmetric—that is, when some individuals know something that others do not (which is almost always the case)—the economy is inefficient. Firms can use their informational advantage over others to exploit them and to gain market power. The limits of information help explain other major market failures, like why individuals often are constrained in the amounts they can borrow and why individuals cannot buy insurance against many of the important risks they face.

■ The market is inefficient in the production of knowledge and the translation of that knowledge into advances in productivity, as embodied in new products and new production processes. We think of today's economy as being an innovation economy, yet almost all innovation rests on publicly funded basic research. We often celebrate some of the important innovations done by the private sector, yet firms often invest too much in some areas to enhance market power, and too little in others, such as climate change, where there could be true public benefits. Particularly worrisome today are the threats to competitive markets that arise from platforms like Amazon, Google, and Facebook. While Europe has done a better job than the United States at curbing these behemoths and their anticompetitive and antisocial practices (including invasion of privacy), there is no reason to be content.

■ Behavioral economics helped explain systematic deviations from behavior predicted by models that assumed a world populated by fully rational individuals with unbounded capacity to calculate.

■ The standard competitive model underlying neoliberalism ignores the costs of adjustment, and hence the challenges posed by structural adjustment. Markets and individuals on their own sometimes failed to adjust—to globalization, for instance. Thus, there is a need for active labor market and industrial policies.

■ Globalization and technological change, while improving GDP, can leave large fractions of the population—sometimes the vast majority—worse off. This is especially true as Europe has expanded trade with countries where wages are much lower and from whom it imports labor-intensive goods. The resulting decrease in demand for labor, and especially unskilled labor, inevitably drives down wages and increases unemployment unless government takes counteracting measures. Too often governments do nothing, guided by mistaken notions of trickle-down economics. A rising tide does not necessarily lift all boats.

Taken together, theoretical advances have undermined the notion that markets are efficient and stable on their own so long as the government keeps out of the way and keeps its own house in order. They have also helped us understand why, even as GDP increased, so many people were worse off.

If an economic model provides a poor description of the economy, policies predicated on it stand little chance of succeeding. However, so much of the construction of Europe, its economy, and the thinking of the dedicated civil servants and politicians who tried to make it work sprang from faulty premises. Bad theory in Europe took the form of beliefs held strongly despite a wealth of evidence to the contrary. Among the key beliefs that have shaped Europe's economic framework are the following nine:

## REWRITING THE DOCTRINE AND CHANGING THE PARADIGM

**1. *The Austerity Doctrine*** dictates that governments need to keep deficits below 3 percent of GDP. Large deficits undermine confidence, so it was believed, and the reduction in confidence undermines investment and weakens the economy. Bringing deficits under control increases confidence and restores the economy to health. A Europe-wide commitment to this doctrine is essential because the failure of one country to keep its deficits in order imposes costs on others through runaway inflation.

**The evidence** is to the contrary and is discussed in Chapter 1. No economy in a recession has recovered through contractionary policies. There is no evidence of spillovers, especially of deficits in one country leading to Europe-wide inflation. Large deficits in Greece had no impact on its neighbors and no effect on Europe-wide inflation. Any cost was borne solely by the people of Greece. What was needed was fiscal stimulus, not an aversion to deficits. The 3 percent number was conjured from thin air and not based in theory or evidence.

**2. *The Debt Doctrine*** holds that government needs to keep debt below 60 percent of GDP, otherwise growth will slow. As with the austerity doctrine, the failure of any one country to do so imposes costs on others. The commitment to keep debt and deficits below the 60 percent and 3 percent limits is known as the Stability and Growth Pact.

**The evidence** shows scant links between debt and growth. Indeed, causality may go the other way. Countries that experience a misfortune (the demand for their natural resources declines, for example, or they are afflicted by civil conflict) grow more slowly and wind up with more debt. In other cases, some factor leads simultaneously to low growth and more debt. In making investment decisions, policy should aim for returns that exceed the cost of capital, as we discuss in Chapter 3. The debt doctrine focuses on only one side of the balance sheet, the liability side, but we should examine the asset side as well. The result of this oversight is that productive investment is curbed, which lowers growth and living standards from what they otherwise would have been. Like the deficit number, the 60 percent number was conjured from thin air, with no basis in theory or evidence.

**3. *The Price Stability Doctrine*** holds that government should keep inflation below 2 percent. In recent years, as country after country has faced the threat of *deflation* (falling prices), this doctrine evolved to say that monetary authorities should ensure that inflation remains at about 2 percent. Where did this number come from? As in the case of the other two key numbers, the answer is: out of thin air. It was predicated on the largely ungrounded fear that if inflation rose too high, it would accelerate into hyperinflation, or if it fell too low, it might accelerate into deflation.

**The evidence** has shown that economies can tolerate a much higher inflation rate and may actually perform better with an inflation rate greater than 2 percent, especially in periods of fast change. In such periods, there have to be changes in relative prices. But markets are characterized by what economists call downward rigidities in nominal wages and prices; for a variety of reasons, it is difficult for workers to accept wage cuts. Higher rates of inflation can thus lead to faster adjustments. Moreover, in a recession, faster rates of inflation mean that the real interest rate, which is the interest rate adjusted for inflation, is lower. That lower rate encourages investment. Even the chief economist of the usually conservative IMF argued in 2010 that the target rate of inflation should be increased to 4 percent. In Chapter 2, we argue that rather than a single-minded focus on inflation, the European Central Bank should pursue a more balanced approach that considers not only inflation, but also growth, employment, and financial stability.

**4.** *The Markets-Know-Best Doctrine* argues that what emerges from the fierce competition of firms within market frameworks will serve society best. Government seldom needs to step in.

**The evidence** is that many of our society's ills, from air and water pollution to excesses of inequality, stem from markets. Without strong government actions, competition will erode as firms create barriers to entry by other competitors, often via questionable practices, and work hard to reduce competition through mergers and acquisitions. In key new technologies (including social media and internet search), for instance, a small handful of companies dominate the global landscape. Here the issue is not so much rewriting the rules but simply writing the rules to protect competition in new industries. The issue here is whether those rules will be effectively written by and for these corporations or by and for the interests of society. In this arena, the European Union is ahead of the United States, where the political influence of big corporations, especially in technology policy, may have led to softer antitrust approaches.

One of the reasons that large corporations have led to more inequality in recent years is that there has not been a balance of countervailing power: in earlier decades, powerful unions provided some check on powerful corporations, both in the marketplace and in the public sphere. But today, in most countries, the power of unions has been eviscerated. While there are a variety of reasons for this development, one reason is the rules: they have been and are being rewritten not only to water down worker protections, but also to weaken the unions themselves. We discuss these challenges in Chapter 9.

**5. *The Banks-Know-Best Doctrine*** holds that banks and other financial intermediaries can properly assess the risk of, and manage, credit intermediation if governments simply step out of the way. In short, financial firms will self-regulate, managing their own risk. There is no need to worry about the short-term focus of markets.

**The evidence** is that underregulated financial markets engage in excessive risk taking, focus far too much on the short term, and engage in market manipulation, insider trading, predatory lending, and other abusive practices. Most of the regulatory reform has focused on preventing the financial sector from imposing harms on others, with less concern for ensuring that the financial sector does what it is supposed to do. The failure of the financial sector to provide finance for small- and medium-sized firms is one of the reasons for the weaknesses in macroeconomic performance of many countries in Europe.

The financial sector used to help money flow from households into firms to be used for investment. Today, the financial sector often moves money out of firms to buy back shares and pay larger dividends. It focuses on the short term—and has encouraged firms elsewhere in the economy to do likewise. With such myopia, it is hard to make the long-term investments that are essential for Europe's long-term growth. The financialization of the economy, or the tendency of the nonfinancial sector to respond to the demands and imperatives of finance, is rightly blamed for many woes of economies on both sides of the Atlantic and is discussed more extensively in Chapter 5.

**6.** *The Shareholder Capitalism Doctrine* posits that firms should maximize the value (profits) of shareholders. In the United States, this notion was popularized by archconservative Nobel Prize–winning economist Milton Friedman, and it replaced a broader vision of corporate governance that still survives (at least on paper) in much of Europe: stakeholder capitalism. In the *Stakeholder Capitalism Doctrine*, firms are seen as being concerned with all stakeholders, including workers and the communities in which the firms operate.

**The evidence** does not bear out the claims. Shareholder capitalism gained currency just as economic theory showed that, on average, shareholder capitalism does not maximize the general welfare, which is especially true when shortsighted shareholders focus on quarterly returns. The private equity firms that take public companies private, load them with debt, pay out large amounts to investors, and set the scene for bankruptcy a couple years later, also illustrate how myopic capitalists can impose high costs on society.

**7.** *The Privatization Doctrine* holds that state-owned companies are per se less efficient and should therefore be privatized. The triumph of this doctrine drove the mass privatization efforts in eastern Europe, but also the more nuanced privatizations in western Europe, such as in health care and retirement programs.

**The evidence** is clear that privatization is not at all a panacea. Some privatizations were successful. Others, like British Rail, far less so, to the point that governments have discussed reversing their decisions. Some of the "privatizations" were, to say the least, peculiar, like Greece selling its airports to a consortium in which public bodies in Germany composed a major part. Administration and transaction costs for publicly provided annuities (pensions) are a fraction of those in the private sector. In general, Europe's largely public health insurance system is far more efficient than the largely private system in the United States.

**8.** *The Markets-Will-Provide Doctrine* holds that we can rely on markets to not only be efficient, but to also take care of basic individual needs—from housing to pensions, health care to education. This doctrine claims that Europe overbuilt its system of social insurance and protection, which was, in any case, less efficient than the private sector. In its most extreme form, it even argues that markets will take care of the environment and other sectors in which there is concern about externalities and the production of public goods, such as in basic research.*

**The evidence** (as noted above) is that government is often as or more efficient than the private sector. Markets pay no attention to social costs like pollution, which is why governments must regulate pollutants or impose costs on those who pollute. Markets failed to provide insurance against the risks individuals care the most about, such as job loss or elder care.† Even today, private retirement insurance typically leaves key risks such as inflation uncovered. Because of higher administrative costs that are partly due to efforts at cream-skimming—insuring only the best risks—private insurance is more expensive. Chapters 7, 8, and

---

* There are some who go so far as to contend that if only the government assigns property rights clearly, even problems of externalities can be addressed within the market. This is sometimes referred to as the Coase Conjecture, and is only true under unrealistic assumptions about information and transactions costs. In practice, regulation can be both fairer and more efficient, as the work of Nobel Prize–winner Eleanor Ostrom demonstrated.

† Economic theory (in particular, theories of asymmetric information) has explained why the private sector often fails to provide insurance for important risks.

9 lay out some general related principles, which are set in the context of social policy.

What must or should be provided by government? The answers to what should be the role of the government—when should it provide finance, when should it be at the center of production—may differ from country to country. For instance, the success of a modern innovation economy rests on highly educated researchers, basic research provided by the government, and research and development by corporations. Too many countries have put too much focus on the latter (the corporations) and too little on the key roles played by government.

**9. *The Free-Trade Doctrine*** posits that removing barriers to trade leads to an increase in the overall well-being of all (or at least most) citizens. This is one of the most widely held economic beliefs. The free-trade doctrine is part of the broader *globalization doctrine:* that globalization of all markets leads to an increase in the well-being of all citizens.

**The evidence** shows that this thesis is generally not true. The advocates of free trade exaggerated its growth benefits and underestimated its distributive consequences. Even when there was growth, the losers got such a smaller share of the pie that they were worse off. Economic theory predicted that this would be the case.

At the very least, societies require government programs to help those who otherwise would have been hurt by globalization, both with financial assistance and assistance in moving from jobs that have been destroyed to new jobs. In the absence of job assistance and a strong macro-economy, old jobs can disappear faster than new jobs can be created, resulting in a decrease in GDP. In the absence of mechanisms to share and manage risk, everyone can be worse off if greater openness increases risk to the point that firms and individuals move from high-return, risky activities to safer activities with lower returns.

Even in the best of circumstances, though, opening trade between advanced countries (in northern and western Europe, for example) and less-developed countries (in Asia and eastern Europe, for example) leads to lower wages for unskilled workers in the more advanced countries. While those who gain might be able to fully compensate those who have lost, they typically do not.

Under the right conditions and with the right policies, global trade agreements that expand trade might work well for everyone, but this possibility presupposes a quality of politics and governance that seldom prevails. Too often, trade agreements have really only advanced special interests. Too seldom have governments provided adequate assistance to those who have been harmed.

Likewise, financial globalization, like trade globalization, is not associated with an increase in either growth or stability in Europe or elsewhere. Indeed, financial globalization enabled the US financial crisis to move quickly across the ocean and almost instantly become a global financial crisis.

Europe's leaders, in an attempt to defend their seemingly inhumane austerity policies, frequently made this last desperate appeal in moments of crisis: there is no alternative. In other words, there was no alternative to austerity, no alternative to the harsh policies that Europe imposed on the countries in crisis, and no alternative to Europe's existing rules and regulations. But there are alternatives. There are alternatives even within the current legal and institutional framework. In some cases, there may be a need to reinterpret the rules. In other cases, it may be necessary to supplement or to revise them. The following chapters further explore the misguided doctrines and resulting policies that Europe has embraced. We then establish that there are alternative policies—alternative rules, regulations, and institutions—that will yield better outcomes.

There are overarching questions for many areas of policy: What should be the rules for the EU? What should the EU require of each of its members? How much harmonization is necessary? How much is desirable? In this respect, Europe has already adopted a principle that makes enormous sense—the principle of subsidiarity. This principle holds that decisions should be made at the lowest possible level and therefore closest to the people. The decisions that should be made in Brussels, Strasbourg, and Frankfurt are those in which the actions of one country have significant effects on others. Activities with negative externalities—spillovers across borders, for example—should be discouraged or proscribed. Activities with positive externalities should be encouraged or undertaken jointly. While this principle makes enormous sense, it has often been poorly implemented because externalities were imagined where they did not exist and ignored when they were significant.

## THE CHALLENGES FACING EUROPE

This book is divided into four parts. In Part I, we turn to the high-level decisions Europe faces in economic policy: its macroeconomic framework, monetary policy, and public investment. Part II examines what well-regulated markets should look like and what government can do to make markets work. Here we outline policies on corporate governance, financial markets, intellectual property, competition, and taxation.

In Part III, we sketch out what a welfare state for the twenty-first century in Europe would look like by first looking at Europe's worsening inequality. Then we discuss social insurance systems and how regulations affecting workers and labor relations have led to lower wages and more inequality. The final chapter, Part IV, argues why Europe can and should fight for better global rules to improve the management of globalization in a way that does not compound the challenge of inequality.

Konrad Adenauer, Altiero Spinelli, Charles de Gaulle, Alcide de Gasperi, Paul-Henri Spaak, Robert Schuman, and Jean Monnet all launched the European project at a time of great uncertainty, with much of Europe still in ruins, and when the world was dividing into two opposing camps that threatened to clash catastrophically. None of these founders expected that European integration would be easy, but they were all convinced it was feasible and urgently necessary.

The European project of greater economic and political integration would help ensure peace in Europe, they reasoned, in part by promoting shared prosperity. Fortunately, they bequeathed to their successors a European identity whose main pillar remains a sense that going it alone will not work. That conviction can be the basis for a fresh start. Rewriting the rules will not be any easier than creating them. But the crises of today's Europe demand bold action and a commitment to renewing the promise of the European project that began more than 60 years ago.

# PART I

# Achieving Full Employment, Rapid Growth, and Economic Stability

*Chapter 1*

# Employment, Not Austerity

**A meltdown in** the financial sector in 2008, at first barely noticeable and then overwhelming, kicked off what became an economic and then a social crisis in Europe. Every crisis eventually passes, but we should measure an economic system on the length of time until it fully recovers, the pain inflicted on its citizens, and its vulnerability to another crisis, not on the fact that the disaster itself has finally ended. The effects of the financial crisis and recession in Europe were unnecessarily deep, long, and painful. The disparity between where the economy was and where it was going (should the crisis not have happened) reaches into the trillions of euros. Even now, a decade later, growth is anemic and fragile.

Nothing sums up the effects of the 2008 financial crisis in human terms better than unemployment, which rose almost everywhere and skyrocketed in the hardest-hit countries. Even a decade later, joblessness remains unacceptably high across much of the EU, and European leaders are still concerned with possible future costs of debt and deficits, both of which rose significantly in many countries. They continue to give short shrift to the devastating effects of the crisis on so many Europeans. Even though Europe is now on the mend, we must remember this dark period in economic history.

Long periods of unemployment have destroyed human and social capital.

Young Europeans who should have been acquiring skills through on-the-job training were at home, idle and angry. Citizens' trust in European institutions has eroded, as has trust in their leaders, many of whom promised that the euro would bring shared prosperity. Instead, the euro, or rather the insufficient structures and inadequate policies around it, created a deep downturn that brought stagnation for some countries, severe recessions for others, and for some, worse economic conditions than they experienced during the Great Depression.

The underlying problems in Europe's economic structure and policy framework that gave rise to the crisis have not changed enough, making Europe vulnerable to another crisis. The system is not designed to withstand another large shock—and there will almost surely be further shocks. That is the lesson of economic history.[1]

Decades earlier, Europe had made a set of critical wrong choices in the formulation of their agreed-upon economic framework, called the Stability and Growth Pact. By stability, they did not mean the stability of the economy, but the stability of prices—a commitment to keep inflation levels low and stable. It was not called the *Employment*, Stability, and Growth Pact. Given the absence of emphasis on employment, perhaps the outcome—unconscionably high levels of unemployment in many countries for long periods of time, and especially among the youth—is understandable. The policies and strictures to implement that pact brought neither growth nor stability, to say nothing of employment.

Years after the crisis, unemployment levels were still strikingly elevated, especially in the worst-hit Eurozone countries. The most notable examples are Greece and Spain, whose unemployment levels at the end of 2017 were 21.5 percent and 16.5 percent, respectively. These numbers were admittedly better than the peak levels of 27.5 percent (Greece) and 26.1 percent (Spain) seen in 2013, though still untenable. Large fractions of the unemployed were jobless for an extended period; long-term unemployment reached 18.5 percent in Greece and 13 percent in Spain. Altogether, at the end of 2017, about 17.8 million people in the Eurozone—roughly equivalent to the populations of Austria and Bulgaria combined—were out of work.[2] By the end of 2017, almost 22 percent of the workforce in the Eurozone as a whole also had to make do with part-time employment, a number that had not budged in the previous five years.[3]

Today, large numbers of young people are unable to find secure or rewarding work in accordance with their skills and aspirations. The unemployment rates for people under 25, and job seekers without upper-secondary education, are twice as high as the European average—18.5 percent and 17 percent, respectively.

Mass joblessness became both a cause and effect of inequality during this decade of lost opportunities. Older workers who might have contributed to society did not; younger workers did not receive the early, formative period of skill development that increases lifetime earnings; children stood a lower chance of having their dream careers. The lack of decent, secure work also brought outright poverty to levels many western Europeans never expected to see in their lifetimes, a subject we tackle beginning in Chapter 7.

Elections in 2016 and 2017, notably in Poland, Spain, the Netherlands, France, and Britain demonstrated that European leaders can no longer assume broad citizen support for the EU. In many countries, there is now active opposition to it.[4]

While there are many causes for this discontent, including the migration crisis that broke out in 2015, an underlying cause in many places is poor economic performance—the joblessness, the inequality, the sense of economic precariousness. And while there are many causes for the poor economic state of many of the countries, including globalization, financialization, technology, the EU, and especially the euro, their rules, structures, and policies are central to the problem. The promise of the euro—that it would deliver unprecedented, shared prosperity that in turn would enhance greater European solidarity—has gone unfulfilled.

The electorate may yet give a mandate to leaders with the courage to rewrite the rules and reform the structures that are not working. This book is written in the hope that it will, and to provide some guidance on what needs to be done. The effort should start with a commitment to attaining full employment throughout Europe, one that is based on new macroeconomic strategies.

At the foundation of the euro, clear hopes were mixed with realistic fears. Could a region with such diversity adopt a common currency with a single central bank and simultaneously achieve widespread prosperity? Or would policies aimed at the economic well-being of the German-dominated core leave some peripheral countries in recession or even depression? The history of the euro so far has confirmed the worst fears. But this failure need not have been the case, and it can be reversed in the future.

The new set of rules that we outline in this book are intimately related and mutually reinforcing. But none looms as large as Europe's approach to growth, employment, and debt. If the EU does not get the macroeconomic framework right, the efforts we sketch out on monetary policy (Chapter 2) and investment (Chapter 3) will surely fail to achieve their objectives of stability and higher long-term growth. Promoting greater economic equality and security in Europe, the subject of later chapters, will then prove a near-impossible task.

The current macroeconomic framework dates to the Maastricht Treaty of 1992. This outlined a set of criteria, called the *convergence criteria*, by which the EU would judge a country's suitability for adopting the euro. Behind this banal term lay a theory that if individual European countries did certain things, then they would cohere in a manner conducive to sharing a common currency. Earlier research, such as by Nobel laureate Robert Mundell of Columbia University,[5] had explained that countries could share a common currency—and jointly achieve prosperity—only if they were sufficiently similar. European countries recognized that, as of 1992, they were not sufficiently similar. The hope was that if they satisfied the convergence criteria, they would become sufficiently similar to make a common currency work.

Those criteria included a fiscal straitjacket of a budget deficit not exceeding 3 percent, government debt of no more than 60 percent of GDP, low inflation, a stable exchange rate, and low long-term interest rates. There was, however, no well-developed economic theory that suggested these rules would promote convergence in growth rates or levels of income, let alone in the structures of the economy. Nor did theory support the notion that convergence in these variables would suffice to enable the single currency system to work well.

There was, however, ample evidence that these arbitrary numbers, virtually pulled out of thin air, could have very adverse consequences during a severe downturn. The limits on fiscal deficits, in particular, meant that countries could not engage in counter-cyclical fiscal policy (cutting taxes and increasing spending in a downturn, for example), which economists since John Maynard Keynes have recognized is essential to pulling an economy out of a deep recession. These counter-cyclical measures are all the more important within a common currency area in which monetary and exchange-rate policies cannot aid in restoring full employment. Without these tools, countries are unable to lower their exchange rate to encourage exports, for example, or lower their own interest rates to encourage investment.

The convergence criteria became instead a mechanism for divergence, and especially so as a result of the Single Market, the set of policies promoting commercial integration that allowed funds to move more freely across borders. When recession hit a part of the Eurozone, the common currency let money easily move from economies in recession to well-performing economies. In the aftermath of the crises of 2008 and 2010, money rushed out of countries that needed it the most, thus contracting credit, exacerbating the downturns, and fostering divergence, not convergence. The fiscal rules also barred weaker countries from making the important public investments that the strong countries undertook, fostering greater long-run divergence.

The Stability and Growth Pact came about in 1997 as the enforcement mechanism. It was a mixture of naming-and-shaming measures and possible fines meant to ensure that countries obeyed the fiscal rules. It was distinctly political, giving expression in particular to German wariness of supposedly profligate southern neighbors. With the pact, the architects of the euro reasoned, pressure for the new European Central Bank to stoke inflation to bail out free-spending governments would simply vanish.

The debt and deficit provisions of the convergence criteria and Stability and Growth Pact were based on a fundamental misunderstanding: that managing public finances was comparable to doing so for a family, thus subject to ironclad restrictions and dire consequences for those who spend beyond their means. Chancellor Angela Merkel invoked the mythical "Swabian housewife," the tight-fisted southwestern German matriarch of lore, to scold other countries. By the early 2000s, the experience that borrowing in an economic downturn could drive aggregate demand and restore full employment seemed to have been forgotten, at least in Germany and in many of the higher circles of the EU. The convergence criteria and Stability Pact were articles of faith, not products of sound analysis.

This journey away from what economists had learned in the twentieth century took a particularly sharp turn for the worse when the crisis came, and the Stability Pact—the *Growth* part of which was often forgotten—begat an ugly offspring: austerity. It was not inevitable that, given the convergence criteria and the pact devised to enforce them, austerity would be the EU response to the crisis, but they surely smoothed the way. Faced with a precipitous drop-off in aggregate demand, government spending that would fill the gap was well-nigh unthinkable for an EU that had dedicated itself to the "3 and 60" rule.

The 2008 crisis and its aftermath hit Europe's peripheries— Portugal, Italy, Ireland, Greece, and Spain (infamously called the "PIIGS")—very hard. The porcine moniker applied to these countries reflects criticism of their domestic policies and the large deficits that some had before the crisis. But Spain and Ireland had been the best students of Europe's conventional wisdom. They had fiscal surpluses and low debt-to-GDP ratios—that is, until the crisis. The crisis caused their debts and deficits to soar.

Compliance with the convergence criteria and the Stability Pact hardly inoculated countries from crises. The convergence criteria were neither necessary nor sufficient for growth and stability. Even countries with seemingly reasonable macroeconomic policies can face severe downturns, though now we more fully appreciate the need to guard against extreme events, particularly through proper regulation of the financial sector, something we discuss in Chapter 5. The costs of regulating the financial sector are small compared to the consequences of not doing so.

The crisis meant that many countries could no longer borrow money at a reasonable interest rate, which effectively shut them out of international capital markets. Countries like Italy that did have access to markets worried that they too would lose it. For most of these countries, this isolation was a new experience, brought on at least in part by the euro and how it was being run. The countries could not devalue to stimulate their exports, nor could they use monetary policy to stimulate growth. Outsiders understood their predicament and knew that without help from the stronger countries of the EU, growth in these countries would falter. With no such help forthcoming, it was no wonder that these countries could not borrow a euro.

With the crisis-afflicted countries shut out of capital markets, thus hampering their ability even to meet current debt obligations, they felt they had no choice but to turn to their supposed friends in the EU for assistance. Help was offered, but only under stringent conditions that strangled growth in the afflicted economies. Deficit spending without the permission of those whom they turned to for help became a literal impossibility for countries like Greece, Ireland, Portugal, and eventually Spain. The countries getting assistance were kept on a very short leash.

Together, the EU and the IMF assembled rescue packages for affected countries. As it turned out, the rescue package for Greece was more aimed at saving the financial systems of France and Germany, whose banks had lent heavily to crisis countries, than to rescuing the hard-hit Greek economy. The European Commission, the ECB, and the IMF (known as the Troika) managed the crises jointly. The Troika imposed the austerity measures that contributed to particularly harrowing recessions. They provided enough assistance to Greece to save the French and German banks, but not enough to restore Greek economic growth, as was promised.

The conditions included in rescue packages were at least in part politically determined—to convince voters, especially in Germany, that the crisis countries, which many viewed as profligate free riders, would not take advantage of German largesse. It would be more accurate to say that the reality cut in the opposite direction. Ordinary Greeks paid a huge price to save German and French banks.

Part of the problem, though, was a gross failure in economic analysis. The Troika thought that a dose of austerity accompanied by the kinds of structural reforms that could be done in short order would quickly restore prosperity. Their projections for Greece, for instance, showed such a quick and robust recovery. These models were consistently wrong, and by a large measure. The same simplistic models, ones that had not foreseen the financial crisis or the real estate bubble, failed spectacularly in Greece, Spain, and the other crisis countries.

Similarly, the Single Market did not perform as hoped. Its advocates expected, based on simplistic ideology, that the Single Market would result in money flowing from the rich parts of Europe to those in need. They ignored the wealth of evidence suggesting that as capital markets open up, capital flows typically move pro-cyclically, not counter-cyclically, thus exacerbating downturns. The reality was that money flew out of the banking systems of the crisis countries, further impairing lending to small- and medium-sized enterprises upon which the crisis-dependent countries relied. Moreover, defaults weakened the banking sector and led to further decreases in credit availability and still-higher interest rates.

## PROBLEMS

### The Stability Pact Did Not Work, in Theory or Practice

Two decades after European leaders hammered out the Stability and Growth Pact, we can conclude that it was a failure on its own terms: it did not lead to either growth or stability, or to any of the other ingredients of societal well-being. Instead, it fostered high levels of unemployment.

Compliance with, or deviation from, the "3 and 60" rules turned out to be a very bad predictor of how well a country would manage over time. Defenders of the pact often frame its goals in the context of buffers—countries should limit deficits and debts in good times so they can still comply with the rules in thin years. But whether or not that is good policy in the long run, it makes no sense to plunge a country into a depression today so that it has the fiscal space to avoid a downturn sometime in the distant future.

Spain and Ireland more than complied with both the Maastricht criteria and the Stability Pact and still found themselves in crisis after 2008, with little room to maneuver.* Even mighty Germany took a breather from the rules in the early 2000s as it struggled with a brief cyclical downturn, an episode often effaced from current political memory by Germans who urged Greece and other southern Europeans to look north for guidance. This double standard, in turn, undermined the political legitimacy of demands placed on the crisis countries.

The only possible way to effectively stimulate the economy was through fiscal policy. Advocates of the pact argued that curbing spending for Europe as a whole would not have much effect on growth, even during recessions, since it was assumed that the ECB could come to the rescue and restore full employment with lower rates. But in the years after 2008, as rates hovered near zero, monetary policy was unable to compensate for the lack of an activist fiscal policy, thus exacerbating Europe's recessionary spiral.†

The Stability Pact thus amplified downturns. The Banque de

---

* Part of the reason is that private debts quickly morphed into public debts, which suggests that surveillance of an economy should include not just a look at the government debt-to-GDP ratio but also the private-sector debt-to-GDP ratio.

† When short-term interest rates hit zero, there was still some room for monetary policy through "unconventional measures," such as quantitative easing. These, too, had only limited impact—not enough to restore Europe to full employment quickly.

France concluded that 2012 was a particularly brutal year in which deficit reduction, in excess of the pact's requirements in some countries, knocked 1.5 percentage points off Eurozone growth.[6] At that time, the southern European countries, such as Spain and Italy, were shrinking their fiscal footprint, but so was Germany, which did not need to. The German export machine, however, helped Europe's largest economy chug ahead, aided by a euro that was weaker than it otherwise would have been because other countries were in such a deep rut, and far weaker than the exchange rate Germany would have faced without the common currency.

The fundamental problem with any single currency system is that it takes away the ability for different countries to adjust their exchange rate (their prices relative to those of their trading partners) to stimulate net exports. In theory, crisis countries could lower their unit labor costs, either by lowering wages or increasing productivity to make exports cheaper. This move would lead to greater sales abroad, as well as renewed growth.

Increasing productivity in the short run is always difficult, but especially so when downturns impose constraints on public and private investment, an issue we address in Chapter 3. The only recourse, then, is lowering wages and other costs, in what is called *internal devaluation*. But in most countries, wages are downwardly rigid—at most, they can decrease at only a small amount each year. But a decrease in wages hurts GDP as demand for nontraded goods falls in tandem. And even as wages decrease, the cost of capital increases because suppliers of capital rightly perceive increased risk as a country goes into recession.

In Greece, Italy, and Spain, lower wages mainly translated into a contraction of demand, lower output and incomes, and consequently lower imports. Policymakers hoped increased exports would offset lower domestic demand, but this did not happen to the extent required to sustain GDP, let alone to spur growth. In Greece, exports of goods as a share in GDP increased by a mere 3.5 percentage points between 2011 and 2015, which was about half of the increases seen in Slovenia or Slovakia, for example, and not far from the Eurozone average increase of 2.2 percentage points. Put another way, Greece gained little or no ground vis-à-vis its neighbors by cutting wages. In 2007, just before the crisis, the amount by which Greece's imports exceeded its exports reached €29 billion. The crisis brought down this unsustainable trade deficit, not so much by expanding exports, but by contracting imports as a result of the depression caused by Troika policies imposed on Greece.

A large body of economic literature predicted this outcome. The Troika analysis sought to blame unemployment on workers, on the theory that if only real wages would fall, full employment would quickly be restored. But such analyses forget that the demand for labor is a *derived demand*—derived from the ability of households to buy goods and services. If real wages fall, families will feel distress and will find it harder and harder to make ends meet. And this is especially so if there are obligations, such as debts, fixed in euros. In such scenarios, families may be forced to the point of bankruptcy, may lose their homes, and may be unable to pay for basic medicine or the education of their children.

Lower real wages did not necessarily close the gap between the demand and supply of labor because the contraction in aggregate demand reduced the demand for labor at any given level of wages. This shift occurred faster than the downward movement along the demand curve that resulted from lower real wages.

This was also the case for firms. The decrease in aggregate demand had a direct and obvious effect on the demand for investment to produce more (nontraded) goods. The worsening recession meant that there was more spare capacity. Many firms relied on retained earnings to finance investment, and smaller profits lowered retained earnings, thus driving investment down further. But the decrease in demand also forced many firms into bankruptcy, which not only drove job losses but also reductions in organizational capital that further decreased the economy's future economic potential. Since firms are interconnected, the bankruptcy of one firm contributed to that of others. The bankruptcies also weakened banks, forcing some of them into distress and most to curtail their lending. Especially in crisis countries, interest rates on loans increased, even as the ECB lowered its own interest rate. With investment thus curtailed and the cost of capital increased, the contractionary policies did not even have the hoped-for benefit of increasing competitiveness.

## Crisis Countries Could Not Bear the Burden of Adjustment Alone

The attempt at internal devaluations within crisis countries themselves brought a far worse contraction than expected because it savaged the sector of modern economies that did not engage in trade. In essence, Europe asked the crisis countries to strangle the largest sectors of their economies for the purpose of stimulating exports, an illusory solution to the crisis if there ever was one. The declines in the nontraded sector—the roughly two-thirds of the economy that did not engage in trade, including restaurants, dry cleaners, and other local service providers—could not be offset by increases in the traded sector. Yet, these two parts of the economy are not really segregated from each other. Banks, for example, lend to both. Because of this relationship, the bankruptcies in the nontraded sector weakened the financial system and had knock-on effects on the availability of credit in the traded sector.

There is one more reason that internal devaluation and austerity had such disastrous and unanticipated effects: it amplified the credit crunch, with impacts on both demand (investment) and supply (firms without access to working capital had to contract). When the crisis hit, as we have noted, money fled the weak countries for the strong ones. Among the reasons for this migration was a lack of investor confidence that the banks within debtor countries could stay afloat or be successfully bailed out by their governments in the event of failure, an issue we address in Chapter 5. Bank credit is especially important for the small- and medium-sized enterprises that remain the backbone of the European economy, especially in the crisis countries. The crunch created a negative feedback loop. In reality, small-company productivity increases over time through learning-by-doing and building trust with clients. Revenues flow back into research and development and investment, but R&D expenditures are particularly vulnerable in a crisis. In short, austerity itself may have impeded exports because even as wages fell, productivity declined from what it otherwise would have been.

For a few years after the financial crisis, ECB president Jean-Claude Trichet preached an inaccurate and long-discredited doctrine of expansionary austerity—the flawed idea that rapid fiscal consolidation would generate greater confidence in the future and thus a rapid recovery. Nothing the Eurozone experienced in the subsequent years validated this theory, and there is now a wealth of evidence from around the world that discredits the idea.[7]

Many in Germany thought their economic success was partly a result of following the prescription that they had pushed on the rest of Europe. In fact, Germany had recovered from a dark period in the early 1990s. After reunification in 1991, eastern German firms struggled to plug into globalizing markets, pressure rose for tighter reins on spending as the costs of knitting the East and West together multiplied, and the Bundesbank gave no quarter in its fight against domestic inflation.* However, only 15 years later, Germany was again a vibrant and dominant European economic power. It had succeeded in getting workers to accept cutbacks in their overall compensation, which was ultimately viewed as an essential ingredient in its recovery.

But each country within the EU is different, and policies that work in one country may not work in another. What gave rise to Germany's relative success may not have been so much its fiscal fortitude and wage discipline as its fortune. For example, Germany specialized in capital goods, the demand for which was soaring from China, while other places in Europe specialized in the very goods that China was itself producing. Furthermore, the low exchange rate to which we referred earlier, which was far lower than would have been the case without the euro, helped Germany even more.

Also, the fact that a smaller percentage of Germans purchase their own homes than in other countries means that fewer Germans are indebted, which in turn makes adjustment to lower wages easier. In countries with high rates of fixed indebtedness, lowering wages is a sure road to impoverishing large parts of the population. Moreover, the role and organization of unions differ among countries. In many countries, adjustments of the kind that Germany accepted, which were fostered by durable institutions and a decent level of trust between management and labor, would be politically and socially unacceptable.

The German internal devaluation had itself severe consequences for Germany. It resulted in Germany having one of the highest levels of market inequality in the advanced world. What made this bearable, and what prevented the markedly negative effects to the nontraded sector observed elsewhere, was that the Social Market Economy, as Ger-

---

* Ironically, one of the reasons that reunification was so costly was that Germany made a critical mistake in setting the exchange between East and West German marks at the wrong rate. Germany paid a high price for misguided exchange rate policies after 1990 and forced the crisis countries to do the same nearly 20 years later.

mans like to label their system, entailed strong support for those at the bottom, including part-time workers. In contrast, the straitjacket imposed on the crisis countries meant that these countries could not mitigate the adverse effects of austerity policies.

## Europe's Focus on the Wrong Spillovers Curbed Aggregate Demand

The thinking behind the Stability Pact and Maastricht reflected a fear that inflation, rather than recession, was the main danger for Europe and the euro. But, as Greece was facing default, it was searing recession rather than galloping inflation that brought the Eurozone close to cracking. Budget deficits in one country did not automatically lead to system-wide, rampaging inflation.*

At the same time, something else spilled over across the borders within the Eurozone: the effects of Germany's slow, deliberate effort to suppress wages in its effort to preserve its employment and improve its own competitiveness. From 1999 to 2008, German unit labor costs declined by 9 percent in the export-driven manufacturing sector. Between 2000 and 2005, domestic demand actually declined in real terms in Germany. Predictably, the average annual nominal growth rate of revenues from exports to Germany by other Eurozone countries fell sharply in the same period.

The German approach resulted in an internal devaluation of its own, spread out over a decade and imposed by broad social consensus. Labor unions saw wage restraint as a means to preserve the absolute

---

* Of course, some may claim that the reason that the ECB did not give in to political pressure to monetize the debt of profligate governments was that strong strictures had been imposed on the ECB. But even in the United States, where in effect the national debt was monetized in quantitative easing, there was not inflation, largely because there was so much excess supply of goods and labor.

number of jobs, even if they paid less. Business harvested the results in higher sales. The German public reveled in the world's recognition of the country's export machine. And while EU laws do not allow subsidies to particular companies, they did not forbid Germany's strategy, which was to provide broad-based help to those who were in need. This assistance smoothed the way for wage and income cuts, policies that in turn had effects outside Germany. With government buffering society against the untoward effects of low wages and income, the effects were little different from what would have resulted from outright subsidies to firms, something that would itself have been labeled as unfair competition and perhaps even been outlawed by European rules on state aid.

Deep fissures within the Eurozone were all but preordained. The German stance was a new version of the beggar-thy-neighbor policies that vexed European currencies in the 1990s (and likewise vexed the world in the aftermath of the onset of the Great Depression). However, instead of devaluing its currency to juice exports, Germany now devalued something it could still control even with the euro: the price of its own labor.

This approach suppressed domestic spending that might have gone toward exports from Greece, Italy, or Spain, a spending reduction that substantially hit aggregate demand in these countries, as Germany is by far the largest Eurozone economy. And the strategy that worked for Germany—export your way to growth—would not and could not work for others. By definition, not all countries in the world can increase their net exports; not all countries can have a trade surplus; some countries must run deficits. Indeed, globally, the IMF and others have recognized that Germany's large trade imbalances represent a threat to global stability. And of course, for Germany's trading partners in the south of Europe, attempts to export more may be thwarted if Germans do not spend more.

In the years before the crisis, as German surpluses piled up, banks recycled them into loans southward, creating the problem of massive credit expansion in Eurozone countries on the periphery. In short, German practices enabled the buildup of the debt in Greece, Spain, and elsewhere that German policymakers would later forcefully deplore. For every debtor there is a creditor who deserves as much or more blame for a bad loan, since the creditor is typically expert in risk management. But Europe chose to single out the debtors for blame, and to force them to bear the costs of adjustment. The problems with the Eurozone were thus at play long before the crisis revealed what could no longer be ignored.

## The Macroeconomic Framework Created a Cycle of Limited Demand and Greater Inequality

Even before the financial crisis, Europe's economies faced some major challenges. There was steady pressure on middle-income Europeans that stemmed from global market forces, such as globalization creating downward pressure on wages from trade with low-wage developing countries, and from technological change, which seemed to be skills-biased, thus increasing demand for high-skilled workers but lowering it for those with less marketable skills.

The growth of inequality weakened aggregate demand. Those at the bottom spent all that they earned and those at the top did not. This upward redistribution from the bottom to the top weakened aggregate demand. When there is a high level of unemployment and excess capacity, what limits output is aggregate demand. If demand grew more rapidly, then output and incomes would also grow more quickly.

Far graver developments in inequality have followed the crisis and recession in southern European countries than elsewhere. Indeed, part of the argument for austerity was that it would contribute to internal devaluation by forcing wages down and making exports more competitive. In fact, all measures of inequality now show widening gaps. For instance, from 2007 to 2015, the Gini coefficient (before any transfers of income) increased from 49.4 to 60.7 for Greece and from 45.4 to 50.8 for Spain.[8]

And the pressure on state finances meant that Greece, Spain, and others could not cushion the losses through the standard welfare state; even after-transfer Gini coefficients rose.[9] Indeed, in many countries, there were cutbacks in the provision of public services, which hit those in the middle and bottom of the income scale particularly hard. In turn, rising inequality in the EU chipped away at aggregate demand and, by extension, employment. It was part of the vicious cycle into which Europe had fallen.

Of course, there are well-known fiscal and monetary policies that governments could have used to respond to the decrease in aggregate demand caused by growing inequality. For example, if governments spend more and tax less or if interest rates fall and credit availability increases, aggregate demand can be restored to a level that ensures full employment. These standard tools, however, were not available to the afflicted countries in Europe. Monetary policy had been delegated to the European Central Bank and was focused on inflation, to the point where it raised interest rates at a time when an employment focus would have led to lower rates. The Stability and Growth Pact not only prevented afflicted countries from using deficit spending to stimulate their economies, but it also forced these countries to take more contractionary actions. The economic slowdown in these countries, on its own, reduced taxes and increased spending (for unemployment and welfare payments). Thus, the 3 percent deficit limit forced governments either to raise taxes or to cut back spending, which further exacerbated the downturn.

What was bad macroeconomics turned out also to undermine the European project, as citizens questioned the worth of policies and structures that had not delivered promised prosperity. Arguably, Europe's policies and structures had deepened the downturns. Had these countries had more control over their own economic destiny, they could have taken more aggressive actions to stimulate the economy. They might even have been able to stem the outward flow of money that did so much to weaken banking systems.

## Economic Divergence Led to Political Divergence

Europe's failure to respond effectively to the crisis has also made it more difficult for Europe to deal with problems that might arise in the future. For example, it weakened European solidarity. The fact that those in the countries doing well, most significantly Germany, constantly castigated the crisis countries as being lazy and profligate contributed to feelings of resentment and division. In reality, data show that Greeks, on average, actually worked 45 percent more hours than Germans in 2012.[10] And, for countries such as Spain and Ireland that had previously been running large surpluses with low debt-to-GDP ratios, the accusation of profligacy seemed grossly unfair.

The macro-dynamics described earlier also led to a divergence of interests and perspectives within the EU, especially between the debtor countries (the crisis countries in the south) and the creditors (namely, Germany). Debtors and creditors often see the world through different lenses. The convergence criteria were supposed to lead to a Europe with countries that were more similar, and therefore more likely to share similar views. As we noted, the strictures, in fact, led to divergence in economic circumstances that led to a greater divergence in political perspectives.

## Assessing the Impacts of the Downturn

As the crisis fades—though in fact, it has been only a few years since its worst effects began to ease—there is a tendency to move on without much reflection. The crisis may not have been managed optimally, goes the argument, but we have emerged from the crisis; growth, admittedly anemic, has returned. The reality is, though, that Europe will face another major shock sometime in the future and there is little reason to believe it would handle the next shock better than it did this one. Besides, the scars from the crisis are deep; it will take a long time for the wounds to fully heal.

Measuring the impact of the crisis and recession in lost GDP or periods of unemployment significantly underestimates the damage done. Hard-to-measure losses in skills and knowledge that would otherwise have been acquired means that Europe's productivity is lower than it otherwise would have been. The skills not gained through on-the-job training due to high youth unemployment, which exceeded 50 percent in the worst-afflicted countries, diminishes productivity. Those workers, even when they eventually find employment, will have lower lifetime earnings. Furthermore, bankruptcies result in a loss of valuable knowledge embedded inside firms, which again impairs future economic performance.

There is another adverse effect of austerity: high levels of unemployment among marginalized groups. While we may strive to create inclusive growth, low-growth environments are historically not inclusive. Minorities, for instance, often have unemployment rates that are significantly higher than that of the country as a whole. And noninclusive growth generates not only inequality but also a sense of distrust in societal structures writ large, whether in the political system or civic institutions. Economists are just beginning to understand how a lack of trust undermines economic performance. It is one of the reasons that economies with greater inequality perform more poorly.[11]

There are also political consequences: mistrustful voters may become radical voters who look for scapegoats in other marginalized populations.

It follows that what Europe did and did not do for the countries in crisis has a range of societal consequences that go far beyond the short-run impacts on output and employment. Europe should not have imposed such severe austerity and should have done more to help the crisis countries. In the following sections, we more fully describe the necessary changes needed in Europe's policy framework and structure.


## SOLUTIONS

### Break from Austerity and the Rigid Application of the Stability and Growth Pact

Europe often looks to large countries for leadership, but sometimes smaller countries have provided models that might be emulated elsewhere. The case of Portugal proved that growth, not austerity, is the best way forward. Eschewing the tightfisted ways of its predecessor government, a leftist coalition in Portugal, elected in 2015, forged an agenda for growth and jobs. As a result, the country crawled out of recession and began growing again, thus leading to much lower unemployment. This case showed that the best long-run solution to improve public finances is to promote growth. In fact, Portugal's budget deficit fell below 3 percent in 2016.

The EU urgently needs an *Employment*, Stability and Growth

Pact—a plan that takes seriously governments' obligation to ensure that the economy provides jobs for those able and willing to work.

The benefits to Europe of focusing more attention on employment should be obvious. Jobs are important for individuals' self-worth and their sense of well-being.[12] And the increased output that results can be used to increase well-being not only today, but also in the future, through higher investment. Increased government spending on social protection increases well-being by increasing security. Similarly, tighter labor markets will help drive up wages and reduce inequality. The divides that have opened up as a result of increasing inequality can be reduced, with all the social and political benefits that follow.

At the time the Stability and Growth Pact was agreed to, the world had just emerged from a period of rampant inflation. But the problem in today's world is unemployment, not inflation. The central fear that inspired the pact, inflation, shows no sign of appearing, while the dangers of long-term and youth unemployment, in particular, are clearly chipping away at people's faith in the system.

There is simply no evidence that more expansionary policies and higher deficits would automatically lead to runaway inflation, especially if spending is aimed at productivity-enhancing investments (which increase the supply of goods and services on the market), and if there are high levels of excess capacity.

At the time the Stability and Growth Pact was formulated, a simplistic theory dominated in macroeconomics: that inflation was always and everywhere a monetary phenomenon. This pervasive belief was the reason monetary policy was supposed to focus on inflation. The idea also held that if countries ran large deficits, there would be pressure to "monetize" the debt and that the only way to stop this was to prevent countries from having too much debt.

More than a third of a century later, the ideas that formed the basis of the pact are largely discredited. The huge increases in central bank balance sheets during the crisis, in the United States, Europe, and Japan, did not lead to inflation; more often, the worry was about deflation. Moreover, global prices are an integral part of the domestic inflation story, a fact that the Stability and Growth Pact neatly ignores. At the very least, the ability to purchase goods abroad tames domestic inflation.

One of the reasons for not focusing on employment was an excessive faith in markets: if only government played its role, say in limiting inflation, deficits, and debt, the market would play the role of ensuring growth and employment. Again, there is overwhelming evidence now against these hypotheses. Low debt, low deficits, and low inflation are neither necessary nor sufficient for strong, equitable growth; in many cases, they work to undermine what should be these shared objectives.

Instead of building policy around the fear of inflation, it is worth refocusing the debate on how to foster equitable economic growth with full employment. Providing jobs for all requires ending austerity, correcting the exchange-rate misalignment in a more equitable and efficient way, and moving toward more and smarter investment, a subject we address in Chapter 3.

Even within the Stability and Growth Pact, there is more that countries can do. For instance, even within a balanced budget framework (or a 3 percent budget deficit cap), countries can simultaneously increase taxes and expenditures to stimulate the economy. This is called the *balanced budget multiplier*, where GDP goes up a multiple of the increase in government spending. If the taxes and expenditures are chosen carefully, the multiplier can be quite large.

In particular, we should not overlook the growth effect of public investment, which stimulates the economy in the short run and increases long-run productivity. When interest rates are low, the enhanced growth in GDP from such investment will almost certainly offset the increased cost of government borrowing, thereby lowering the ratio of debt to GDP.

Public and private investments are often complementary. For instance, one of the main spurs to investment is the discovery of new technologies, the result of government investments in R&D and especially in basic research. An increase in public investment can "crowd in" private investment, making the multiplier from increased spending on public investment all the greater. Better social protection systems can increase individuals' sense of security, allowing them to spend more in an economic downturn, which again leads to a high multiplier.

In fits and starts, driven sometimes by political pressure from large countries or by an urgent crisis, the EU has tweaked the Stability Pact. However, the EU has not taken decisive steps to distinguish between consumption-oriented public expenditures and investments that open the door to stronger growth in the future or that promote follow-on investments by the private sector, two subjects we address in Chapter 3. That is, restraints on the deficit should be interpreted as applying only to public consumption and not public investment.

At the very least, the EU needs to carve out an exception to the pact when the ECB cannot lower interest rates further. As we have noted, one of the reasons for the seeming lack of concern about the macroeconomic implications of the deficit rules was that monetary policy could be used to restore Europe to full employment. But the ECB cannot ride to the rescue when growth stalls with interest rates near zero. Especially in these circumstances, policy has to allow sufficient fiscal stimulus to restore full employment.

## Recognize that Burden-Sharing Is the Essence of Greater European Integration

The authorities imposing austerity and the other extreme policies that resulted in such suffering often said there were no alternatives. But there were. Greater coordination of policy, a common refrain emanating from EU summits and policy papers, will not do much good if the policy framework itself is flawed. EU strategy remains preoccupied by the need to scrutinize national budgets and police levels of debts and deficits.

Cooperation that included more expansionary policies by the strong economies, such as Germany, and more assistance to the weak countries, such as Greece, would have been better. An objective of European Union policy should have been (and should be in the future) to manage that moment of disaster together rather than to leave Greece or any country to manage on its own. With a common currency, cooperation in adjusting to shocks has to take precedence. At that moment, the EU could have sought a balanced strategy that efficiently and equitably spread the burden between Germany and southern European countries. Instead, the way the burden was shared was unfair, inefficient, and counterproductive. The crisis countries were asked to cut back their spending, not to default on debts, and to cut wages and prices. Alternative policies would have asked the strong countries to increase their spending, wages, and prices, which would have allowed more debt restructuring by the debtor countries. In effect, Germany demanded that the crisis countries bear a disproportionate share of the costs.

If the European project is to succeed, and if the EU is to succeed, there has to be a modicum of solidarity. Economically, solidarity means help for countries in crisis, whether it is in the form of assistance with their unemployment payments, help for their banks, or a loan fund for their small- and medium-sized enterprises. Now, this is where the household metaphor—Merkel's reference to the Swabian housewife— is relevant: members of a family help each other. Families function as a kind of mutual insurance society that helps its members in times of need.

Europe *does* understand these principles. Richer countries generously gave what they called "solidarity funds" to poorer entrants each time the EU expanded. Germany called its tax to rebuild the former East Germany the "solidarity surcharge." What is needed now is a solidarity fund for stabilization to help countries in macroeconomic management—a recognition that the euro took away critical tools that countries could and would have used before they joined the euro. This cross-border help is essential. Without such help, countries having to pay more money for unemployment will have less money to spend on public investments, and thus will fall further behind—a pattern of divergence that has been all too evident over the last decade.

The exact form that such help could take is discussed in various chapters throughout this book. For instance, in Chapter 3, we discuss how the European Investment Bank can be used more extensively to sustain investment in the crisis countries.

## Share Risks and Avoid a False Debate over Debt Mutualization

There are several principles that should guide Europe in thinking about sharing the burden of adjustment, including *equity*: the relative ability of countries to bear the adjustment. Another is *efficiency*: the costs associated with different allocation of adjustments.

It should have been obvious that rich Germany was in a much better position to bear the costs than poor Greece. But it would probably also have been more efficient if more of the burden were imposed on Germany. For a variety of reasons, markets are marked by downward rigidities in wages and prices. Upward adjustments are easier. Thus, putting the burden on Greece by requiring it to lower wages (rather than on Germany) had, overall, much higher costs.

There is another fear, besides inflation, that has animated much of the political debate in Europe—especially in the aftermath of the euro crisis: Germany has worried that in one way or another, it will end up picking up the tabs for other countries. The slogan for this fear is "Europe is not a transfer union." It has taken on the meaning that not only should one country not help another directly, but also that there should not be any risk sharing. The problem was that Greece cannot borrow on its own. It could borrow through the ECB, but the fear is that if Greece defaulted, the rest of Europe would bear the costs.

Between the extremes of full legal mutual responsibility for debt and doing almost nothing, there is a range of options that would fortify cross-border solidarity. There are measures that could help countries facing difficulty, without encouraging the rampant overspending that skeptics seem to assume is inevitable any time the subject arises. The choice is not between Germany paying all Greece's bills and Germany doing nothing. We have more to say about this subject in Chapter 2.

The former German finance minister, Wolfgang Schäuble, took a parting shot at the notion of shared responsibility for government debt in the Eurozone by calling it "complex and expensive financial engineering."[13] But it is essential to understand a crucial point: Eurozone members have already, in the critical moment of the bailout, taken some mutual responsibility for debts accrued by their weaker members, and they did this as much to save German and French taxpayers as to help Greece. If Europe had not helped Greece, there would have been severe consequences for the French and German banking systems. The Rubicon has already been crossed.

Schäuble and others who argue similarly are fixated on what they call the "moral hazard" issue: the risk that the debt mutualization will incentivize countries to become overindebted. This belief is based to a large extent on a total mistrust of the other countries in the EU. But these concerns are grossly exaggerated for at least two reasons. First, no country would put itself through the suffering that Greece has gone through just to get a few more euros transferred from Germany. Countries do make policy mistakes, and events that could not be fully anticipated (like the financial crisis) do occur. Sometimes countries do wind up becoming overindebted, but no country takes on debt in a deliberate attempt to get transfers from its economic partners. Second, Europe can impose constraints both on the amount of lending and the actions of borrowers. Indeed, it already does this extensively.

What is at stake is not so much, as Schäuble suggested, the mutualization of debt, but how much suffering the EU will impose when a European country cannot meet its obligations. Every country recognizes within its borders that when a debtor cannot meet its obligations a debt restructuring is needed. In fact, each country has adopted a bankruptcy code that helps ensure that debt restructuring is done fairly and efficiently. To achieve a more humane balance, the EU has to facilitate this kind of debt restructuring for governments that become overindebted. It needs to recognize overindebtedness is as much a problem of irresponsible lenders as it is of irresponsible borrowers. Lenders typically understand risks better than borrowers, but often they actually encourage excessive indebtedness because they focus on the short-term gains and ignore the long-run risks that are often borne by others.

Indeed, in some circumstances, debt restructuring can be beneficial to both the creditor and the debtor. Debt restructuring allows growth to resume so that the debtor can pay creditors more than what they would, in reality, have otherwise received. Some suggest this is the case for Greece. For instance, a large debt restructuring by Greece would have changed its fiscal position by lowering its interest payments. In the end, it grappled with more than one debt restructuring.

At the time, though, political leaders both in Greece and elsewhere in Europe worried that such a debt restructuring could precipitate a financial crisis in France and Germany, whose banks held many Greek bonds. At the moment of the crisis, leaders in Europe were not sure that German and French citizens would countenance a bailout of their banks. In effect, Greece had to pay a high price for political expediency elsewhere by being forced to buy time for French and German banks to dump their Greek bonds.

The magnitude of the necessary debt restructuring would be reduced if Europe had committed itself to the full employment policies described earlier. It would also be reduced if the creditor countries assumed a bigger role in other aspects of adjustment.

## Address the Most Pressing Externalities

In designing Europe's economic framework, there was much concern about cross-border spillovers, particularly over worries that inflation would spill over from one country to another. That was why, it was argued, each country had to restrain its deficits and debt. As we have explained, however, the assumed link between deficits and debt on the one hand, and inflation on the other, simply was not there.

Europe, however, ignores more important spillovers. Countries with inadequate aggregate demand are imposing costs on others. Germany's current account imbalances, with German exports consistently exceeding its imports over the last two decades, are a symptom of a country that consumes too little and saves too much. This dynamic leads to a higher exchange rate that creates current account deficits in other European countries. These current account deficits, in turn, hurt the other countries' aggregate demand and increase unemployment. Thus, there are significant adverse effects from German policies that lead to sustained trade surpluses.

Ending austerity without an adjustment of real exchange rates will lead to unsustainable current account deficits (trade deficits) in crisis countries. Thus, if there is to be full employment in all countries, there has to be an adjustment—an adjustment that would have been easy to make outside the single currency but difficult to achieve within the Eurozone. Looking back, there was no reason why the deficit countries, including Greece, Spain, and Italy, should have been the only ones required to adjust. Surplus countries like Germany need to participate in the effort as well. Indeed, some economists suggest that putting the burden of adjustment on the surplus countries would have been good for Europe as a whole. An increase in wages in the surplus countries would have reduced imbalances without introducing a deflationary spiral across the whole of the Eurozone. Doing so would have reduced inequality in Germany as well.

There are several ways that Germany could have done itself and all of Europe a favor. For example, a higher minimum wage would have boosted consumption by a socioeconomic group that tends to spend, rather than save, additional earnings. Higher pay for civil servants, long a demand of Germany's public-sector unions, would foster domestic demand as well. Changes in bargaining structures, which we discuss in Chapter 9, would also promote higher wages. Most importantly, stronger government spending will put upward pressure on wages and thus both directly and indirectly lead to increases in aggregate demand, thereby reducing Germany's trade surplus, weakening the euro, and strengthening growth in the crisis countries.

Germany has a medium-term interest in shifting away from its export-heavy economic model. For much of the last decade, it benefited from a historical happenstance. As its neighbors fell into recession or stagnation, Asian economies, above all China, were in the market for a German specialty: machines that make things. However, this voracious appetite for capital equipment will, over time, turn into competition in that very same sphere as Chinese firms learn how to manufacture what they used to buy. More vibrant domestic demand, coupled with healthy European economies, can cushion this inevitable shock.

## Adopt a Macroeconomic Framework that Works

A rethinking of the European Union's macroeconomic framework necessarily involves a recalibration of what is properly the responsibility of EU policy and national, regional, or local authorities. In general, areas that do not give rise to effects on other countries can reasonably remain the subject of policies below the European level. For example, there is no reason Brussels needs to enmesh itself in decisions about local schools, highways, or policing.

The EU did not get the balance even close to reasonable in its response to the economic crisis. The Troika reached deep into the affairs of the most affected countries in ways EU members would never have countenanced in other contexts. A macroeconomic approach based on stimulating aggregate demand, both across Europe and within each country, would have rendered this erosion of the European principle of subsidiarity, the idea that matters are best handled by the lowest-level competent authority, entirely unnecessary.

The EU demanded structural changes that it said were necessary to revive growth in the crisis countries. A closer look at many of these policies—whether it is about the size of loaves of bread, the pricing of drugs in pharmacies, licenses for taxicabs, or definitions of "fresh" milk—reveals they had little if any macroeconomic consequence. Some of these measures, even if successful, would have deepened the downturns by opening markets more to foreign competition, exacerbating current account imbalances, leading to lower incomes for ordinary citizens, and weakening further aggregate demand. This is especially true of reforms in collective bargaining that would have tilted the balance, already skewed, further against workers.

## CONCLUSION

That Europe could do more to stimulate overall European aggregate demand is clear. But even if it did so, there remains the question: What happens in a currency union like the euro to a country that is facing recession? It cannot lower its own interest rate; it cannot devalue its currency. This chapter has outlined a broad set of approaches for how Europe can achieve full employment, or at least steer toward that goal in all countries simultaneously.

Solving Europe's macroeconomic problem, namely ensuring that aggregate demand is sufficiently strong so that there is full employment across Europe, is a condition for achieving shared prosperity. Higher incomes and low unemployment would open up greater possibilities for public investment, directly reduce inequality, promote growth, and create the fiscal space adequate to test new ideas to achieve the inclusive, equitable, and sustainable growth that Europe seeks. This chapter has focused on one key set of instruments: fiscal policy to ensure full employment. The other major instrument is monetary policy, to which we now turn in Chapter 2.

# Chapter 2

# Monetary Policy: Prioritizing Employment

**Before the euro,** Europe had not shared a single currency since Emperor Charlemagne's coinage around the end of the eighth century. It is unsurprising, then, that the euro became a symbol of modern European integration. However, the currency—more particularly the way the Eurozone has been managed—now threatens to discredit or even destroy the European project that birthed it.

The fateful 1992 decision to create the euro was not wholly wrong, but the failure to create institutions that would make it work most certainly was. European leaders did not (or refused to) fully grasp what was required to make a currency arrangement work, especially for such a diverse set of countries. The Eurozone stripped individual countries of two key instruments of adjustment: the exchange rate and the interest rate. But it did not put anything in their place to compensate.

Even worse, the Stability and Growth Pact imposed further strictures that made adjustment even more difficult. A well-designed currency arrangement cannot ensure prosperity, but a poorly designed system like the Eurozone's is a near-guarantee of economic difficulties. Although many economists predicted that the euro would face difficulties if Europe were confronted with a shock, the 2008 financial meltdown, originating from across the Atlantic about a decade after the creation of the euro, turned out to be a deeper crisis than anyone had expected. Even the critics did not fully understand how the deficiencies in the common currency arrangement and the Single Market would deepen and lengthen downturns and result in divergence rather than convergence between the strong and weak countries of Europe.

The euro's architects hoped to entrench the currency as an important source of European identity. It would, they anticipated, help bring a prosperity that would reinforce a commitment to the European project. Instead, the euro and the manner in which the euro crisis was managed, especially in the peripheral countries, resulted in increasing (though by no means fatal) antipathy to the euro and the entire European project. In many countries, anti-euro parties grew in popularity even if they failed to achieve a majority. Some parties found that commitment to the European project, which was once a political advantage, was now the opposite.

In Italy, the euro and the associated strictures are being blamed, rightly or wrongly, for the country's long stagnation. Indeed, many citizens around Europe believe they gave up their economic sovereignty—something leaders did not prepare them for when the euro came into being. Moreover, citizens feel that they sacrificed their sovereignty to entities that do not share the same values or understanding of what makes for good economic performance. If the Troika, in administering their distasteful medicine to Greece, had brought about a quick recovery, that would have been one thing. Instead, the policies it imposed only drove Greece deeper into depression.

Now, vital questions loom over the euro experiment. Does the euro advance prosperity and stability? Are the problems we have seen in the decade after the euro crisis the fault of the individual countries, of the policies that the Eurozone has followed, or of the very structure of the Eurozone itself? What is to be done to ensure there is shared prosperity with full employment throughout Europe?

The process the European Union embraced to establish the euro was deliberative and reasoned, but it took place in the late 1980s and early 1990s at a time when an unfortunate economic perspective dominated the mindset of global central bankers: above all, control inflation. Parts of the world had experienced high inflation and low growth or even stagnation in the 1970s. This stagflation, as it came to be known, helped instill an inflation phobia among central bankers, who subsequently made two incorrect inferences: that the high inflation had caused the low growth and that if one kept inflation low, growth would be high. By the early 1990s, central bankers settled on solutions involving a strong legal mandate for price stability, independence of the central bank from control by elected officials, and sustained communication to markets that they would keep inflation muted.

Thus, the European Central Bank states unequivocally: "The primary objective of the ECB's monetary policy is to maintain price stability. This is the best contribution monetary policy can make to economic growth and job creation." The ECB defines price stability as "a year-on-year increase in the Harmonised Index of Consumer Prices (HICP) for the euro area of below 2 percent. In the pursuit of price stability, the ECB aims at maintaining inflation rates below, but close to, 2 percent over the medium term."[1]

The belief held that if the central banks played their role in macroeconomic stabilization, especially by muting inflation, then the market could do the rest and ensure high growth and efficient allocation of resources. There never was strong theory or evidence behind these doctrines, even at the time when they helped shape the ECB's framework.

There were countries that grew rapidly with high inflation and others that kept inflation low but did not do well. In reality, the 1970s' stagflation was caused by the oil price shock—two successive large increases in oil prices—that simultaneously hurt real incomes and spurred inflation. But the years after the crisis provided even more evidence against inflation fears, as Japan faced low growth and persistent deflation.

The founders of the euro should have realized that the central macroeconomic problem changes from one period to another. They should also have understood the folly of structuring an institution around the problem of the moment, even though it was supposed to ensure Europe's prosperity for decades to come. Unemployment had been the central problem in the past and would turn out to be the central problem for most of Europe in the first decades of the Eurozone. An excessive focus on inflation hampered the ability to restore Europe to full employment. As a result, a massive amount of productive resources went to waste, and even ten years after the crisis, growth rates had not been restored to precrisis levels.

This devotion to bad doctrine also has much to do with a misreading of history, especially in the case of Germany. The 1970s was not the first episode of inflation, though it may have been the first on such a global scale. Germany had experienced hyperinflation in the 1920s, and this event cemented a post-1945 political consensus that the new Bundesbank had to ensure price stability above all else. In the eyes of many, hyperinflation was to blame for the weakening of Germany's embryonic democracy. Yet Hitler and the rise of fascism were born, in an immediate sense, as a result of the high level of unemployment that was part of the global Great Depression of the 1930s—not of Germany's hyperinflation of the 1920s.

But given the consensus on inflation in Germany and some of its northern European allies, any European agreement on a common currency had to be rooted in a commitment to price stability. Moreover, these countries obsessed over fears that fiscal profligacy in southern Europe would somehow lead to EU-wide inflation and demanded the constraints on debt and deficits discussed in Chapter 1.

The first presidents of the ECB, Wim Duisenberg of the Netherlands and Jean-Claude Trichet of France, anchored the singular focus on inflation control during their tenures at the infant central bank. Trichet, in particular, formed a tacit alliance with Berlin, even as some French politicians, supported by many French academics, began questioning the wisdom of the ECB's independence and obsession with inflation.

Trichet turned the Stability and Growth Pact into a religion and used his pulpit—probably the most visible European office the EU had yet created—to go well beyond monetary policy. He preached fiscal rectitude and wage flexibility, both matters that exceeded his remit. The strategy may have steeled the ECB for a crisis that Germans dreaded—massive pressure on the central bank for inflation to bail out profligate governments one after the other—but it left the bank unprepared for a crisis in which the central problem was unemployment. In reality, inflation could have helped deleverage debt-wracked economies. Instead, austerity led to economic contraction.

Even after it was clear that the initial phase of the financial crisis (September and October 2008) would cause a terrible contraction in 2009, Trichet refused to pivot from precrisis orthodoxy. "We would destroy confidence if we blew up the Stability and Growth Pact," Trichet said in December 2008.[2] In fact, Trichet raised interest rates twice in 2011 based on unfounded fears of inflation and all but ignored rising unemployment.

The leadership of the ECB then passed to Italy's Mario Draghi, a man whom Berlin endorsed, via Germany's leading tabloid, as "very German, even downright Prussian."[3] The changing of the guard created room for monetary policy to evolve. As the Greek sovereign debt crisis got underway, Draghi announced the ECB's determination to do "whatever it takes" to ensure Eurozone governments could borrow. This pivot bought valuable time. The massive defaults that could have come from countries being cut off from credit markets were averted. Since then, only Greece and Cyprus, which are among the Eurozone's smaller countries, have had major debt restructurings.

But no one believes that the problems of the Eurozone have really been solved. Not only is Greece still registering weak economic growth and unemployment near 20 percent, but now questions are also being raised about Italy's long-run economic viability, as its new right-wing populist government wrestles with Brussels over government spending. Any major global slowdown, whether originating in the United States, China, or the emerging markets, could trigger another euro crisis. A stronger recovery in the United States could also lead to higher interest rates. If either scenario happens, Italy may be thrown into a crisis, given its already high debt-to-GDP ratio of 133 percent in 2017. In this case, Italy will face a dilemma. It could cut back other expenditures to service the debt, which will further weaken its already shaky economy. Raising taxes would have the same effect, though such a move is politically less likely. The only way out would be for Italy to restructure its debt—a clinical way of saying that the country will never repay what is owed in full—or for the ECB to become the lender of last resort.

Under the current EU framework, Draghi's "whatever it takes" strategy—or at least the conviction that the ECB would follow such a strategy—would be the only tool for preventing a Greece-like panic situation. "Whatever it takes" has typically meant buying up the country's debt when no one else will, in an effort to contain the difference between what interest rates other countries have to offer compared to the benchmark, Germany. Italy's debt is ten times that of Portugal's and far larger than any of the other countries that were in crisis. Would the ECB be willing to buy the requisite amount of Italian bonds to prevent a crisis? Would Germany look the other way as the ECB effectively moves Italian debt onto the ECB's balance sheet—an act that many Germans would view as little different from moving the debt on to their own balance sheets? At the very least, many Germans would object vociferously.

Hopefully, Europe will not have to find out whether the ECB could or would manage an Italian crisis. The likelihood that it would have to come to the rescue, though, depends on whether Europe changes its policies in other areas discussed elsewhere in this book, including greater fiscal flexibility, a banking union, greater cost-sharing for programs like unemployment, better regulation of the financial system, and so on. These reforms would reduce the likelihood, depth, breadth, and duration of a crisis, thus increasing the ability of Europe to cope.

But even with reforms outside the area of monetary policy, European central banking still needs a course correction that makes room for new ideas in the ECB's strategy, governance, and tools.

Also, to an overly large extent, Europe tried to blame the crisis countries for their own travails by suggesting that it was not a problem with the Eurozone's structure or policies, but with the way individual countries had managed their economies. It was another instance of blaming the victim. If only one country had had a problem, that interpretation might have had some plausibility. However, with enough crises in the recent past and the prospect of still more, we must seriously consider that the euro itself, including its underlying rules and governance, may be part of the problem. We must acknowledge that the structure of the Eurozone weakened crisis countries by facilitating capital flight. We must admit that the policy of austerity, and the refusal to consider sufficiently large debt restructuring, and the so-called structural reforms imposed on the crisis countries that were neither well-timed nor well-chosen, combined to deepen the downturns.

While this chapter focuses on monetary policy, a brief discussion of structural policies will help set the scene. In standard macroeconomics, unemployment typically arises when there is an insufficiency of *aggregate demand*, which is the sum total of the demand for goods and services from households, firms, and governments. Monetary and fiscal policies, when appropriately designed, help resuscitate the economy by increasing demand, which leads to higher output and employment.

Structural policies affect the behavior of particular sectors or factors by making an industry more competitive or the labor market more flexible, for example. They affect both aggregate demand and aggregate supply. In well-functioning economies, aggregate demand and supply are balanced. But often, at least for a while, one falls short of the other. When aggregate demand exceeds supply, there will be strong inflationary pressures. More common is that aggregate demand is less than supply, a situation Europe has experienced for a better part of a decade. In that case, of course, firms only produce what they can sell. (They may try to sell more by lowering prices, which is why periods of excess demand are often associated with deflationary pressures.) Well-designed structural policies, those that make the economy more productive at any level of wages and prices, increase the supply. However, if demand does not move in tandem with supply, structural policies have no effect on output since there is already excess supply. In such a case, policies can simply exacerbate the gap between demand and supply. Over the long run, such policies may have a positive effect on standards of living, for if and when aggregate demand increases enough to restore the economy to full employment, output at full employment will be higher. But an economy has to get to full employment first.

For that reason, we are focusing on the short-run impact here. In the short run, structural reforms increase output if they increase aggregate demand and decrease output if they decrease aggregate demand.

A review of the structural reforms imposed by the Troika in the euro crisis makes clear that most of them worsened the downturn. The labor market reforms enabled firms to lower wages, the immediate impact of which was a lowering of demand. Indeed, demand could have been lowered even before the policy took effect, simply because households realized that their incomes would be decreasing. The hope was that lower wages would translate into lower prices, and then lower prices into more exports. That process, however, was long and uncertain.

In the case of Greece, exports only barely increased. Part of the reason for this small change was that the cost advantage that lower wages provided was more than offset by the adverse effects on access to funds that resulted from Troika policies.

(Here, we might mention a peculiar measure of the Troika: the demand that milk be considered fresh so long as it is not more than 10 days old. Some argued that the reason for the change was to enhance sales of cheaper milk that had to be shipped from the Netherlands. But if that happened, the income of Greece's dairy farmers would decrease, thus lowering aggregate demand in Greece and exacerbating its depression. Moreover, Greece's trade deficit, already a major problem, would also increase.)

Thus, the critical issue facing the Eurozone is the reform of the Eurozone itself. To be sure, there are reforms within the individual countries that would enhance the overall performance of the Eurozone. Moves such as easing professional licensing requirements would facilitate cross-border migration by creating a true Eurozone-wide labor market for these professionals. However, such a reform might actually exacerbate downturns in individual countries, since a negative shock to one country would lead to both capital and professionals leaving, thus hollowing out the economy. Moving professionals to where the returns on their skills are highest maximizes Eurozone GDP but lowers that of the crisis country—once again promoting divergence rather than convergence. Even in the United States, attention is paid to how policies affect particular states. In the European Union, surely concerns about policies that further weaken fragile democracies should be of concern.

As we noted in the last chapter, the key challenge to make a common currency function is to achieve full employment in every country simultaneously when one no longer has two critical tools—exchange rates and interest rates—to differentiate policy among the countries. Fiscal policy (government expenditures) are among the key instruments. That is why in the previous chapter we called for a solidarity fund for stabilization, which would help those countries that are hit by a shock to attain full employment without taking on excessive deficits and debt. But, so far, the EU budget is too small to provide this kind of assistance. In the last crisis, monetary policy was the only available instrument and it did not differentiate among countries in different circumstances. An excessively narrow focus on inflation resulted in the ECB worsening the crisis and increasing divergence under Trichet. Later, a broader interpretation of the ECB's remit enabled Draghi to contain the crisis.

In spite of the kudos given to the ECB for eventually containing the crisis, there is deservedly much dissatisfaction with its overall conduct of monetary policy. Inevitably, as we have noted, every country eventually recovers, so recovery itself is not a sign of whether a policy works. Instead, the efficacy of policy is a matter of how long the downturn lasts, how deep it is, and how much damage it causes. Europeans are right to seek a better way. ECB actions did not contribute enough to shortening the crises and making them less deep. They arguably made crises worse in several instances, namely in Ireland and Greece. Afflicted countries will take years to recover from these poor ECB policies. In the following pages, we describe in greater detail the problems with the structure and conduct of the ECB, and what can be done.

## PROBLEMS

### *The ECB's Inflation-Fighting Mandate Has Proved Badly Counterproductive*

As Europe set about creating the Eurozone, the prospect of a money-printing ECB feeding inflation became the risk that EU leaders sought to avoid. As a result, they gave too little thought to the role that monetary policy could play in sustaining higher growth and employment, as well as to the downside of excessively tight monetary policy reducing growth and employment. In fact, the damage done by the financial crisis and subsequent recession has been enormous, with trillions in lost output. The EU, in short, designed the ECB for a problem of the past (inflation) and did not give it enough flexibility to fight twenty-first-century problems (employment and stagnation).

The inflation-only mandate of the ECB had still other effects. For example, when inflation crept upward in 2005 due to high energy or food prices, the buying public suffered the consequences. Raising interest rates under these circumstances may have reduced inflation somewhat, but at a high cost—lower growth and higher unemployment. Workers thus suffered triply, from higher food and energy prices, from higher interest rates, and from lower growth and employment.

Indeed, all of these ripple effects from a mandate that was fixated on price stability, which had no focus on employment, inevitably meant that the average unemployment rate was higher than it would have been otherwise, regardless of whether there was a financial crisis. In this scenario, there would always be a greater gap between actual and potential output. Inflation targeting, entailing increasing interest rates whenever inflation exceeds or even approaches the 2 percent target, ensured this outcome.

Three widespread beliefs dominated thinking of the time. The first we have already noted: if only monetary authorities stopped inflation, the private sector could take care of the rest by ensuring high growth and full employment. The second was that monetary authorities should be given simple rules to implement, rules like inflation targeting or the even simpler monetarist rule that prevailed for years, before it was discarded: just increase the money supply at the rate of growth of the real economy. And the third was that the best way to run macroeconomic policy is to assign different institutions different targets, with central banks setting the target of price stability (to be achieved through the simple rule described above).

Each of these beliefs has been widely, though not universally, discredited in the subsequent decades. Inflation has been tame in the advanced countries, but this low inflation led to neither sustained and equitable growth, nor stability. More was needed, but the ECB was hard put to deliver, even if strong action by the ECB under Draghi played an important role in preventing a total financial collapse. Its mandate primarily proved more of a constraint around effective macroeconomic management than a benefit. Perhaps Trichet even felt this way when he raised interest rates at a time that, from a broader economic perspective, could not have been more inappropriate.

The world has proven more complex than the one for which these simplistic rules were designed. The truth is that inflation can arise from many different sources, including from excessive aggregate demand or from a shock to costs, such as an increase in oil prices. These different shocks necessitate different responses. But a simplistic policy that responds to every problem in the same way is not going to lead to growth with stability and full employment. Moreover, the idea that good macroeconomic outcomes could be achieved without close coordination between fiscal and monetary policies, as well as between policies conducted at the European and the national levels, was also based on simplistic and unrealistic models.

## Deficiencies in ECB Governance

There was another idea that was fashionable at the time that infected the governance of the ECB: a central bank should be "independent," which in practice meant "free of political control." The idea was to give the ECB a clear mandate (price stability) and leave the rest to technocrats. It also followed that if those lacking specialized knowledge would simply step aside, people trained in the task could steer monetary policy in an optimum direction. Underlying this assumption was again the fear of inflation and fiscal profligacy, that politicians would presumably be incentivized to overheat the economy to win elections, and also have the central bank buy their bonds to finance irresponsible government spending. There was a distrust in democratic accountability.

Not surprisingly, central bankers loved this doctrine. It gave them unfettered powers within their limited remit, and they could and would expand their remit in many ways. But perhaps the most appealing part of the doctrine for them was that being at the center of the Eurozone economy gave them a bully pulpit from which they could comment on every other aspect of economic policy—government spending, the flexibility of labor markets, and even the welfare state.

Ironically, bankers were extraordinarily critical of direction from others. Trichet was quick to slap down any national official outside the European system of central banks who tried to push the ECB in one direction or another. Jean-Claude Juncker, later president of the European Commission, once commented that Trichet "speaks of the need for an independent central bank in an almost erotic manner."[4]

The EU endowed the ECB with virtually total independence. Decisions are made by a council consisting of the six executive board members and, on a monthly rotating basis, the heads of four of the five largest Eurozone countries' and 11 of the 14 smaller countries' central banks. The executive board members, in turn, are appointed by the heads of government of the Eurozone countries for an eight-year, nonrenewable term. Each of the central banks within each country is required to be independent. The ECB was ensconced in Frankfurt, away from the hurly-burly of Brussels, with its politicians and Eurocrats. The bank assumed new quarters in a handsome twin-skyscraper construction designed by an avant-garde Austrian architect.

The 1992 Maastricht Treaty legally ticked all the boxes to fence off the ECB from political pressure. The treaty barred politicians from even attempting to influence the ECB's conduct of monetary policy. Of course, the decision to make the ECB independent, to give it a single-minded focus on inflation, and to leave out adequate political accountability, was itself a political decision.

The decisions of the ECB have consequences for the creation and, most importantly, the distribution of wealth, something that ought to be a political question. Because all policy is conducted in the presence of uncertainty, ECB decisions affect who bears what risks. If self-government (democracy) means anything in the twenty-first century, it is sovereignty over important factors in our economic lives. Here, it should be noted that the conduct of monetary policy affects different groups in various ways.

Higher inflation reduces the value of debt held by creditors, who seek price stability above all else. Fighting inflation typically entails raising interest rates, which lowers growth and employment. This hurts workers in particular (at the very least in the medium term) by discouraging investment. Moreover, lower interest rates decrease the income of retirees who depend on interest from bonds for part of their income, and they also typically increase the value of equities, which are disproportionately held by the more well-to-do.

The focus on inflation was thus a political decision. Had the ECB been given a different mandate, say, one with greater emphasis on employment, inflation would have almost surely been higher but so too would have been the average level of employment.* But even within the bank's inflation mandate, there are decisions that have to be made that also have distributional consequences.

If the mandate and structure of the ECB revealed a bias toward a certain type of policy, then the central bank's actions during the crisis that exhibited greater responsiveness toward concerns of certain constituencies should also give us pause. Though one might want to believe that the ECB reflects only the broad interests of society throughout the Eurozone, its handling of the financial sector evinced a particular concern for the industry's well-being over that of other segments of society. It sought to ensure the well-being and stability of the financial sector, but there might have been other ways to protect the flow of funds to the economy without narrowly bestowing such largesse on that sector, inflicting so much pain on the rest of society. The ECB's actions, particularly in Greece and Ireland, however, are there for all to see.†

To bring banks through the most intense phase of the financial crisis, hundreds of billions of euros flowed to commercial banks in the most massive government–private sector assistance program ever launched in Europe. Much of this money came from the ECB in the form of loans at below-market interest rates and were made without any decision by elected governments or even EU leaders. It is import-

---

\* At the time of Maastricht, a particular economic doctrine called the natural rate of unemployment was fashionable. This doctrine claimed that if one tried to push unemployment below this natural rate, then inflation would accelerate, growing ever faster. Thus, if one did not want to have ever-accelerating inflation, one couldn't push the unemployment rate down below this natural rate. In this view, then, there was, at least in the long run, no sustainable trade-off between inflation and unemployment. The technical task of the ECB was simply to ascertain the natural rate and devise the best policies for making sure that the economy kept it. This theory has largely been discredited since; if there is such a natural rate, it is not stable. But even if the theory were correct, there are still trade-offs, say, between a higher unemployment rate today and a lower one in the future, with distribution effects of the kind that should not be left to technocrats alone to make.

† It is worth noting that similar criticisms can be raised against other central banks, including the US Federal Reserve.

ant to note that this program dwarfed any welfare program ever constructed to alleviate the suffering of ordinary citizens. Eventually, the ECB even went on to buy bonds issued by large corporations, in Germany for example, putting small- and medium-sized enterprises at a disadvantage—companies that play such a crucial role in periphery countries like Greece and Portugal.

Perhaps the most disturbing episodes of the ECB's performance during the crisis involved the use of its leverage (its power) to force policy changes far afield of its remit of monetary policy. One might expect a corollary of the ECB's legal insulation from democratic politics to be that its influence is restricted to monetary policy. However, the central bankers felt no such constraint.

In 2010, the ECB pressured Ireland not to impose losses on bank bondholders as part of a financial restructuring, thus saddling Irish taxpayers with costs that should have been borne by the banks' borrowers and bondholders. Similarly, it demanded a detailed list of wage-reduction and deregulation measures from Spain in 2011 in exchange for financial assistance. And the central bank leaned on Greece in 2015 to accept a high budget surplus requirement even as the IMF warned that a debt restructuring was what was urgently necessary.

The ECB had enormous power with which it could leverage demands of its partners in the Troika (the European Commission and the IMF) during the crisis, something seen most clearly in the case of Greece. Within its powers, the ECB could paralyze the financial system, and it did. Greece had to severely limit withdrawals of cash from banks during the peak of the confrontation between the Troika and the Greek government in the summer of 2015. The fact that these levers of power were in the hands of an institution with limited political accountability, whose mindset was too close to that of the financial sector, and whose mandate and governance was already being questioned in many quarters, was disturbing.

That the ECB made mistakes during the crisis is not prima facie evidence of an inherently flawed design; human beings are imperfect. But policy decisions that over time bend toward the interests of the financial sector and creditors, and that also reflect a particular mindset and set of interests, should prompt us to think about why. The answer lies in the governance behind the policy. A different governance, for instance, one in which workers had a greater voice, could lead to different decisions. In this case, more attention would be paid to employment and growth and less to the erosion of bond value. The result of this would be more vibrant economic performance from the standpoint of ordinary citizens.

## The EU Needs Instruments Beyond the ECB to Make the Euro a Success

The biggest challenge in creating a framework for the common currency was posed by the need to respond to *asymmetric shocks*, a term that describes how a single event (a financial crisis, for example) can affect individual national economies or parts of an economy differently. If a shock affected everyone in the same way, then the ECB could return everyone to full employment by simply lowering interest rates.

The ECB also did not consider what would happen if the benchmark interest rate fell to zero amid excessively high unemployment, which is exactly what happened. If it had, it might have proposed revising the Stability and Growth Pact in the way suggested in Chapter 1: when the interest rate hits zero, then governments should be allowed to stimulate the economy through fiscal policy, even if doing so would breach deficit targets.

Architects of the euro and the Stability and Growth Pact anticipated that debt-to-GDP constraints would not prevent countries from being able to respond, even to an asymmetric shock. The thinking among some was that countries would run budget surpluses in good times so that they could spend extra in bad ones. However, the crisis occurred too soon after the establishment of the euro for most countries to have amassed the economic buffer necessary.

The crisis also showed the flaw in this reasoning. Ireland began the crisis with a very low debt-to-GDP ratio, and under the theory behind the pact, should have been well positioned to respond to the shock. Yet, as the crisis progressed, private debts quickly became public because the government assumed responsibility for paying back the bondholders of the banks that were going bankrupt. This was done in part at the insistence of the ECB itself. Ireland's debt ratio rose to an unsustainable level almost overnight, well beyond the strictures of the convergence criteria.

The crisis demonstrated one further point: the stricture of a deficit-to-GDP ratio of less than 3 percent was too tight.* Of course, even before the crisis, Germany and France had violated this restraint. But the 3 percent limit simply provided too little stimulus, especially in the absence of adequate assistance from European partners and within a poorly designed Eurozone working within a poorly designed Single Market. In short, the limit condemned the crisis countries to unacceptably high levels of unemployment.

In its attempt to compensate for the absence of effective instruments with which to respond to asymmetric shocks (notably greater government spending) and with the short-term interest rate already at zero (even as most European countries had unacceptably high interest rates), the ECB got creative. First, it undertook aggressive *quantitative easing*, the name given to monetary stimulus that goes beyond low-

---

* Recall our earlier discussion that the numbers used to define good behavior—2 percent inflation, 3 percent deficit-to-GDP ratio, 60 percent debt-to-GDP ratio—were essentially pulled out of thin air. It's important, accordingly, to assess the consequences: What would happen if they were, at least at the margin, tightened or loosened?

ering benchmark short-term rates to zero. It means buying not just short-term notes (the conventional approach of monetary policy), but also long-term bonds, and in some cases, bonds that were issued by the private sector. The bonds purchased via quantitative easing amounted to an average monthly pace of more than €60 billion from 2015 to 2017. The policy did lower long-term borrowing costs, especially for the countries that had been facing a debt crisis. Interest rates on Greek bonds fell to 4.4 percent and on Spanish bonds to 1.4 percent at the end of 2017. In 2014, the ECB went even further by lowering interest rates on overnight deposits in the central bank to negative 10 basis points, then lowering them to negative 40 basis points in 2016.

But the effects on the real sector of these innovative policies were both muted and much delayed. Borrowing conditions for smaller enterprises typically differ markedly from those of governments. Indeed, interest rates on government bonds can go down even as the interest rates that small businesses pay go up. If the economy is moving into recession and depression, lenders will worry about the ability of these small firms to weather the storm. They may even refuse to lend to small businesses.[5]

The small impact of lowering interest rates below zero should not have come as a surprise. Lowering interest rates from 4 percent to 0 had not resuscitated the economy. Why should one think that lowering another 10 or even 40 basis points would do so? Indeed, there are reasons that such policies could even lead to reduced lending if not well designed. The negative interest rates were like a tax imposed on banks on money they kept in reserve at the central bank. This tax adversely affected banks' balance sheets, which had already been weakened greatly by the crisis. Accordingly, banks grew more cautious in their lending, even though the negative interest rate was designed to incentivize them to lend. But if expected returns to lending are low, because of the recession, this balance-sheet effect could outweigh the incentive effect.

It would be months and years before borrowing conditions for small- and medium-sized enterprises eased significantly, which exerted an enormous toll, especially on the crisis countries. And in those countries, the real issue was the availability of credit. With capital (in the form of deposits) leaving the crisis countries for the stronger countries, banks had to restrain their lending.

Monetary policy is one of the critical tools for maintaining macroeconomic stability. What matters is not only low and stable inflation, but overall stability in the economy and full or almost full employment in every country. In the aftermath of the 2008 crisis, monetary policy alone was not able to do this, neither in Europe nor the United States. The United States, however, used monetary policy to greater effect. Why did Europe fail to do so?

# SOLUTIONS

## Broaden the ECB Mandate

Europe needs a vibrant debate about the merits of the Maastricht framework for the ECB and whether that framework is in accord with current thinking about macroeconomics. Both economic understandings and the European economy have evolved over the more than quarter century since Maastricht.

The most important reform for the ECB is to broaden its objectives to include an employment goal. But changing an EU treaty is a long haul, even under the best of circumstances. The ECB under Draghi has demonstrated, though, that there is some flexibility within the current rules as it has exhibited more creativity than the prior decade under Trichet and Duisenberg. What follows are some ideas that might create the flexibility that the ECB and European monetary policy so desperately need:

■ *Use the discretion that Maastricht does provide.* Price stability at the ECB currently means below but close to 2 percent. But this number is not specified by the Maastricht Treaty; it is an interpretation. Why is it not zero? Why not 3 percent? There is no legal answer to these questions. It is a matter of judgment. Setting a higher inflation target could help close the deep fissures between the European core and periphery. It could also broaden the interpretation still further to state that price stability means inflation "not below 1 per cent and not above 4 per cent," thus providing more room within which it could exercise discretion.

■ *Use core inflation metrics.* Unlike the Federal Reserve, the ECB bases policy on *headline inflation* (the rate of increase in overall prices) rather than on *core inflation* (inflation in the economy that excludes the volatile food and energy sectors). The ECB approach poses great problems when there are supply-side shocks, such as the particularly sharp spikes in energy and food prices before the crisis. Such shocks also often have adverse effects on domestic demand because consumer spending is diverted to pay more for imported oil. In these circumstances, focusing on headline numbers could lead to higher ECB rates, even though tighter money will not reduce oil prices and will not even reduce inflation, except via the blunt instrument of reducing demand and increasing unemployment. The increases in food and energy prices that Europe experienced just before the crisis did indeed prove transitory, obviating the need for rate increases. The Federal Reserve has demonstrated for years that core inflation is not just a viable metric for central bankers, but a preferable measure for attaining economic stability.

■ *Shift the focus to include, and under current circumstances emphasize, the risks of low inflation or deflation.* At the time the Maastricht Treaty was signed, memories of high-inflation episodes were still fresh in European minds. Today, however, the problems are deflation, disinflation,* and unemployment. This means the ECB should be particularly attentive to the risks that these problems pose. It once attempted to nip nascent inflation in the bud, recognizing that because of long lags, it was important to act preemptively. Now that Europe is in an era of weak demand, and that the threat has shifted to deflation, and disinflation, the ECB also needs to think ahead.

■ *This greater balance in focus should also be reflected in the ECB's research agenda.* Just as ECB research used to dwell on the reasons behind persistent inflation in certain sectors or geographies of the European economy, the central bank should now spend more time researching the causes of unduly low inflation and what can be done about it. The ECB undertook a valuable research exercise in 2015 and 2016, which showed that unorthodox monetary policy (such as quantitative easing) helped to expand aggregate demand in these periods of economic weakness.[6] If central bankers can anxiously scan the horizon for wages that rise too fast and threaten to push prices higher, they can surely do so for persistently low inflation, deflation, and disinflation.

■ *Make any inflation target symmetrical, or even biased toward preventing deflation, since periods of high unemployment are associated with deflationary pressures.* If inflation dips too low, market participants need to understand that the ECB will react as strongly as it would if inflation threatened to rise, by providing strong monetary stimulus. For too long since the financial

---

* Deflation occurs when (average) prices fall; disinflation when the rate of increase of prices is reduced. Unanticipated disinflation can have strong adverse effects. Firms that had anticipated higher prices in order to pay back loans can find themselves in distress, even bankruptcy.

crisis, deflation has stalked the European economy, but the ECB dithered in making its goal to raise inflation clear. This must be a permanent feature of ECB policy.

■ *Use banking supervision and regulation creatively to encourage growth and stability, thus enhancing productive investments and discouraging risky speculation.* A common refrain of hawkish central bankers was that too-easy money creates asset bubbles and other distortions in lending. Sensible supervision could address such problems by restricting lending in areas where there are nascent bubbles, especially in real estate. This action would encourage more lending to more productive activities. Some central banks take an even more proactive policy by setting minimum levels of lending, say, to small- and medium-sized enterprises. These policies allow more lending without the creation of bubbles, even at low interest rates. They ensure that more of the credit that is created goes to stimulating the economy.

■ *Manage supervision in ways that do not exacerbate economic downturns.* Now that the ECB has a larger role in bank supervision, it needs to acknowledge fully that the way it engages in banking oversight can have significant macroeconomic consequences.* It is one thing when an isolated bank has a problem, but quite another when the banking system of a region or a country is facing difficulties. Both inferences about the underlying causes and concerns about the consequences of actions are markedly different. Even when banks have lent prudently, loans will sour in the face of a prolonged downturn, such as

---

* One of the central messages of Stiglitz and Greenwald, 2003 (*Towards a New Paradigm in Monetary Economics*, Cambridge: Cambridge University Press) is that one cannot separate out regulatory policy from macroeconomics. This is now widely recognized with macroprudential regulation; but other, even more micro-oriented policies, e.g., those associated with forbearance, also have macroeconomic consequences.

what faced large parts of Europe in the aftermath of the crisis. And overly tight supervisory actions, such as forcing banks either to cut back lending or raise more capital, have macroeconomic consequences and may well backfire. Especially in deep downturns, raising new capital is a virtual impossibility. In this case, the only alternative is to cut back on lending; but when many banks do so simultaneously, the economy sinks deeper into recession, which weakens banks' balance sheets. To remedy this dilemma, careful forbearance is required, which may imply that different standards are applied in different countries. Thus recognizing that when the circumstances are different, the consequences of supervisory actions should also be different, and accordingly what the supervisors do should differ.* This differentiated supervision can play a key role in addressing the greatest challenge posed by the common currency: the achievement of simultaneous full employment in all countries after the Eurozone has been hit by an asymmetric shock.

■ *Use whatever powers the ECB has to encourage small-business lending.* It could make access to ECB refinancing dependent on a bank allocating a minimal percentage of its asset portfolio to small-business lending, much as the United States pushes banks to lend equitably through the Community Reinvestment Act.†

■ *Stick with monetary policy and bank regulation.* Under Maastricht, the ECB's remit is limited to monetary policy. Now it

---

* This is consistent with the policy recommendation made in Chapter 1 entailing providing more scope for different countries within the Eurozone to take different actions, reflecting differences in economic circumstances.

† The ECB implements monetary policy through its weekly refinancing operations (the "repo" process) in which banks swap collateral for credit from the central bank. It could use this channel to promote lending to small- and medium-sized enterprises, possibly through explicit restrictions on its dealings with banks that lend insufficiently to small businesses.

also has a role in banking supervision. There is no reason central bankers should use these powers to advocate for fiscal policies emphasizing spending cuts, weaker labor-protection rules, a weaker welfare system, or trade policy.

## Reform ECB Governance

There is nothing God-given about an independent central bank of the sort that the European Union created. Different bank structures hold out the possibility not only of better economic performance, with more concern about growth and employment, but also of greater democratic accountability. There are a wide range of degrees in the de jure or de facto independence of a central bank. In Britain, for example, the government sets the inflation target and the Bank of England must execute a strategy to achieve it.

The British recognize that the trade-off between inflation and employment and growth is a quintessentially political one, a decision that should not be delegated to technocrats or to an independent body, and especially one in which the mindset of the financial sector predominates. The issue of governance becomes even more important as central banks have taken on roles that go well beyond simply setting interest rates, such as we have seen in the context of the interventions in the euro crisis.

Other countries have had independent central banks, but their central bank governors have realized that even though independent, there has to be some degree of political accountability and sensitivity. Echoing this sentiment, Paul Volcker, chairman of the Federal Reserve from 1979 to 1987, famously said, "Congress has created us, and Congress can un-create us."

Both during the crisis and in the run-up to it, some of the best-performing central banks included those with less independence, such as in India and Brazil. Here, what matters is not only de jure independence, but also how central bankers and governments behave (the norms and customs). In a broad sense, the EU needs to foster an environment in which the ECB follows the right norms. That means having mechanisms that keep the ECB focused on monetary policy, open-minded as to how to achieve the desired outcomes, and aware of the necessity of coordination. Wise monetary policy realizes that there is, accordingly, discretion in both targets and instruments.

Too many central banks disproportionately reflect the particular perspectives of the financial sector. The interests of workers are under-represented at best, but mostly not represented at all. This mindset creates a bias toward higher interest rates, and a greater concern about the well-being of the bankers, the banks, their shareholders, and their bondholders. In turn, it generates less concern about employment and stability, and more about inflation.

Given that monetary policy is so complex, it is understandable that central bankers should have expertise. And there are, moreover, dangers from politicization. But the same can be said for many other areas of policy that are run perfectly well without central bank–style independence. The struggle of modern democracy has been to combine democratic accountability and representativeness with expertise. Policy may entail government setting broad goals to be implemented by technocrats, but within a democratic review process. Maastricht did not strike this balance. Part of the problem was with the remit, since monetary policy has broad effects, but the ECB was instructed to focus only on inflation.

Some countries have tried to rectify this bias by restricting representation from the financial sector on the governing bodies of central banks and ensuring some representation of workers. This type of governance is difficult within the structure of the ECB, whose board is composed of representatives from each country. Still, there could be a commitment to broader representation in the choice of the six members of the executive board.

Changing ECB governance, like changing the ECB mandate, will not be easy. The central banking establishment would no doubt rally against any changes. Here are some ideas of what might be done short of a wholesale change in ECB governance:

- *A debate involving all stakeholders.* The ECB would take a step in the right direction if it simply encouraged a public debate on what, precisely, "price stability" entails. There is nothing magic about 2 percent inflation. There is no cliff to fall off of if inflation exceeds that, and no reason that only central bankers should have a say in that debate. It is more of a political decision than the technocrats want to admit. Britain has admitted this and so has the United States. It is time for Europe to also break the taboo.

- *Improved oversight by the European Parliament.* The ECB president already testifies before European legislators, but a vibrant culture of oversight has yet to take root. In today's world, central banks do far more than just change interest rates; they intervene in the economy in a multitude of ways, especially in crises. During the euro crisis, the ECB engaged in numerous activities that were highly political, and in retrospect seem at a minimum questionable, especially in Ireland, Greece, and Spain. In a democratic society, there has to be some accountability for an institution with so much power.

- *Better oversight by the European Council.* The council represents the EU countries. It meets at the leader level but more frequently at the minister level. Top ECB officials should report regularly to those ministers, and not only finance ministers (who often reflect the views of the financial sector). Labor and economy ministers deserve a seat at this table. Monetary policy is too important to be left to finance.

■ **Enhanced transparency.** The ECB's actions during the crisis, which ran far afield of monetary policy, often came to light only through dogged journalism or revelations by ex-officials. At the very least, the European public deserves to know in real time what the ECB is doing, including if the ECB is trying to influence policy that is not directly related to its mandate.

■ **Debate other aspects of ECB policy, including what it accepts as collateral.** The collateral that the ECB accepts affects the loans that banks are willing to make; it can affect the relative competiveness of different countries and companies. Thus, what collateral the ECB accepts merits a public decision; the decision should not be made behind closed doors.

■ **Analyze unorthodox measures used during the crisis, based on deeper research into their consequences.** These and possibly other instruments should be added to the toolkit. The ECB embraced quantitative easing long after the Federal Reserve and the Bank of Japan did, and only then after a fraught debate. How these policies are implemented can also make a great deal of difference,[7] and there needs to be more of a public debate about that.

■ **Facilitate a vibrant discussion of the role of monetary policy in fostering inequality.** Especially in an era marked by large and growing inequalities, monetary policy needs to be sensitive to its potential impacts on inequality and the relating differential impacts on various segments of society. What one *measures* affects what one does. More closely monitoring impacts on distribution might affect decision making. At the very least, it will help inform other parts of the government on what policies or actions might need to be taken to offset the increased inequality that results from monetary policy.*

A proper reform of the ECB necessarily includes limitations on what the central bank can demand of governments. As the ECB has taken on a central role in ensuring governments' access to financial markets and in buying government bonds to bring down the interest rates they have to pay, it has de facto increased its powers. It now has the power to demand much of governments, as was evidenced too clearly in Ireland and Greece. What was demanded of these countries particularly reflected the interests and perspectives of the financial sector. It should be deeply disturbing that an unelected and unrepresentative body has such powers, which it used and abused, to make such demands.

## Create an Improved European Stability Mechanism and a Banking Union

There will be shocks in the future, and Europe needs to learn from the failures of the past to design a better way to respond to them. Under the extreme pressure of the sovereign debt crisis, the *European Stability Mechanism* (ESM) was created in 2012 as a €500 million fund to provide fiscal support to members of the Eurozone that are facing financial difficulties. It was a start: big enough to handle a crisis in a small country, but far short of what would be needed were there a banking crisis in a large one.

Europe also realized that the lack of a common deposit insurance played a big role in exacerbating the euro crisis, as money fled the crisis

---

* Taking into account the effects on inequality is especially important for the EU, given the paucity of instruments available to counteract them.

countries. Creating a system of common deposit insurance is part of a broader agenda of creating a banking union in which all banks in the Eurozone would also have a common supervisor, and in which there would be a common procedure for bank resolution (for dealing with insolvent banks). While there is now an agreement to gradually move forward with a banking union, the delay may prove costly, especially if another crisis hits before it is fully established. Without common deposit insurance, given the Single Market, money could once again freely flow out of a crisis-hit country and its banks, creating cutbacks in lending that would deepen the downturn. The Eurozone is still inherently unstable in the presence of asymmetric shocks.

Mutual support in times of crisis should be the default scenario, and not a grudgingly granted gift from northern Europe's fiscal curmudgeons to their profligate wards. Without cooperation and trust it will be virtually impossible for the single currency system to be successful, and the Eurozone will drive further economic divergence and political resentment rather than help individual countries manage asymmetric shocks.

Currently, obtaining assistance from the ESM amounts to a formalization of the hat-in-hand process that the Troika oversaw during the crisis. To receive assistance, countries must agree to specific fiscal rules and various policy changes. To date, the ESM has been used to aid a bank recapitalization in Spain and a sovereign bailout in Cyprus.

The issue of conditionality has long been central in aid debates. What conditions should be imposed on a country for it to receive aid? The worry is that with no conditions, the money would be wasted, and that citizens in the benefactor country would find such aid unacceptable. On the other side, demanding too much amounts to the country giving up its economic sovereignty. Moreover, because donor countries are often not fully apprised of all the relevant circumstances in the recipient countries, conditionality has not worked well. It would be far better to provide aid based on trust: on an agreement by both parties on how the assistance will be used, and a mutual understanding about safeguards and benefits of such aid. Such a level of trust should be particularly important among countries in the EU. Severe conditionality imposed to get access to ESM funds not only undermines that trust, but it also signals there is none.

Within certain countries in Europe, there is a fear that without stringent conditionality, one country or the other will take advantage of the ESM, a problem we alluded to in Chapter 1. There is much hand-wringing over this moral hazard, and the risk that because money is being made available for countries in crisis, governments will run their country in such a way merely to access it. The answer revolves around one basic fact: it will never be advantageous, in either a political or economic sense, for a national government to follow economic policies that lead to such a severe downturn that it can request assistance from a European stability fund. Politically, seeking help from fellow Europeans is embarrassing, painful, and in some cases, fatal. Economically, a request for assistance is bound to dent business and consumer confidence, while the existence of a strong backstop could actually support both. The fear of "moral hazard" is a self-serving excuse of some potential well-off countries not to help their neighbors in their times of need.

A silver lining of the crisis is the creativity demonstrated by the ECB in expanding the instruments it is willing to use, such as negative interest rates and quantitative easing. But its powers to intervene in financial markets and to regulate and supervise banks can be used still more effectively. The ECB showed its power when it went well beyond conventional monetary policy by forcing Spain, Ireland, and Greece to do things that were not in their own interests.

Stronger macro-prudential regulations—realizing that when an asset bubble is forming, one needs to lean against the wind by reducing access to credit for bubble assets and by increasing the cost of credit—

can be an important crisis-prevention tool, and one that simultaneously puts banks in better stead when the crisis occurs. Such regulations may entail having higher collateral requirements on real estate loans, or higher risk weights in assessing capital adequacy.

Some critics of the euro criticize it not only for exacerbating the crisis, but even for helping create the crisis.[8] In truth, asset bubbles have been a feature of capitalism since its origin. Supported by an underregulated financial market and a herd mentality, speculators flow into one market or another; the resulting increase in value of the assets attracts still more funds; the bubble increases. At some point, the returns on the asset in question look uncertain, especially when compared to other potential investments. As prices become more and more untethered from reality, the bubble eventually bursts.

Thus, in the early days of the euro, the current account surpluses of Germany and other northern European countries found rising returns on the periphery, especially in the real estate markets in Spain, Ireland, and other crisis countries. These surpluses spurred growth in the countries that had been lagging, and it seemed as if the euro were working, when in fact, the euro and the Single Market were helping to facilitate a bubble. The bursting of these bubbles (in tandem with the real estate crash in the United States) was the origin of the crisis.*

There has been a presumption that government should not intervene in the allocation of credit. Convention held that the market knew

---

* In the United States, both Alan Greenspan and his successor Ben Bernanke argued that you cannot tell a bubble until it bursts. That is wrong. It may not be possible to be entirely sure that it is a bubble. But no policy is conducted with perfect certainty. When median house prices relative to incomes reached levels never before seen, it should have been a warning. For housing prices to have been sustained and for housing to have yielded returns commensurate with other assets, it would have been necessary for the typical family to spend an unacceptable amount on housing. That there was a bubble was especially obvious in places like Nevada, where land has little intrinsic value (there is no scarcity), and accordingly, where the price should have been capped at reconstruction costs, so they could not continue to grow exponentially.

best and that it allocated scarce capital to where returns were the highest. But we know that financial markets are rife with failures. Indeed, it is precisely because there are such large disparities in private and social costs and benefits that regulation is desirable, even necessary. The social cost of a burst bubble is enormous. On the other hand, the social benefit of lending to a small business may well exceed the cost, which is why governments all over the world have special programs for lending to small- and medium-sized enterprises. Since these firms rely heavily on banks for credit (because they are too small to get access to capital markets), bank volatility has particularly large consequences for them.

The implication of large discrepancies between social and private returns is that the ECB should do what it can to encourage some types of lending, whether to smaller firms or minorities, and to discourage other types of lending, such as to property speculators, or for mergers and acquisitions. The ECB could also restrict bank lending portfolios—a maximum lending in some areas, a minimum in others. Especially in a deep economic downturn, it is important that credit flows to where it can best resuscitate the economy.

## CONCLUSION

Now that the intense phase of the Eurozone crisis is past, and Europe has regained a measure of stability, it is clear that monetary policy and the ECB did not just fail to prevent the crisis, but that, at certain moments and in some ways, they also amplified it. It is clear, too, that the policies and structures of the EU made Europe particularly vulnerable to asymmetric shocks. The money would flow from those more adversely hit to those who were better off, aggravating downturns. Counterfactual history is always difficult to write. However, there *were* alternative policies and actions that would have done more to prevent the crisis or limit its scope, and that would have done so in ways far more beneficial both for the afflicted countries and Europe as a whole.

Economics cannot be separated from politics, though. In the early days of the Greek crisis, French and German banks had to be saved, and for politicians from these countries, it was preferable to do this on the backs of the Greek citizens rather than on the backs of citizens of their own country. The hypocrisy of an institution claiming to be above politics, and then engaging in such intense politics, has planted bad memories in the minds of people across Europe. This widespread dissatisfaction is all the more reason for changes to European monetary policy and structures.

But even better monetary policies and policy responses to crises will go only part of the way to protect Europe against the adverse effects of asymmetric shocks. There must be changes in the mandate and governance of the ECB, a broadening of the instruments at its disposal, and further reforms to the structure of the Eurozone. Better fiscal and monetary policies, as well as reforms to the structure of the Eurozone, will allow the ECB to help Europe maintain full employment. On their own, however, these changes may not lead to the restoration of rapid growth. Such improvement will require more investment, both public and private. On that topic, the next chapter discusses what Europe can do to increase the level of productive investment.

*Chapter 3*

# Investing for an Equitable Future

**Full employment, achieved** through fiscal and monetary policies of the kind described in the first two chapters, does not ensure rapid growth. Future standards of living rise or fall based on productivity increases, which are largely the result of new investment, especially in research. Productivity increases in Europe, measured in output per hour, are now far less than in the years immediately after World War II.

And even if a country is at full employment and growing well today, it can still be profligate by consuming so much and despoiling the environment so badly that future generations will not enjoy the same standard of living. Sustainability requires smart investment and careful treatment of the environment.

Progressive economic thought has always been about the future, about securing an intergenerational compact that promotes prosperity for those not yet born. It has recognized that private markets can fail to strike a proper balance between today and the future. It holds that private markets tend to be shortsighted, which has especially been the case in recent years, as firms have focused on returns in the next quarter. Moreover, people at the bottom of the socioeconomic pyramid often do not have the resources to invest in themselves or to realize their full potential. Accordingly, progressives see an important role for government in managing and promoting public and private investment, including in education, technology, and infrastructure.

The Stability and Growth Pact has helped to stymie any truly progressive agenda on investment in the years since the crisis. The pact led to an excessive focus on deficits, constraining borrowing even for investments with very high returns. It also led to austerity as a policy response to the crisis, as we saw in Chapter 1. And when budgets are cut back, it is often investment, including research and development, that suffers the most because the effects will be felt only in the future. In contrast, budget cuts in other government programs are felt immediately. Politicians, like the private sector, tend to be shortsighted. In some cases, for example, the austerity measures implemented were so severe that they forced large cutbacks even in the most basic investments, such as education and health.

Critics of government spending often contrast the performance of the public sector with private firms to paint a picture of tightfisted companies that do not spend unless they absolutely must. However, smart businesses distinguish between capital expenditures (money spent on assets like land, buildings, and factories) and other outlays. Young, fast-growing enterprises know that it would be a mistake to limit investments to current profits, so they borrow, sometimes heavily, to finance their expansion. In assessing the economic strength of a firm, we always look at its balance sheet and not its debt in isolation. It makes sense for a firm to borrow to finance productive investments that yield returns far higher than the interest it must pay. The same logic also applies to governments.

Because the EU did not absorb this lesson, a misguided perspective is built into the Stability and Growth Pact: the imperative of limiting debt and deficits regardless of the availability of productive investments yielding far higher returns than the cost of capital.

A capital budget can be an important instrument of government, ensuring that enough of government spending is devoted to spending that enhances future standards of living. But a narrow conception of investment leads to distorted patterns of investment. Europe should not have too much spending on bricks and mortar, roads, and bridges, and not enough investments in research or in people's health and education.

There is often, too, a concomitant bias in favor of private over public investment. This conviction is predicated on the belief that the private sector is more efficient. Evidence, however, calls this belief into question. For instance, the administrative costs that are associated with public pensions and health care are far smaller in public programs than in private ones. And no government ever has wasted resources on the scale of the private financial system, for instance, in the case of the United States during the run-up to the financial crisis. During this time, homes financed through unaffordable mortgages birthed a real estate bubble. European finance got in on the action by buying securities backed by those loans. The long series of real estate and other bubbles, dating back to the Dutch tulip mania of the seventeenth century, testifies to the extensive history of private financial sector misallocation of scarce resources in faddish, boom-and-bust cycles.

Of course, all human institutions are fallible. We seek to learn how to be more productive, to identify waste when we see it, and then cut it out. Even so, there is waste in both the public and private sectors. The only relevant questions, then, are which sector best tackles a particular challenge and how can money be spent most effectively. Sustained growth requires both public and private investment, and an appropriate balance between the two, with decisions about both based on the goal of increasing productivity.

The myth that the private sector is always more efficient than the public has resulted in the turning over of much of the public sector to the private—a process called *privatization*. Around the world, this process has achieved mixed results. In some countries, in areas where there are reasonable levels of competition, privatization has worked well. But in many areas of activity, like in the provision of electricity, water, or rail service, sectors in which competition is naturally limited, the results vary. Sometimes there is an increase in productivity, especially when investment in the sector has been limited by government budget constraints. In fact, the excessive focus on deficits has sometimes circumscribed governments from allowing public enterprises to borrow money, even when the investment-return ratio is favorable. In these cases, the move to the private sector removes the credit shackles and enhances productivity. However, because of insufficient oversight of monopoly providers of electricity and water, for example, the private sector often increases charges, which may impoverish some citizens and often impedes private investment in other areas.

There is another enduring myth that has played a role in circumscribing public investment. Not only do critics of greater government spending claim that the returns on public investments are lower than on private, but they also suggest that greater public investment crowds out private-sector investment because government borrowing leads to higher interest rates, thus making finance for private investment less available and more expensive. This idea is clearly wrong when unemployment is high and the economy is operating far below its potential, as was the case after the 2008 financial crisis.

In such circumstances, the expansion of output will not lead to an increase in inflation. Even a central bank with a single-minded focus on inflation should not raise interest rates in this case. There is simply no crowding out. To the contrary, public spending increases incomes today, and this increase in incomes provides encouragement for the private sector to invest more. Rather than crowding out, there is crowding *in*. Private investment may be stimulated for another reason: public investment increases incomes in the future, which stimulates consumption today, which can prompt private investment.

More public investment can crowd in private investment for still another reason. Projects in energy, transport, or telecommunications, when executed correctly, create new opportunities for businesses to invest. A simple example: improved roads make efficient delivery of new services possible and profitable. Private and public investment can be complementary.[1]

In addition, investments in education also lead to a more productive labor force, which in turn can increase the return on capital. Furthermore, much of the investment in dynamic industries is based on government-sponsored research. Silicon Valley, for example, would not have the dominant position it has in many areas of advanced technology were it not for the US government's heavy investments in research and development. Likewise, the European business landscape is dotted with beneficiaries of government support for advanced research and new product development.*

Finally, the increased productivity that results from the increased public (and associated private) investment means that output can be

---

* When the economy is at full employment, more public investment, unaccompanied by taxes to finance it, will increase inflationary pressures, which will lead the central bank to raise interest rates. Then, the net effect on private investment depends on the strength of the consumption response to higher interest rates. But even in cases where there might be, as a result, some crowding out, the appropriate public response to sustaining high levels of investment is not to cut back on public investment, but to raise taxes on consumption.

larger without inflationary pressures, thus allowing the ECB to have a looser monetary policy at any given level of output than would otherwise be the case.

Though obtaining precise numbers on the returns from either private or public investments is difficult, it appears that marginal returns to public investments, especially in R&D and education, are very high. They are higher, in fact, than marginal returns on private investment, and this is especially so for public investments in the many European countries where public-sector spending has been tightly constrained. The returns on investment are sufficiently high that it makes sense for a country to sacrifice consumption today to achieve higher living standards in the future.

## PROBLEMS

### *Austerity Squeezed Already Too-Low Public Investment*

For some time before the crisis, the EU had experienced relatively low levels of investment, reaching only 22.5 percent of GDP, for example, in 2006. In emerging and developing economies, investment was 26.7 percent in the same year. The crisis, however, dragged EU investment further downward. By 2017, total EU investment had fallen to 20.1 percent of GDP. It should be noted that this fall in the investment-to-GDP ratio since the financial crisis was most pronounced in the Euro area, and especially in the crisis countries.

Lagging investment has various negative impacts. It means that many technological breakthroughs through research and development will come later, if at all. Even the ability to absorb new advances from elsewhere is reduced. It means that deployment of innovations in industry will lag. Europe may suffer especially if efficient production methods come online only after competitors elsewhere have already adopted them. In our globally competitive economy, there is often a large first-mover advantage. This is evident particularly in the case of the American technology giants.

The squeeze on public investment in Europe has been especially grave, with serious long-run implications. For example, fraying infrastructure undermines productivity. Because of the complementarities between public and private investment that we noted earlier—with public investments increasing the returns to private investments—underinvestment by the public sector induces underinvestment by private enterprises.

Underinvestment in education and health lowers the productivity of Europe's labor force in the future and will keep it from reaching its potential. To take one example, underinvestment undermines the ability of Europe's research universities to function as they should, by inhibiting the bridging of the pure science of the academy with the applied science of industry.

These effects have been particularly severe in the aftermath of the crisis, and especially so in the hardest-hit countries. To grasp what has been happening, we can define a category of public expenditures whose objective is to promote growth and sustainable development. Separating out these investment expenditures from others is an example of what is called capital budgeting, where the government isolates capital (investment) spending from government spending that goes to current consumption, though sometimes the boundaries are blurred.* A rough, but conservative, approximation for public expenditures that

---

* Some, for instance, would include most spending on defense as an investment in our security. On the other hand, health care expenditures that extend the life of a 90-year-old by six months can hardly be called "investments in the future."

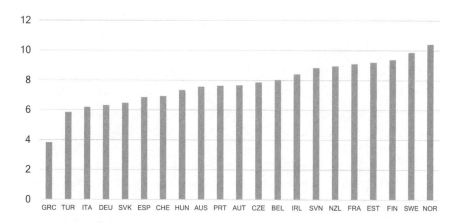

**FIGURE 3.1: FUTURE-ORIENTED PUBLIC EXPENDITURE (% OF GDP)**

Future-oriented public spending represents the sum of public investment, such as public R&D spending, and public education (including childcare) expenditures.

*Source: Based on data from OECD, "Going for Growth" (2016).*

promote growth and sustainable development (what we refer to as future-oriented public expenditure) is the sum of public investment on infrastructure, public R&D spending, and public education (including childcare). This is illustrated in Figure 3.1.*

A noteworthy finding from this public investment metric is that Germany has an investment rate that is very low by European standards. Italy and Greece are the only other EU countries with such a low ratio.

Other measures give similar results. For example, *net public investment*, or gross investment (gross fixed capital formation of the general government, such as in roads or bridges) less the depreciation of such assets, was actually negative in the Eurozone in 2016. These num-

---

* This definition leaves out certain other expenditures that are future-oriented: protection of nature and the environment, subsidies for renewable energy, family support, active labor market policies, and health care.

bers for investment are lower than they were before the crisis. Not surprisingly, the trend was most notable in the crisis-hit countries of the Eurozone. For example, total investment in Greece as a percentage of GDP fell from 23.7 percent in 2006 to 12.9 percent in 2017 (and that was a percentage of a much smaller GDP resulting from a harrowing contraction). For Spain, the ratio declined from 31.1 percent to 20.5 percent over that same decade.[2]

Plunging public investment should be a blot on the record of any politician who professes concern for future generations. Politicians often cite excessive debts and deficits as a terrible burden for future citizens. But what matters for those citizens is not only the liabilities they inherit but also the assets. Cutbacks in investment, especially in a recession when the cost of capital is low, can hurt them far more than the increase in indebtedness would have. (The same can be said for policies that allow environmental degradation.)

Such precipitous decreases stem from poor policy choices, guided by a poor policy framework. Among the crucial defects of the Stability and Growth Pact is its failure to distinguish between consumption and investment. Curbing consumption at a time of inadequate demand is bad enough but cutting high-return public investment is almost unforgivable because it damages both the present and the future. At the time when many countries could borrow at near zero or even negative interest rates, real interest rates had a plethora of investment projects yielding returns high enough so that the increased tax revenues alone would more than service the debt.

Austerity left the crisis-wracked countries with little choice but to enact large cuts in government spending. However, it was impossible to cut many essential expenditures. In no democratic society would it be acceptable to simply throw people onto the street, though in Greece matters went beyond what anyone thought they could. Although the consequences of these cutbacks in consumption manifested themselves immediately, years will pass before the consequences of reduced public investment appear.

But even in countries with public finances that would have permitted greater investment, notably Germany, a small-government and low-deficit ideology prevented the kind of activist role for government that would have taken advantage of the ultralow real interest rates. As the main advocate of stringent fiscal rules since the Maastricht Treaty was negotiated, Europe's largest economy practiced at home what it preached abroad, even though it made no economic sense for Germany to do so.

Following the rules in this manner led Germany to neglect investment, which, as we have explained, is more important for future generations than a balanced budget. For example, Germany has serious deficiencies in transportation and other infrastructure, something the successive governments in Berlin have often recognized but not seriously addressed.

In 2015, the European Commission seemed almost to acknowledge that the Stability and Growth Pact served the Eurozone badly and that the logic of austerity failed, when it published a framework that allowed countries to deviate from anti-deficit rules in order to promote investment. However, the commission layered so many conditions on this exception that it left the practice of austerity nearly intact. And so, the problem remains. The pact curtails productive investment at precisely the time it is needed most and when it would cost the least. This is because when a country goes into recession, revenues decline and expenditures for social support—notably unemployment compensation—increase. Inevitably, in a deep downturn, the country will run against the fiscal constraints even if its finances were in good shape before the downturn.

Austerity curtails productive investment at precisely the time when the social benefit-cost ratio is highest, when the opportunity cost of making these investments is low. When there is significant excess capacity and unemployment, public investments do not displace either private investments or consumption because they can avail themselves of resources that otherwise would be idle. On the contrary, as we have already noted, public investments crowd in private investments, and if done correctly, increase consumption both today and in the future.

Even in conventional commercial terms, economic downturns are the right time to make investments—a point that was clearly illustrated by the periods following the 2008 financial crisis and the 2010 Eurozone debt crisis. With long-term government bond yields close to zero for years, and with real interest rates, taking inflation into account, negative, it would have been very easy to find public investment projects that generated a return significantly in excess of the cost of capital. Ultimately, by failing to increase government investments in this period, Europe missed a golden opportunity.

## Private Investment Follows Public Investment Downward

During and after the financial crisis, European leaders compounded the problem of ailing aggregate demand by creating adverse conditions for private investment in the region—and at a minimum they deserve criticism for failing to address weakening investment in a timely manner. Policy failures, often explicable only in terms of ideological prejudices, were numerous.

The reduction was sharpest in the southern Eurozone countries, with private investment in this region decreasing from 22 percent of GDP in 2007 to 14 percent in 2014. The picture, however, was almost uniformly grim across Europe. Slack aggregate demand, of course, depressed private investment. The increased risk and lower demand for countries' products reduced the demand for investment. However, many firms would have been willing to invest more if only they could have gotten access to funds. Access to outside funds became especially important during the crisis because the deep economic recession reduced the retained earnings that firms had to invest. Unfortunately, bank credit became hardest to get at the moment it was needed most. Since small- and medium-sized enterprises (SMEs), everywhere but especially in Europe, rely on bank credit, a cutback in lending distorts the economy, hurting these firms more than it would the larger enterprises that can turn to bond markets. And the cutbacks in bank credit were especially costly in many peripheral countries (like Greece), because SMEs represent a disproportionate share of their economies.

Even in 2017, throughout Europe, 7 percent of SMEs were reporting "access to finance" as their main concern. There was, however, a great deal of inter-country variation. In Greece in 2017, the percentage was still 22 percent, while in Germany and the UK, it was only 5 percent.*

Of course, firms that were constrained in their investment to retained earnings also had to cut back on investments, since, as we have noted, profits typically fell, sometimes dramatically, during the downturn. Moreover, as firms borrowed to survive, they were less able to access credit for investment. In short, the downturn constrained pri-

* European Commission/European Central Bank Survey, SAFE. In 2014, the percentage of SMEs that applied for a bank loan and got everything they asked for was 78 percent in Austria, 75 percent in Germany, 77 percent in France, and 80 percent for Denmark, but 24 percent in Greece, 54 percent in Italy, and 53 percent in Spain. In 2009, the same figure was 33 percent for Greece, 62 percent for Portugal, and 50 percent for Spain.

vate investment in capital goods (equipment), as well as in intangible assets like intellectual property.

At the same time, the downturn, exacerbated by austerity, hurt firm and bank balance sheets. The adverse effect on banks' balance sheets was one of the reasons for the cutback in credit: banks were less able and willing to lend.* The worsening of firm balance sheets—the decrease in their net worth and in their cash positions—made many less willing to invest (even if they could get access to credit), and sometimes even less willing to produce.†

The combination of weak private investment and sagging public investment meant, of course, that overall investment was depressed. In Greece, gross fixed capital formation—a broad measure of public, private, and household investment as a percentage of the much smaller GDP—went from 26 percent in 2007, to about 13 percent for each of the years from 2012 to 2017.[3]

## Underinvestment in Research and Development

There is one category of investment that is focused on increasing productivity and thus is crucial for the long-run success of Europe's economy: spending on research and development. The data suggest that there has been underinvestment in R&D. In 2017, EU members spent around €317 billion on research and development. As a percentage of

---

* That was why the 2008 recession was often referred to as a balance-sheet recession, but it was, of course, much more than that.

† As we noted in Chapter 2, the Single Market without deposit insurance and other elements of a banking union meant that money flowed out of the crisis countries, and especially out of their banks, necessitating cutbacks in bank lending. Reforms and institutional innovations, such as the ESM and the banking union, have been halting and have still not adequately addressed the underlying problems.

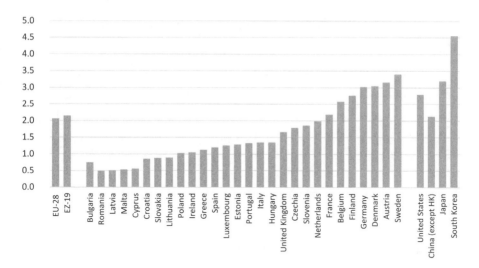

**FIGURE 3.2: TOTAL RESEARCH AND DEVELOPMENT INVESTMENT (% OF GDP)**

The figure shows total R&D expenditure as percentage of GDP for European countries for the year 2017. Comparison of average figures of EU-28 and EZ-19 with other industrialized non-EU countries (on the right) demonstrates the need for an increase in R&D expenditure by European countries.

*Source: Eurostat.*

GDP, a metric known as "R&D intensity," the level stood at 2.06 percent in 2017 (see Figure 3.2).

While this number is larger than it was 10 years ago—in 2005, R&D expenditures were just 1.74 percent of GDP—it is far lower than in other major economies such as Japan (3.20 percent), South Korea (4.55 percent), and the United States (2.79 percent, including both civilian and military expenditure). While a good portion of US expenditures, which were much larger than Europe's, reflect defense spending, the central problem remains: Europe invests too little in R&D.

Moreover, the differences among countries' R&D investments are striking. When Sweden invests well over 3 percent in R&D and Greece invests just over 1 percent, we can identify yet another fissure within the European project—a warning that the divides in Europe are likely to be even greater in the future.

The challenge facing Europe, then, is how can it increase both public and private investments, particularly in areas like R&D and infrastructure where returns seem especially high, and particularly in countries where investment lags behind the EU average?

## SOLUTIONS

### Encouraging Public Investment

We have seen how the Stability and Growth Pact has constrained investment, just as it has limited the flexibility of countries in crisis to restore the economy to full employment. The EU needs a framework for fiscal policy that safeguards, and even increases, fruitful investment even when public finances come under pressure during downturns in the business cycle. In 2015, the EU acknowledged the need to make better use of the flexibility that the pact currently provides.[4] But this move was half-hearted at best, and badly hamstrung by numerous caveats. In practice, fiscal policy has been strongly pro-cyclical, exacerbating boom-and-bust cycles.

We propose a different policy trajectory, along the lines of the changes already discussed in Chapter 1. First, debt financing of government deficits should be permissible when used for *productive investment*, defined to include not only infrastructure but also investments in education, health, and innovation. This approach makes particular sense in a recession, when resources would otherwise be idle and when real interest rates are often negative. These expenditures determine future growth and yield very high returns. Sustaining, or even increasing, these investments is both good politics and good policy.

Short of excluding all investments, there could also be a "positive list" of expenditures that could be removed from Stability and Growth Pact calculations. This concept would create a clear benchmark that anything not explicitly excluded from the pact would be included and would assure skeptics that changes—new exceptions–will not happen by stealth. Countries should, of course, prioritize categories on the positive list that offer the greatest benefits to future generations, such as improved climate protection and better early childhood education.

## Capital Budgeting

Capital budgeting provides governments and citizens alike with a better view of the extent to which government spending is future-oriented. Capital budgeting also helps shift the focus of public finance away from the size of the deficit and toward an approach that asks how, each year, the government adds to both sides of the balance sheet (to both liabilities and assets). The government is in a stronger position if its assets increase at least as much as its liabilities, just as a firm that sees its assets increase more quickly than what it owes is in a better position. (We would say that its balance sheet was stronger, and that its net worth had increased.) Information affects how we perceive the world. If we measure investments, we may think more about the future and therefore do more for future generations.

As a start, each of the EU member states should publish accounts that distinguish between public expenditures for consumption and investment. (Initially, one might focus on a narrow definition of investment.) The United Kingdom already publishes such a report and France has started to do so. German skepticism of the idea should not stop other countries from making it a reality. Over time, countries should publish a full capital budget that identifies all investments, including those in human capital.

## The European Fund for Strategic Investments

But accounting for changes in the government's balance sheet only begins to hint at the kind of fresh thinking Europe needs to encourage overall investment. The European Fund for Strategic Investments (EFSI), which is the core of the Investment Plan for Europe (usually referred to as the Juncker plan), hopes to encourage up to €500 billion of additional, mainly private investment by leveraging €33.5 billion in public funds.* (Originally, the plan envisioned only €300 billion in additional investment. It was subsequently increased by €200 billion.) A quarter of the funds under the Juncker plan will support small- and medium-sized enterprises, and another quarter will target research and development. The remaining half will be spread among energy, digital, transport, environment, and social investment areas.

### Additionality

An important question is to what extent EFSI public resources are genuinely additional, given the fact that a large part of the resources come from other parts of the EU budget and do not represent additional contributions by EU governments. Even if overall EU spending is not increased, the Juncker plan may constitute a small shift in resources toward investment. Similarly, even if there is no additional EU spending, the plan may still stimulate GDP. European authorities argue that the multiplier effect of EFSI is significantly larger than that of the budget programs from which resources were taken, given the higher leverage of EFSI funds. Preliminary analysis by the European Parliament reveals that EFSI succeeded by speeding up the time frame

---

* EFSI resources are made up from a €26 billion guarantee funded from the European Union's budget, complemented by €7.5 billion of the European Investment Bank's capital. The intent is to leverage these funds enormously.

for the implementation of projects, boosting market confidence around a project by providing a first-loss guarantee, reaching new clients who have no history or track record of activity with the European Investment Bank (discussed further below), and raising the economic impact by funding smaller shares of the total investment cost for a higher number of projects.

### *Targeting*

The EFSI investment agenda prioritizes sectors in which investment is likely to have good returns. As of March 2018, 29 percent of funds had been allocated to support small- and medium-sized enterprises, 23 percent for research and development, 21 percent for energy, 11 percent for digital, 8 percent for transport, 4 percent for social infrastructure, and 4 percent for environment and resource efficiency.[5]

There are some sectors where additional resources might particularly yield high returns, such as digital infrastructure and energy efficiency. Because investment in these areas has lengthy payback periods and low financial returns, especially in underpopulated areas, public investment is necessary.[6] However, the extent to which more risky and innovative projects in new sectors such as electric cars have been funded is less clear.

### *Limitations*

Perhaps the most important limitation of the EFSI is its inadequate size, especially in countries such as Greece, where a continuing credit crunch means additional lending is needed, particularly for smaller firms. Even if the goal of stimulating €500 billion in additional investment over five years is attained, and even if this growth in investment is additional to what would otherwise have occurred, it would only increase the investment-to-GDP ratio by less than 1 percentage point.

Similarly, the EFSI is more prone to support those economies in which greater investment opportunities already exist, thus leading to uneven geographic distribution of support. Clearly, richer economies have greater capacity to develop viable projects. By mid-2016, almost all financing granted under the EFSI (92 percent) had been allocated to older, mainly western European member states, among which the largest beneficiaries were Italy, Spain, and Britain.

In contrast, the newer member countries, mainly from central and eastern Europe, accounted for a mere 8 percent of disbursements. Support per capita in these countries stood at just €7 (or €370 per €1 million of these countries' GDPs),[7] while in the older member states it was €20 per capita (or €631 per €1 million of those countries' GDPs).

Fortunately, more recent data suggests the situation may have improved. Countries harmed by austerity, including Spain, Portugal, Italy, and Greece, now rank among the highest receivers of EFSI investment, as a percentage of GDP. In investment per capita terms, the investment rates also remain high.

One of the reasons for the deficient investment in poor countries is that they lack the institutional capacity to put forward good projects. Capacity building to overcome discrepancies in these allocations must become one of the key objectives for EFSI. Technical assistance and help in defining strategic sectors in each member state are a means to this end. Special attention must be given to countries in central and eastern Europe, but also Greece, where a special EU investment initiative appears to be indispensable.

Despite the shortcomings of the Juncker plan, the extension of the timeline for the Juncker plan (announced in September 2016) to 2020 was a move in the right direction. The extension has enabled an additional €200 billion in further investment. Furthermore, the EU has now committed to a successor of the Juncker plan, called InvestEU, which it hopes will generate an additional €650 billion of additional investment in the seven years after 2020.

## The Lighthouse Initiative

A more decisive approach toward the deficit in European public investment is the initiative that we refer to here as the *Lighthouse Initiative*, which signifies the brighter future on the horizon if European policymakers do the right thing. It is a clarion call for greater and more carefully planned public investment in Europe, and a decisive break with the austerity-driven past that would add to, rather than replace, the Juncker plan. We propose this initiative for the Eurozone only, bound as it is by Maastricht Treaty rules on debt and deficits, though a strong case could be made for its application to the entire EU.

- The annual size of actual spending on the Lighthouse Initiative should be around 1 percent of Eurozone GDP for a period of at least five years—a total of approximately €500 billion.
- The program should continue until the marginal returns on public investment are roughly equal to those on private investment. Economic circumstances should dictate its duration.
- National governments should fund the initiative. The EU should exclude these expenditures from national deficit calculations, as is the case with the Juncker plan.
- The plan should be implemented as soon as possible. As this book goes to press, interest rates remain low, but will eventually rise.
- The member states would have to demonstrate that the funds are used to finance growth-enhancing expenditures. This European Commission would police adherence to this criterion. In reclassifying spending as investment in these categories, it will be desirable to avoid complex accounting procedures.
- Projects that crowd in private investment would enjoy priority, as would projects that show potential for fulfilling unmet social needs, including those arising from market failures.

■ Governments should experiment with new risk-sharing mechanisms to maximize the crowd-in effect.

## Support Public Development Banks to Boost Investment

One of the key constraints for an increase in private investment in the European Union is a lack of private finance, and especially of long-term finance for infrastructure and for investment in smaller firms. Around the world, public development banks have proven to be effective institutions in supplying the necessary credit, correcting what is now recognized as a key market failure. Because of their long-term perspective—in marked contrast to the short-term perspective that dominates in private financial markets—development banks can help design, fund, and coordinate expertise in specific areas of investment.*

By working with the private sector and appropriately designing financial instruments, development banks can engender financial support, especially for long-term projects, that is a multiple of the amounts spent by the development bank itself. In the wake of the financial crisis, there has been renewed support for development banks, as the limitations and problems of a purely private financial sector have become more evident.

The private financial sector has been pro-cyclical, over-lending in boom times but ruthlessly rationing credit during and after crises. Again, small- and medium-sized enterprises have suffered acutely, especially in downturns. Even in tranquil times, but more so in turbu-

---

* A key malfunction of the financial markets is related to *credit rationing*: the inability of a borrower to get access to funds at any interest rate, even though similarly situated borrowers do get credit. It is caused in turn by imperfect information and information asymmetries. Such market failures are particularly pervasive in the provision of long-term credit. Another related market failure is the lack of a full set of risk (insurance) markets. By now, there exists an extensive literature explaining how government, even when it faces similar limitations, can improve societal welfare.

lent times, the private financial sector has also not sufficiently funded long-term investments, including in innovation, infrastructure, renewable energy, and energy efficiency.

During and after the crisis, many development banks in Europe especially (but not only) provided counter-cyclical finance. For instance, the German development bank KfW greatly aided smaller firms during and after the crisis, and thus has aided the growth and structural transformation of Germany. Today, development banks are beginning to play a more important role in developed, emerging, and developing economies. The World Bank, which in the past was quite critical of national development banks, has increasingly viewed these institutions favorably.

There are now a whole array of development banks at every level. Globally, of course, there is the World Bank, while regions have the Inter-American Development Bank, the Asian Development Bank, and the African Development Bank. Likewise, many countries have their own development bank (Brazil's, BNDES, is even larger than the World Bank) and some subnational jurisdictions have development banks (state banks in Brazil, the Bank of North Dakota and the Development Bank of Puerto Rico in the United States). Each of these banks deploys a variety of instruments, including direct loans, loan guarantees, and equity investments. They are also channels for government subsidies to activities that yield significant societal benefits.

The European Investment Bank (EIB) is among the largest and most important development banks in the world. The EIB has had a long track record of successfully playing a key role in funding intra-European infrastructure projects (including in renewable energy), SMEs, and innovation, as well as European national public development banks. The 2012 increase in EIB resources (paid-in capital) was doubled with contributions from all member states. This change led to significant increases in lending and equity operations by the EIB Group.

Recent evaluations of EFSI show that around one-third of its operations involved cofinancing from national development banks. However, some national development banks report that for larger projects, EFSI still behaves as if it were their competitor. This feeling of competition undermines trust, free exchange of information, and effective collaboration. It also calls for, once again, emphasizing the EIB's commitment to collaboration with national development banks.

National development banks play an important role in leveraging private investment, but too often these institutions are simply too small to exact needed changes. These banks need to grow in size. One important step in this direction would be to exclude capital increases of development banks from the deficit targets of the Stability and Growth Pact.

## CONCLUSION

Higher investment in the European Union, both private and public, is needed to achieve increases in productivity and structural transformation. This is particularly urgent in the countries hit badly by the Eurozone crisis, and in the poorer countries of the EU.

Because of the complementarity between public and private investment, an increase in public investment would also stimulate private investment. Perhaps more than anything else, an increase in public investment would help to promote Europe's growth today and in the future. These increased growth prospects would stimulate further private investment—a virtuous circle of prosperity.

Aggregate demand and employment, monetary policy, and investment remain the central challenges of macroeconomic strategy in Europe. Together, they occupy the commanding heights of economic policy. Without a credible plan at this level, no strategy to revitalize

Europe or the EU can succeed. At the same time, the right macroeconomic strategy alone cannot ensure success.

However, the finer mechanisms of Europe's market economy, including those that ensure that competition thrives, that finance goes to where it should, and that taxes are fair and efficient, have also not worked as well as they should or could. Markets, the subject of our next section, can be made to work much better than they currently do.

# PART II

# Making Markets Work for Fairness and Efficiency

*Chapter 4*

# Promoting Competitive Markets: Incentives, Regulations, and Innovation

**Among Western nations,** markets have long played a central role in organizing the production and distribution of goods and services. Europe has maintained a mixed economy—a balance between private enterprise, government (at many different levels), and a mix of other institutional arrangements, including foundations, cooperatives, and not-for-profit organizations. However, the aggressive free-market approach of Margaret Thatcher and the fall of the Berlin Wall resulted in a major change in this balance, based on an excessive confidence in markets. In the clash between two competing systems, Communism and capitalism, the latter seemed to have triumphed absolutely. Some, like Francis Fukuyama, went so far as to proclaim "the end of history," prophesying that the entire world would eventually appreciate the wisdom of liberalism, capitalism, and democracy. This triumphalism paved the way for a shrinking role for the state.

This confidence in the market has taken more than a few body blows since 1989. Above all, the 2008 financial crisis laid bare deep structural shortcomings. In the West, even in the decades before the financial crisis, few economic gains have accrued to the bottom half of households, or even the bottom 90 percent. Large numbers of European households saw their incomes stagnate or decline over long periods of time. And China's brand of state capitalism has performed remarkably well—to the point where by some measures, China is now the largest economy in the world.

Moreover, the triumph of the West over the former Soviet Union had more to do with the failures of an authoritarian political system, combined with central planning, than anything else. Also, the success of the West did not rest solely on its affection for markets. A whole array of institutions, including government, nonprofit institutions, and civil society writ large, contributed to the strength of Western countries.

A major objective of this book is to encourage a rethinking of this economic ecology—a fresh evaluation of the appropriate mix of state, private-for-profit, and nonprofit institutions and how these relate to each other. Much of the thinking over the past 30 years saw these as antagonistic institutions, with a cutback in the state necessary to help the private, for-profit sector flourish because that sector was viewed as the foundation of economic success. Today, however, we are aware that with an appropriately designed framework, these various entities can work in a complementary way; in particular, without an appropriate regulatory framework, unfettered markets can lead to disaster. In truth, better financial regulation might have spared the world from the 2008 financial crisis.

Moreover, in many instances, the private sector could not have performed as well as it did without prior government investments, notably in research and development. Today's global technology sector would not be what it is without earlier government investments to create the internet. In her influential book *The Entrepreneurial State: Debunking Public vs. Private Sector Myths*, Mariana Mazzucato argued that the state has often fostered important innovation by acting with a more far-sighted mindset than does the typical capitalist.[1]

Even accepting that the best way of organizing production puts markets at the center, we must ask about the many forms of the market economy, with their different rules and methods for balancing the role of private markets and government power. American, Nordic, and Japanese capitalism are all different and employ different means to balance the role of the state and the market.

Even within Europe there is an assortment of market economies. Some of these countries and regions performed better than others and demonstrated greater resiliency after the 2008 crisis. These successes are at least in part because those countries chose different forms of capitalism, with different institutions, rules, and regulations.

Of course, what works well for one country, with its particular history and culture and norms, may not work so well for others. Moreover, it may not be possible to easily transplant institutions and arrangements from one country to another; individual solutions are frequently bound to individual cultures. Nonetheless, we can look for general principles. We can try to identify which institutional arrangements contribute best to growth, equality, and stability across the board. Countries that design their rulebook in accordance with the general principles and insights gleaned from analysis are more likely to succeed.

Market advocates often say, "Leave it to the market." However, such simplistic statements obscure the essential question: What *kind* of market should we leave it to? As we have emphasized, and repeatedly will, markets do not exist in a vacuum. They have to be structured. Different countries have differently structured markets, with unique rules and regulations that result in a diversity of outcomes. Policy choices, including decisions about how markets are structured, bear much responsibility for the differences in outcomes. That fact also offers clues leading toward a better way forward.

Europe needs to draw from experiences that have worked well, but also from those that have not. And in assessing what has worked well, Europe needs to take into account not just impacts on GDP, but also broader measures of societal performance.[2] Questions that should be asked include: What is happening to the standards of living of ordinary citizens? What is happening to their health and education? Is the growth sustainable—socially, environmentally, or economically? The answers will help Europe craft an economic model that is both sustainable and equitable.

Some places in Europe have been quite successful in advancing the well-being of their citizens. Indeed, once inequality is taken into account, 12 out of the top 20 countries in the UN's Human Development Index (a broad measure of well-being incorporating income, education, and health) are in Europe.[3] In comparison, the United States occupies the 26th spot.

But even in Europe, the failure to make markets work as they should—competitive markets with the private interests of key decision makers such as CEOs aligned with society's interests—has resulted in a less productive and less equal Europe. There are policies that can help Europe's private sector work better, not only for itself in the long run, but for all of society. The chapters in Part II of this book describe some of the key ways in which this can be done.

The worst manifestations of dysfunctional markets are those in which some entities make money by taking advantage of others, whether through market power or information asymmetries. Any new rulebook that does not address these instances of market failure will be incomplete, and no sector has failed to perform as it should so much as the financial sector. We devote Chapter 5 entirely to it.

The efficiency of all sectors (including finance) and their ability to serve society depends on robust competition. Firms with market power use that power to exploit others by raising prices to garner more profits for themselves. Thus, market power is bad for overall economic performance, but it is also recognized as one of the biggest sources of inequality. Accordingly, we begin the discussion in this chapter with a discussion of what can be done to ensure that markets in Europe are more competitive.

We follow this with a discussion on how to make firms, which are the basic unit of production in our economies, serve society better. Firms today are far different from the simplistic textbook models in which an entrepreneur owns a firm and makes decisions to maximize long-run profits. Large and influential corporations today have large numbers of shareholders, and there is a separation of ownership and control. Control is in the hands of a CEO and a coterie of managers. Getting this group to act in ways that maximize societal welfare, or even the wealth of shareholders, is the central problem of *corporate governance*, the rules and regulations pertaining to how firms are run. Corporate governance is concerned with what the objectives of the firm should be and whose voices should be heard during decision-making processes. These considerations, in turn, affect the incentive structures of executives.

Chapter 5 shows how this particular issue played out in the financial sector. The 2008 crisis exposed its perverse incentive structures, which served the interests of the bankers but not the banks' shareholders, bondholders, or customers, let alone those of the broader society. Short-sightedness, excessive risk taking, and exploitation of banks' customers (whether they deposited money, borrowed from the bank, or turned to the financial sector to manage their investments) characterized precrisis finance activities and too often still do.

Finally, intellectual property is a central asset of European firms as Europe moves from manufacturing to an innovation-based economy. Here too, current rules have done more to promote narrow corporate interests than to encourage innovation. In the third part of this chapter, we highlight what Europe needs to do to create a more innovative economy whose fruits are shared broadly.

## COMPETITIVE MARKETS

A somewhat shopworn saying in postwar Europe posited that "what happens in the United States happens in Europe, too, only later." If there is even a grain of truth in this glib notion, then competition policy is one area in which Europe can and should get out ahead of a problem that threatens Western economies: the concentration of market power in too few corporate hands. Fortunately, the signs are promising that European authorities recognize the challenge. They should sustain and expand their efforts.

Changes in the power of corporations relative to workers have played an important role in the increase in inequality. Worker compensation has not kept pace with productivity, so the share of income going to workers has decreased. So too, working conditions have, in many places, deteriorated. Workers are contracted without any certainty about the hours they will work, the income they will receive, or whether they will be pushed to work overtime without additional compensation. Moreover, online platforms for workers to sell their services, such as Uber or TaskRabbit, fragment the labor force and mute their voices. Chapter 9 discusses the key issue of the weakening of worker bargaining power.

In this chapter, we focus on the market power of firms over their customers. We see it everywhere in the limited choices individuals have. One example is the vital information technology sector. This industry is dominated by only a few American corporations: Google, Apple, Facebook, Amazon, and Microsoft. Of course, not every sector is marked by market power (domination by a few firms), but many are. The privatization of key public utilities, including telecom, water, gas, and electricity, has also often led to a concentration of market power in these sectors. Robust competition is hard to come by in these parts of the economy.

Increases in market power contribute to inequality in multiple ways. For example, they lead to an increase in prices above what they would be in a competitive market, thus lowering the living standards of ordinary workers just as would a decrease in wages. Also, not surprisingly, these monopolies and oligopolies can be very profitable. Rates of return in many sectors remain substantially above what they should be in a competitive economy in which new entrants drive rates of returns to a low competitive level.* These incumbents have created entry barriers to discourage other firms from entering and driving down their returns. Furthermore, these high profits accrue naturally to the owners of capital, who are disproportionately the rich, leading to an increase in income inequality.

One of the anomalies observed in many sectors is that investment can be weak even when profits are high. Market power provides a persuasive explanation. Monopolists (or more broadly, firms with market power) worry that increased investment, by increasing output, will require lower prices to sell the additional output, thus adversely affecting profits. Of course, there are large negative externalities associated

---

* That level is typically the safe interest rate plus the risk premium, or the return to compensate for the extra risk associated with owning productive assets.

with curtailing investment. Unless there are strong offsetting macroeconomic policies, it results in lower output, lower growth, higher unemployment, and lower wages.

Europe may not have to grapple with the levels of monopoly and oligopoly that the United States faces, but the trends that drive the weakening of competition straddle the Atlantic. Large networks created by online behemoths like Google and Facebook raise their value to users but have an anticompetitive and even abusive side. They have an enormous ability to exercise market power and violate privacy rights—and have a track record of doing so. They have also allowed the use of their platforms for political manipulation, thereby potentially affecting the outcomes of elections and undermining confidence in democracy.

Interestingly, competition policy in the United States was originally motivated as much by a concern for the danger of excessive concentration of economic power in politics as in economics. Late-nineteenth- and early-twentieth-century Progressive Era advances in antitrust enforcement in the United States mirror policies that were aimed at reducing the political influence of cartels in postwar Germany. Both efforts reflected the conviction that accumulated wealth distorts democratic politics. It was true then, in both cases, and it is true now. Unfortunately, over the nearly 70 years that have elapsed since antitrust laws were last updated in the United States (the Anti-Merger Act of 1950), competition policy has narrowed to a focus on economic impacts on the competitiveness of relevant markets and, in particular, on the prices and choices that consumers confront.

With this narrowing of focus has come a change in presumptions. By and large, US courts presume that markets are competitive, and that what firms do is to enhance how they serve their customers, thereby deriving greater profits. Given this prevalent belief, a heavy burden is placed on those who want to show that what the firm is doing is actually reducing competition and that the resulting adverse effects outweigh any positive benefits that consumers get from such anticompetitive practices.

The importance of competition is seen most keenly in the telecom sector. This sector employs much the same technology worldwide and requires relatively little labor—so prices around the world should not differ greatly. Yet at times, prices in Mexico have been ten times that of the United States, and those in the United States have been far higher than in India. The difference in prices is largely explained by differences in competition: the Indian market has been highly competitive, the Mexican market has almost no competition, and the American market very little.

The European Commission and European governments have proved willing to take on the new challenges of platform monopolies like Facebook and Google. Google, for example, was using its dominant position in the search engine business to destroy competitors in the separate business of comparison-shopping services. By raising the profile of its own service in search results, Google committed classic breaches of antitrust law, and as a result, received a €2.4 billion fine in 2017. It earned another €4.3 billion fine in 2018 for using its mobile phone operating system to fortify the domination of its internet search engine.

But the task of policing the marketplace will not end with stopping classic breaches. As platforms like Amazon, Facebook, and Google have gained dominance, they have often imposed conditions on customers that operate within their own ecosystem, thereby abusing their dominant positions. Amazon, for example, forces sellers to provide it with the best prices they offer to any online marketing platform. Such provisions undermine competition from other platforms, and even the entry of new competitors, as competitors know they cannot attract business through lower prices because the same terms will have to be offered to Amazon.*

Traditionally, antitrust policy has focused on monopolies and oligopolies in which where there is one, or a few, dominant sellers in a market. But Amazon illustrates something that has become of increasing importance—a *dominant buyer*, called a monopsony. A dominant buyer has the power to drive down prices. British Sugar, for example, purchases virtually the entire British sugar beet crop each year. Likewise, in labor markets, a dominant employer has the power to drive down wages (think of a small town with one or two dominant employers).

In following the example of the United States, European competition law has too often focused on the effects of market power on consumers. Those with market power in buying may share with consumers some of the benefits that they extract from suppliers and other inputs (in particular, workers). However, the exercise of market power nonetheless causes a major distortion in the economy. Especially when there is market power in labor markets, there is greater inequality. Therefore, competition law needs to look beyond market power's effects on consumers, to how it distorts the functioning of market economies more broadly.

For example, even though Google and Facebook offer most of their services, at least for the moment, for free, they have exploited their customers' personal data to build unassailable market positions in the online advertisement market. Moreover, they can also use this information to help others engage in discriminatory pricing, to charge more, for instance, to customers in areas where there is limited compe-

---

* This illustrates a general principle: often, provisions that seem to encourage competition have just the opposite effects. Some stores, for instance, advertise that they will "meet the competition" by charging a lower price than any other firm. While it looks like they are being fiercely competitive, the reality is there's now less competition because no entrant can outbid the incumbent.

tition. This discriminatory pricing is simply a transfer from consumers to the owners of the information; it actually leads to a less efficient economy, since efficiency requires everyone to pay the same price for a good. The barriers to entry for potential competitors in these sectors also increase, with resulting negative effects for competition, and ultimately, innovation.

Europe took the lead in regulating the use of information with its General Data Protection Regulation of May 2018. This step should be but the first. Europe needs to do much more to prevent the abuse of privacy, the potential abuse of such data in the market (e.g., discriminatory pricing) and in politics (through the kind of political manipulation already seen). Moreover, the concentration of market power in the online economy cannot be tackled by an approach to protect individual rights alone, that is, the rights of the "owner" of the data. There are broader societal consequences that have to be addressed.

Google, the credit card companies, and Microsoft have brought attention to another set of concerns: anticompetitive practices by which monopoly power, once acquired, can be leveraged, strengthened, and extended in reach and time. For instance, in many countries, credit card companies charge merchant fees that exceed the minuscule costs of transferring funds from the customers' accounts to that of the merchant, as well as the cost of preventing fraud. They force merchants to honor all cards with the name Visa or MasterCard and do not allow the merchant to pass on the fees to their customers, or even to steer customers to lower-cost means of payment. These companies are short-circuiting the price system. Indeed, American Express has even forbidden merchants from disclosing the fees charged, lest some customers switch to a less expensive debit card. European regulators have curtailed these abuses of credit card companies better than their American counterparts, but similar provisions exist in many industries.

Competition authorities need to understand, too, that market power, once established, is hard to undo. In the 1990s, Microsoft engaged in certain anticompetitive practices, which enabled it to destroy the innovative browser, Netscape Navigator, that had once dominated the market, and then to push its own browser, Internet Explorer. But even long after these anticompetitive practices were proscribed, Microsoft remained dominant.

The entrenched nature of market power is why European alertness is so important. This is especially the case because those with market power have become innovative, not only in the products they produce, but also in the ways by which they extend their market power. Technology giants often buy up potential competitors long before they reach the size at which they attract antitrust scrutiny. Regulators need to be on the lookout for these preemptive mergers and be ready to ask whether a merger or acquisition has the potential to undermine future competition (not just whether it would undermine current competition).

Traditionally, antitrust authorities have focused attention on mergers and acquisitions within an industry and paid little attention to those between firms in different industries. But when competition is limited, such mergers, known as *vertical integration*, can weaken competition further. A cable or telecom company that buys a provider of entertainment services can limit further competition among providers of such services. This is true even if there is an obligation of the cable or telecom company to be neutral, so that it does not give preferences to its own subsidiary. When such a company imposes a high charge for the provision of a service (say, carrying a program over its cables) on its own subsidiary, it is simply transferring money from one pocket to another. The high charges may put its competitors at such a large disadvantage that it drives them out of business. The vertical integration of US cable and telecom companies with producers of media bodes ill for competition in that country in this vital sector.* There are similar forces at play for horizontal and vertical integration in Europe, and hopefully Europe will do a better job at circumscribing these ways of increasing market power.

Some Europeans have suggested that it would do better if Europe were less attentive to competition and focused more on creating European or national champions—the big, multinational behemoths that are supposed to lead the charge against American or Chinese competitors. But these large enterprises can just as easily exploit Europeans as they can conquer foreign markets. Ensuring that markets are competitive requires constant vigilance, especially in a time of rapid technological change, because firms discover new ways to create entry barriers and to circumvent existing regulations and standards.

Europe should build on its experience with fighting former network monopolies in areas such as electricity and gas distribution. The 200 merger and 17 antitrust decisions that were made in the energy markets by the European Commission between 2005 and 2013 were clear successes. They boosted competitiveness and investment, and in at least two prominent cases, one involving E.ON, a German energy behemoth, and the other, GDF-Suez (now ENGIE), a French company, also led to lower wholesale and retail prices.

Changes in economic structure and technology have combined with innovations in the creation and maintenance of market power to create a landscape full of significant threats to competition. What enables a market economy to serve society is competition. European governments, and in particular the EU, must be as innovative as the

---

* The June 2018 decision of the Federal Communications Commission to repeal the net neutrality rules, which limit discrimination by an internet provider, will only exacerbate the problem.

private sector in combating market power, and as committed to limiting it as the private sector is to enhancing it.

## CORPORATE GOVERNANCE

For decades, Europe has debated best-practices for corporate governance. Should European firms simply maximize the value of the firm to their shareholders or should they take into account the (often diverging) interests of other stakeholders? Even within shareholder capitalism (as the first perspective is often referred to) there is a debate: Should the focus be on today's stock market value or on longer-term value? In practice, shareholder capitalism in the United States has led to short-termism. This is a focus on the here and now, or, in other words, how to get today's share price up regardless of the cost to the long-run viability of the enterprise. With this approach, firms have often taken on so much debt that they actually go bankrupt. Stakeholders, by contrast, are a broader group that includes employees, customers, local communities, and society at large. Stakeholder capitalism, by its very nature, has to consider the long term. For most of the last few decades, these two groups have come to symbolize polar opposite approaches.

Germany has been the exemplar of stakeholder capitalism, with this kind of governance being very pronounced in Germany's mid-sized companies, known as the *Mittlestand*, but not only there. Wendelin Wiedeking, the longtime CEO of Porsche, the sports car manufacturer, once heartened his own workforce with a simple line: "First comes the customer, then the employees, then the suppliers and then the shareholder. If the first three are happy, the shareholder will have a right fine time." Porsche, in short, managed to at least articulate a synthesis of the shareholder and stakeholder models of corporate governance.

Wiedeking's formulation is a good start, but it leaves out a crucial stakeholder: the citizen who might not ever buy a Porsche—and there are many of those. Their sense of what is fair and reasonable should also count for something in a democracy. CEOs of multinationals who guide their companies in massive tax avoidance (for which Apple has become the poster child), and companies that flagrantly violate environmental protections (Volkswagen, now the parent company of Porsche, has become emblematic in this domain) illustrate actions where shareholder and societal interests differ. Companies may claim the mantle of corporate social responsibility, but the first responsibilities of any corporation are to pay its fair share of taxes and not despoil the environment. Too many companies thrive off public investments in infrastructure, education, and technology, but are not willing to pay back society.

The view that firms should simply maximize shareholder value is of recent origin, often dated to the influence of Milton Friedman and his right-wing ideology of the 1970s and early 1980s, a time when there was a shift to the right on both sides of the Atlantic. Friedman's stance was ironic because at just the time he was arguing for shareholder capitalism, economic theorists were explaining why, in general, maximizing shareholder value would not lead to societal well-being.[4]

Only in simplistic economic models are public and private interests perfectly aligned. Public policy should aim to bring them into better alignment. But it never does so perfectly, which means that maximizing shareholder interests is seldom itself sufficient to ensure societal well-being. The interests of executives have become decoupled from the interests of the company and of society as a whole. CEO bonuses and starkly higher pay for executives in some sectors, notably in finance but elsewhere as well, have become a lightning rod for public criticism, and rightly so. While the claim is that these bonuses are necessary to incentivize executives, the evidence is that these payments do not even fulfill the stated goal of increasing shareholder value but generate enormous negative side effects. In banking, they encouraged excessive risk taking and short-termism; in the auto industry, they facilitated attempts to circumvent environmental regulations; in some international businesses, they enabled corruption and bribery.

As long as CEOs and other high-level corporate executives have their compensation and benefits linked to stock prices, and particularly stock prices in the here and now, as many currently do, they will be tempted to pursue short-term gains and creative—destructive is a better word—accounting tricks, which are ephemeral sources of growth at best, over adding real long-term value to their companies. CEOs who can manipulate share prices by using creative (or even fraudulent) accounting practices are simply exercising their market power on their own behalf and for their own financial reward. As they do that, there is less money left over for investment, to pay workers, or even for distribution to other shareholders. Incentives matter, though not as much as these CEOs might claim. Too many European firms followed the American model in providing incentives that mainly serve to enrich top executives.

According to Bloomberg data,[5] the CEO pay-to-average-income ratio in Europe is still not as out of control as in the United States, but it is particularly worrisome in some countries. In Germany and the Netherlands, for instance, a CEO earns 136 and 171 times more, respectively, than the average worker. This is about half of the corresponding number for the United States, but Europe should take little comfort in knowing that it has so far not been plagued with the extreme excesses of the United States. In a globalized world, many European executives are pushing in this direction.

## SOLUTIONS

Creating an economic system in which executives act in the public interest and in the interests of all the firms' stakeholders is not easy. There are three critical components: the right mix of decision makers, the right rules for guiding firm decision making, and the right managerial incentive systems. Europe needs rules that bring other voices besides executives to the table, that ensure that firms see their objectives more broadly than the enrichment of shareholders, and that encourage compensation systems focused more on the long term and that are more consistent with the interests of society as a whole.

Ultimate responsibility for a firm's decisions should lie, to a greater extent, with those who are affected by the firm's decisions and whose interests are most aligned with the firm's long-term performance. Workers and the communities in which a company operates are vitally affected by what the firm does, but under shareholder capitalism, their interests have no weight and therefore they have no voice. By contrast, under stakeholder capitalism, the corporation should at least take into account those who have a vital stake in the long-run performance of the company—not only shareholders. That is one of the reasons that stakeholder capitalism, part of the corporate governance framework of some European countries, is preferable to shareholder capitalism.

Systems where workers have some direct financial stake in the company (as in employee stock ownership plans) may also help to ensure the alignment of all interests and may encourage more cooperative behavior. Also, the voices of shareholders who have a greater interest in the long-run performance of the company deserve a better hearing. Loyalty share voting,[6] which is rewarding those who have held on to their shares longer by giving them greater say in the affairs of the company, is one solution. It will, at the same time, weaken the voice of corporate raiders (sometimes from private equity firms) who often buy up companies only to strip away their assets or to load them up with debt that leads to an eventual bankruptcy and loss of jobs.

Executive compensation schemes, too, have to be reformed in a way that provides incentives that promote long-term value, rather than a focus on short-term spikes in share prices.

There have been several proposals for curbing excesses in executive compensation and to better align executive incentives with the long-run interests of firms. As we noted, the effect of distorted incentives was most apparent—and had perhaps the highest social costs—in the financial sector, where it led to excessive risk taking and other forms of anticompetitive, exploitative, and antisocial behavior. This is a regulated sector—government can simply prohibit the kind of incentive schemes that encourage short-termism and excessive risk-taking, and this may be especially appropriate for government-insured institutions. The EU has not yet met the challenge of regulating performance bonuses in the financial sector. Bankers who were responsible for a crisis that cost so many so much continue to be rewarded with outsized compensation through incentive structures that encourage the very behavior that proved so costly. And outside the financial sector, even less has been done.

While the scope for regulation elsewhere is more limited than in the financial sector, there are a number of other instruments that can be used to encourage better compensation schemes. Well-functioning markets require transparency. At the very least, there should be transparency about the compensation provided to executives in publicly listed corporations and about how that compensation compares with that of ordinary workers. From January 2017, a company listed on US exchanges must annually disclose the ratio between the CEO's compensation and the salary of its median worker. A similar measure took effect at the beginning of 2019 in Britain but has not entered into the core of the European agenda. Adopting this requirement would represent a very minimal step toward encouraging good corporate practices.

Giving shareholders some voice in the pay of their managers, who supposedly work for them (a measure called "say on pay"), would also discourage needlessly large pay packages. At least in some places, it has proven effective; and the fact that so many CEOs resolutely oppose this idea suggests that they are afraid that it might be effective.

Tax codes can also have an impact on the design of executive compensation schemes. Some blame exorbitant compensation on a provision in the US tax code that exempted performance-based pay from a tax on excessive executive compensation. This provision encouraged compensation using stock options, which, as we have seen, led to distorted decisions that focused on increasing short-term share value rather than long-term performance. Some have suggested that imposing a surtax on firms with excessive managerial compensation (absolutely, relative to the size of the firm, or to the pay of others within the firm) will discourage these excesses. At the very least, obvious ways by which executives enrich themselves at the expense of other shareholders and the public treasury should be discouraged. Share buybacks, for example, increase the value of each remaining share, and thus benefit CEOs, whose pay is related to share price. But by depriving the firm of needed funds for investment, the long-term value of the firm may decline. Imposing a hefty surtax on any capital gains earned, as part of the executive compensation of a firm that has engaged in a buyback, would almost surely discourage this practice. The United States is now considering an outright ban on share buybacks. So should Europe. Any firm wanting to distribute funds to its shareholders can easily do so through the traditional route of paying dividends.

Another way to combat the pernicious effects of skewed incentives in the private sector is to encourage the formation of businesses with organizational forms other than the joint-stock, publicly listed company. The standard corporate form (seen in almost all the leading companies in every sector, such as Banco Santander, Novartis, or Siemens) is and will likely remain dominant. But forms like the cooperative Mondragon in Spain and the foundation-controlled Robert Bosch GmbH in Germany deserve more attention than they get. Community-owned savings banks in Germany and Italy often faced pressure to privatize from ideologues, especially before the crisis. Instead, these and other alternatives deserve respect for what they are: valuable contributions toward encouraging diversity and competition in the market for corporate organization.*

Worker-owned business models, for instance, directly incentivize and reward workers for their efforts.† Owner-employees are often more productive. Direct ownership puts all the fruits of ownership, including income, capital appreciation, information, and control, in employees' hands as shareholders. With employees as the shareholding beneficiaries, the returns to the firm may be shared more equitably, thus making work more rewarding. Even without full ownership, employee share ownership programs (that can be encouraged, for example, through tax incentives for the purchase of shares) can foster these types of benefits.

Worker ownership is an example of a broader class of cooperative organizations that includes those where other stakeholders, such as consumers, have ownership and management rights. During the financial crisis, cooperatives also often proved more resilient by laying off fewer workers, thus losing less of the human capital that had been invested in

---

* An EU database of business forms administered by the European Commission would be a start for appreciation of the diversity of corporate organization, and for the potential for improvement.

† There is one drawback: the risk that too much of an individual's wealth and well-being is tied to the firm. If it should run into trouble as a result of dramatic changes in market conditions, an employee could lose both job and pension.

the enterprise. This enabled them to bounce back better once the economy recovered. Financial cooperatives, which we discuss more extensively in Chapter 5, also deserve stronger support from policymakers.

In the United States, there has been another development in corporate organization: corporations that are mission-driven rather than profit-seeking (as their only bottom line). Laws in many states have been changed to encourage such corporations (called B-corporations). A few European countries have followed; more should do so.[7]

Small, medium-sized, and large enterprises are all basic parts of the productive fabric of society. Their actions are central to the long-run performance of economies and societies. Society benefits when the enterprises and those who run them behave more responsibly—with a view toward the long-run prosperity of all of their stakeholders. It makes perfect sense for society to encourage organizational forms that are more consonant with the interests of society; at the very least, it makes sense for society to encourage greater diversity in organizational form. Tax preferences are an important tool for encouraging socially desirable behavior, and Europe should extend them to cooperatives, to B-corporations, and to those companies in which employees have more ownership and more voice.

## INTELLECTUAL PROPERTY

As Europe's economy transforms itself into a knowledge and innovation economy, *intellectual property rights* (IPR), or exclusive temporary ownership rights given to innovators and others who make contributions through patents, copyrights, and trademarks, have drawn greater scrutiny. These rights are supposed to foster innovation by ensuring that inventors enjoy the fruits of their creations, whether they are works of art, technological advances, or trademarks and other commercial ideas. At the same time, intellectual property rights introduce inefficiencies in the economy by impeding the free flow of knowledge—they confer monopoly power. Well-designed intellectual property rights regimes attempt to minimize these static harms and maximize the dynamic benefits. Poorly designed intellectual property regimes may even impede innovation, for instance, by making access to knowledge, which is the most important input to any research, more difficult to come by.

"If I have seen further, it is by standing on the shoulders of giants," Isaac Newton famously wrote. Many of today's intellectual property laws make these metaphorical "shoulders" off-limits, by forbidding not only profit from another's innovation but also any research based on it (at least not without providing compensation). Think of all the research that has been based on the discovery of DNA. Imagine how subsequent research would have been impeded if Watson and Crick had barred the use of what they learned or had charged a high fee for its use.

Innovation can also be mired in conflicting patent claims. In the field of technology, innovators often have to wade through what has come to be called a *patent thicket*. A patent thicket emerges when large corporations have the resources to acquire a large number of patents, not to use them for research or to make new products, but simply to prevent other firms from entering the market and competing. Worse are *patent trolls* who acquire intellectual property rights solely for the purpose of making money by suing infringers.

Today's intellectual property regimes in Europe are not well designed. Their poor structure reflects corporate interests more than broader public interests. In a twenty-first-century economy, the market for innovation, or more particularly, for the knowledge behind intellectual property, is one of the most important markets. Rules must be designed to make this market work as well as it can—in the interests not just of corporations but also of society at large. It is simply false to say that policy must protect intellectual property as strongly as possible. Such policies may not even maximize the rate of innovation, let alone balance other societal concerns.

There are multiple ways of promoting innovation, some of which do not have the adverse effects of patents. We can, for instance, promote innovation in pharmaceuticals without rewarding drug companies with outsized *monopoly profits*, the high prices the drug companies charge that condemn to death those who cannot afford them. It is particularly ironic that, while the basic research on virtually all of the advances in modern medicine has been funded publicly, the drug companies demand, through the patent system, that the public pays a second time for these essential medicines. It would be one thing if the pharmaceutical companies were simply rewarded at a fair return for their contribution in bringing to the market the insights of government-funded research. But they have used the patent system and the monopoly power it grants to extract rents far beyond such justification.

That Europe and the United States have tumbled into policies that overprotect intellectual property is not entirely surprising. The entertainment and pharmaceutical industries realized that such policies could garner tens of billions of dollars in profits, and that it was a good political investment to lobby to get an ever stronger, corporation-driven IPR system. The system that has evolved is not one that maximizes the pace of innovation, let alone societal well-being. It is also not one that is supported by those in the scientific community who are concerned with the advancement of knowledge and its use for improving the human condition.

This is not the place for a full discussion of the construction of a well-functioning intellectual property regime, one that would make the twenty-first-century innovation markets work for society. However, four key insights are crucial:

**1.** *Knowledge is a public good.* There is no additional societal cost of someone else having access to knowledge, and there is possibly considerable benefit. Knowledge is fundamentally different from ordinary goods. If one person consumes some food, for example, another person cannot consume that meal. Knowledge, on the other hand, is never reduced by its use. It is therefore in society's interest to have the widest access to, and dissemination of, knowledge. Only if there is a strong case that some restriction will promote the production of knowledge should a restriction that reduces its utilization be justified. Traditionally, the patent system requires full disclosure of knowledge so that others can build on it, even if the patent holder temporarily has the exclusive use of the patent. But today, many corporations want the rights (or protections) of patents without fulfilling disclosure requirements. These disclosure requirements need to be strictly enforced, and if the owner does not make use of a patent,* the knowledge should be put squarely in the public domain.

Because knowledge is a public good, privatizing it, which is effectively what patents do, can be highly profitable even if socially costly. Here, the patent holder sees private gain but not the losses to the rest of society. This creates an incentive for excessive patenting. That is why the government needs to set high standards for granting a new patent.

By the same token, challenging a patent's validity takes something that is in the private domain and puts it into the public. This process creates a public good, and as always, there will be an undersupply of public goods. The intellectual property regime should make it easier to challenge a patent (Europe does a much better job of this than the United States) and provide incentives for doing so.

The length of a patent is also an important consideration. The lon-

---

* These are called sleeping patents and are designed to forestall entry of competitors.

ger the patent, the longer the time before the benefits of that knowledge can be widely shared. Especially in pharmaceuticals, corporations have tried to extend their patent durations through a process called "evergreening," which works by companies making slight and often obvious improvements to a drug, such as developing a time-release version. The patent system needs to guard against such abuses.

**2. Intellectual property rights are only one part of a country's innovation system.** Innovations can be financed and incentivized by public funding and prizes. Europe may have lost a sense of balance and proportion. Public funding is essential, especially for basic research, and it benefits all of Europe. It should be an important part of the EU's budget going forward. Too much of the EU budget is focused on the dominant industry of the past—agriculture—and too little on innovation, the key to Europe's future.

Prizes awarded to innovators are especially important, especially when a need exists, such as for a lightweight, inexpensive battery for cars, a vaccine for a deadly disease, or a cure for HIV/AIDS. Once the discovery is made, society wants the fruits of that discovery to be made as widely available as possible.

The award of a monopoly is also a prize, but it is an inefficient and distorting one. The monopolies that result from patents restrict use to maximize profits. In contrast, the kind of prize system that would reward innovators on the basis of the significance of their social contribution can be largely self-financing. Charging license fees for the use of the patent but still allowing market forces to compete to make the innovation as widely available as possible (and at as low a price as possible) would avoid the distortions of monopoly.

The government can also encourage other legal arrangements for promoting innovation, such as the "collective commons," which promotes open-source programming and innovation.

**3. In intellectual property regimes, details like the length of the patent and the standards that have to be satisfied to get a patent really matter.** Corporations, as we have noted, have every incentive to try to make protection as strong as possible—with wider patents and longer terms, and for a wider range of areas, such as business process innovations. The extremes in America are almost comical, as was the case of Amazon's patent, since expired, of the "one-click ordering process."[8] But here, as elsewhere, European corporate giants would not hesitate to imitate the United States.

**4. Intellectual property rights are a social construction, designed to promote societal well-being, and are a means to an end, not an end in themselves.** When intellectual property rights result in behavior that conflicts with broader societal objectives, they need to be adjusted. For instance, access to life-saving medicines is essential, and no company should have the power to deny the right to their access. To protect against this, governments have introduced the principle of *compulsory licenses*, which compel the owner of the patent to grant its use for a reasonable fee.

Even the US government made use of such a provision when the country faced an anthrax scare, and the owner of the patent on the drug that was most effective against it (Cipro) could not meet the supply required. There may need to be more extensive use of compulsory licenses in the future, not only for public health but also for technology that curbs greenhouse gases. Likewise, when patents result in excessive monopolization of markets and interfere with the workings of competition in broad arenas, as did Microsoft's control of the software for the main PC operating system, they may have to be curtailed. At the very least, policy needs to be sensitive to the incentives to leverage the market power granted by a patent and to extend and enhance that market power.

## CONCLUSION

Too many European elites propagated a myth that unfettered markets, on their own, promote efficiency and lead to societal well-being. Indeed, the very notion of unfettered markets is itself a myth. Markets, as we have noted, do not exist in a vacuum but have to be structured; they have to operate under certain rules and regulations. The relevant question is, therefore, what are the rules and regulations that best advance the long-run interests of society in general? At the very least, markets need laws that govern property rights and contracts, corporate governance and bankruptcy, labor rights, and competitive behavior. These laws, rules, and regulations determine what a firm can and cannot do, as well as who gets rewarded and who makes decisions. How markets are structured has profound consequences for efficiency and the distribution of income.

Textbook economics—whether Adam Smith's "pin factory" or an idealized firm run by its owner—are a far cry from today's twenty-first-century innovation economy, which is marked by imperfections in competition, a dysfunctional financial sector, and managerial capitalism. Today, profits can be enhanced more easily by more efficiently exploiting others.[9] For example, this can be done by unfairly using market power or by taking advantage of the lack of information available to one's customers—the opposite of building a better product or providing a better service at a lower cost. This is one of the reasons that markets are so frequently inequitable—generating such low incomes for some that it causes misery and creates a burden on society, while bringing returns for others that are out of proportion to their social contributions.

Nor do markets on their own lead to efficiency. Without adequate regulation and an appropriate role for government, society will experience massive collateral damage. For example, there will be too much pollution, too many risky financial products, hordes of overpaid executives, insufficient expenditures on basic research, and too little dissemination of innovation. Moreover, markets may not even be particularly stable, as we clearly saw in 2008.

If there were a single set of rules that dominated all others, which made everyone better off than under any other set of rules, life would be simple; everyone, everywhere would want to adopt those rules. In this chapter, however, we have seen multiple examples of trade-offs. Monopolists lose when a country has a good competition regime, and the rest of society benefits. In contrast, a poorly designed intellectual property regime benefits drug companies at the expense of the rest of society. This imbalance of benefits is why writing the rules of the economy is so contentious.

We have argued in this chapter, and elsewhere in this book, that current rules are too favorable to corporate interests, supported by an ideology—a misguided theory—about how the economy functions. Almost a half century of research has exposed the flaws in this ideology, in what we have referred to elsewhere as *market fundamentalism*. And four decades of experimentation in economies around the world that have, to one extent or another, adopted rules guided by this ideology, have shown the ways in which it leads to a distorted economy marked by inequality and instability. In fact, market fundamentalism has not even produced the high growth that was promised.

The fact that there are trade-offs makes the design of rules difficult. Accordingly, each country must choose rules that reflect its own values. Europe faces a particular challenge in enabling individual countries to do this because it complicates another EU goal: cementing the integration of the internal market. Such a goal will sometimes require a harmonization of the rules, or even that the rules be set by the EU.

Here, the principle of *subsidiarity* comes into play. This principle says, in effect, that rules that have no externalities, no cross-border effects, should be set by the individual countries. However, policymakers will need to exercise careful judgment. Often there are some cross-border effects, but they are limited. EU policy has to be strong enough to remove national barriers that impede a proper functioning of the Single Market. Without a single integrated market, EU operators in many key sectors will not be able to serve the citizens of Europe as well as they should.

This chapter has described some of the steps that can be taken to make European markets work as they are supposed to, with competitive companies striving to improve societal well-being through better corporate governance, which includes better executive compensation schemes. We have also seen how government can best promote innovation. An appropriately designed intellectual property regime is part of this answer.

All of the changes in Europe's rules discussed here would contribute to greater equality. They would also, therefore, soften the backlash against the European corporate sector and against a political system that seems to have supported it in an unbalanced way, a backlash that has contributed to political gains of radical groups. In the last several decades, no sector deviated further from what was expected of it than did financial services, which is an industry in need of specific, far-reaching reform. We turn to that challenge in the next chapter.

*Chapter 5*

# Toward a Financial System That Serves Society

**For most of** the last half of the twentieth century, European countries presided over a remarkably stable financial system. The opening years of the twenty-first century, however, bore out the warning of economist Hyman Minsky that the moments of complete stability, when the environment seems perfectly and permanently calm, are the most dangerous, as people take on excess risk on the presumption that the stability will continue. In 2008, the world glimpsed the prospect of how the disintegration of the financial system could have pulled down the entire economy with it.

## A DYSFUNCTIONAL FINANCIAL SYSTEM

Since then, public opinion has firmed behind a strong resolve to avoid anything resembling a repetition of that harrowing episode, and a broad consensus has formed in favor of stronger regulation of the financial sector. But the industry and its lobbyists have met this resolve with resistance to any regulations that would reduce profit margins. For those in the financial sector, the crisis is ancient history, an unfortunate event, a once-in-a-century flood that is best forgotten. They ignore the fact that the crisis did not emerge from nowhere but was caused by what they had done. And if they are allowed to take outsized risks, it might well happen again.

During the few decades before the financial crisis, Europe, though to a lesser degree than the United States, lost sight of the fact that the financial sector is supposed to serve society rather than the other way around, with the interests of society subservient to the interests of finance. No modern economy can function well without a well-functioning financial sector. But this sector worked poorly in both Europe and the United States. Both regions need a financial sector that will perform certain essential services, from managing the wealth of individuals for their retirement, to running a modern payments mechanism, to providing prudent financial intermediation. The financial system must ensure that scarce capital is allocated to the highest-return activities, thus providing the funds necessary for creating new firms and expanding old ones.

Had they performed these services well, those in the financial sector would have been amply rewarded. However, their greed knew no bounds, and they realized that their position of trust gave them an unprecedented opportunity to exploit others. In addition, lack of competition in the financial sector gave them the power to set prices well above the costs of providing their services.

The world's financial system did not efficiently allocate capital. The US housing bubble provides the best example of this, with shoddy homes built in the middle of the Nevada desert. But Europe provides numerous other examples, including the Spanish construction frenzy. Furthermore, European banks provided plenty of the money for America's reckless real estate boom, and the financial sector was indifferent as to whether a firm earned its profits from exploitation or from wealth creation.

As we noted in the last chapter, the financial sector did not play its traditional role of intermediating between households and firms, bringing to enterprises money to make investments that would foster growth and employment. Instead, it did the opposite and helped money flow out of firms. This trend drove lower physical investment, fragile growth, and long-term stagnation in labor productivity.[1]

In the 1950s, economist Joan Robinson[2] said that "where enterprise leads, finance follows." Her statement applies to an ideal: a financial system designed such that it supports the productive sector. In contrast, recent structural changes in the functioning of capitalism mark the growing prominence of financial motives over productive purposes. These changes were supposed to lead to better allocations of resources, especially capital, and to better management of Europe's companies. A superior financial system was supposed to make sure that money went to where societal returns were the highest.

Empirical findings support a thesis of the *financialization* of the economy, namely that the nonfinancial (real) economy is increasingly oriented toward financial activities. A simple example is the increasing reliance of automakers on their financing arms for profits.

Most importantly, the financial sector encouraged other firms to follow their lead in short-term thinking—in maximizing share value today, regardless of the implications for the long term. They also set an example in executive compensation schemes that not only delivered a disproportionate share of corporate profits to executives, which left less to be reinvested in the firm or distributed to shareholders, but also incentivized managers to act in shortsighted ways. The financial services industry's obsession with short-term returns and executive compensation based on incentive pay has spread throughout the corporate sector like a contagious disease. It is no wonder that as the financial sector grew, the overall economy did not match its pace. Overall growth actually slowed.

The excessive compensation in the financial sector distorted the entire labor market. Scarce human resources were not allocated according to where they would contribute the most to society or even to firms. Disproportionately, the most talented workers went into finance and not into fields such as research, education, or social work. Morale for those working elsewhere suffered because they seemingly received a relative pittance for their hard work and high abilities. The result was not greater efforts, but widespread resentment. This dissonance reached its peak during the 2008 crisis, when the bankers, who had brought their banks and the global economy to the brink of ruin, walked away with massive bonuses. What they did in pursuit of their private interests had undermined the efficiency, stability, and growth of the economy.

## The Mantra and Myth of Self-Regulation

The zeitgeist of the 1990s and early 2000s conveyed that Europeans were living in the Age of Finance, which seemed to be a good thing. European events such as the World Economic Forum heralded bank CEOs as the titans of a globalized economy. And Britain's highly financialized economy arguably turned London into the global capital of finance.

The mantra of the age was *self-regulation*, the idea that these leaders of finance knew better how to manage risk than any government official. Adam Smith's dictum—that the pursuit of self-interest would lead (by dint of the invisible hand) to the well-being of society—was often quoted, but without acknowledging the many qualifications that Smith put on it. Contrary to the views of his twenty-first-century acolytes, Smith saw an important role for government.

Unfortunately, the public in Europe became aware of the importance of a stable financial system and the failures of self-regulation only when something went terribly wrong. Before that, the main voices heard were those of the bankers themselves, who had argued that loosening regulations would create a more dynamic financial system, which would contribute to a stronger European economy from which all would benefit. Besides, the bankers argued, there was a global marketplace into which they, their profits, and their jobs would disperse unless there was deregulation. Indeed, around the world, there was a race to the bottom as countries competed to attract the attention of footloose bankers.

As neoliberals talked about the supposed growth and employment benefits of deregulation, they neglected the costs—both the macroeconomic risks that might arise from a poorly regulated financial sector that is engaged in excessive risk taking, and the microeconomic costs arising from the financial sector's exploitation of its market power and consumer and investor ignorance. In the end, deregulation proceeded apace, and the sector expanded. But the promised growth and employment proved illusory, and the risks even proved to be greater than the critics had predicted.

Regulations are necessary when one person or organization can impose large costs on others. Bank misdeeds brought on a financial crisis; the recession that followed the financial crisis amplified the costs that banks imposed on the rest of society. The bankers simply did not take into account these costs, nor would they have been expected to do so, as they focused their attention on their own pay, and on maximizing profits or short-term market value. So, too, as short-term thinking has increased and moral scruples decreased, the financial sector has demonstrated a propensity to engage in exploitation of others to the greatest extent possible, from market manipulation (such as the distortion of foreign exchange markets), to abuse of market power, to predatory lending.

As it turned out, even in a narrower sense the banks showed less economic prowess than they claimed. Part of the reason for this discrepancy was the existence of the perverse incentive schemes that were discussed in the previous chapter. This was a disease that originated in the United States but has now contaminated much of the rest of the world. These incentive schemes typically reward bankers on the basis of short-term returns and without penalizing them for losses, either in the short or long term. Predictably, the incentives led to short-term thinking and excessive risk taking.

### The enormous costs of the financial crisis

During the crisis, governments had to provide enormous support for their banks. By 2013, a point in which most bailout costs had already been incurred, the European Union had plowed billions and billions into its banking sector, which served mainly to avert disaster; bailed-out banks did not generally improve performance in the coming years.[3] All this aid came in addition to the hidden subsidies that were provided by the ECB, as it lent money to the banks at essentially zero or negative (real) interest rates. By mid-2017, banks in the Eurozone had about €760 billion in cheap liquidity thanks to the ECB.[4] By way of comparison, in 2013 the EU sprinkled only €2 billion into a new effort to fight youth unemployment, a crucial problem exacerbated by the banking crisis and the austerity-minded response to the recession.

But these financial costs are dwarfed by the costs that the financial crisis imposed on the rest of the economy. If one compares what

GDP might have been without the crisis (based on historical growth) and what GDP actually was, Europe's cumulative losses were in the trillions of euros.

Of course, the individuals who lost their jobs and homes bore the brunt of the costs of the crisis. And the effects are likely to be long-lived. Even years after the crisis, the level of GDP and the growth rate are far lower than they would have been without the crisis. More-over, the level of unemployment is higher. As we note elsewhere in this book, for years now, many young people have not been able to use their job skills. We saw in Chapter 2, too, how the flawed response to the crisis discouraged the kind of investment that raises productivity and makes future growth possible. Economists refer to these long-run effects as *hysteresis*, the idea that history matters, or in this case, that the loss of skills from the lack of productive employment or the loss of productivity from the lack of investment will not be recouped for a long time, if ever.[5]

## The Challenge of Finance for Europe

Europe will have to create a stable financial system that serves ordinary Europeans, most of whom do not work in high finance. The revenue that the financial sector has garnered for itself comes at the expense of the rest of society, but it is worse than a zero-sum game. The losses to the rest of society are far greater than the gains to the financial sec-tor. For instance, the exercise of market power distorts the economy. But this is even truer when the financial sector exploits its information advantage over others through insider trading, market manipulation, and predatory lending. These behaviors destroy trust in the financial system and thus its capacity to perform essential functions. This trust deficit has also spread to a mistrust in government, which is partially understandable, given the failure of governments throughout the West to adequately hold the financial sector to account.

The pace of reform in the decade after the crisis has been far slower than hoped because, as we noted, the bankers have resisted many of the necessary changes. It would be preferable in a global economy to have a coordinated regulatory response. That, however, has proven possible only to a very limited extent, and even this limited cooperation is now at risk. While there is a general consensus (outside of the financial community) that there is a need for more regulation, the US Congress has already approved a partial rollback of the Dodd-Frank law of 2010, landmark legislation that was, nevertheless, only a first step in addressing the problems posed by the financial sector.

The widespread understanding of the need for financial sector reforms provides a chance to align them more closely with European values. It is imperative that the regulations of the Single Market ensure a well-functioning European financial market. The ideas needed to meet the challenge are at hand. If Europe follows through, it will be an important step forward for the European project.

Europe should draw little comfort from knowing it may be doing a better job than the United States. The American lurch backward under the Trump administration toward a pro–Wall Street agenda only strengthens the case for a different approach by European leadership. The 2008 crisis has made it abundantly clear that the costs of not having a good financial system with adequate regulation are enormous, far greater than the costs of the regulation that is urgently needed.

### *The disparity between social and private returns*

The underlying problem with the financial sector is that private returns are not well aligned with societal returns, either at the level of management or of the institutions. And changes in the financial sector in recent decades have made matters worse, not better. Part of the reason for this disturbing trend is the prevalence of market fundamentalist (neoliberal) ideas, which hold that whatever is profitable is beneficial to society.

Advances in economics over the past four decades have shown, however, that when there is imperfect information, imperfect competition, or an incomplete set of risk markets (which is always the case), this is not true. Firms can increase their profits by taking advantage of others, for example, through market manipulation or insider trading. These activities distort the economy both in the short run and the long. When these schemes are discovered, there is a loss of trust in financial markets, which means that markets will be even less able to perform their essential functions. Market fundamentalism simply ignored the implications of these pervasive market imperfections, these real-world deviations from a textbook ideal. The kind of exploitation that we have seen simply could not occur if everyone was perfectly informed. One of the central roles of financial markets is to gather and process information to best allocate scarce capital. To assume perfect information is to assume away the central function of financial markets.

Because of the often large disparities between private returns and social returns, banks often make decisions that do not serve the rest of society well. The bank focuses only on maximizing its profits or stock market value, giving short shrift to the collateral damage that its actions might cause to the rest of society. An obvious example of such behavior is banks' exploitation of their market power by charging more than the competitive price—in this case, charging more to borrowers even as they pay less to depositors than they would in a fully competitive market. The prices lower the well-being of both savers and borrowers, all for the purpose of enriching the bankers.

When a bank does not do what it should, and too much of what it should not, there are knock-on effects. With banks focused on speculation or predatory lending, less attention is paid to lending to small businesses. The result is that fewer jobs will be created, which, in the absence of government intervention, means higher unemployment and/or lower wages.

Such knock-on effects can occur from virtually any decision the bank makes. For example, if one of two banks closes in a community, the remaining bank will have monopoly power. This lone bank can then (and almost surely will) exercise that market power by raising interest rates it charges to local small businesses. Yes, businesses might be able to establish a banking relationship elsewhere, but because their new bank will know less about them, they will be charged a higher interest rate. At the higher interest rate, the firm may be discouraged from investing and creating jobs. As employment in the community declines, some workers will move away, which will then hurt landowners because of decreasing land values. In a community with only one or two banks, the closure of a branch has broad societal effects that the bankers will not take into account.

## SOLUTIONS

In the following sections, we will examine some of the key problems within the financial sector and what can be done to improve the likelihood that banks serve society in the way they should and reduce the likelihood that they continue to inflict societal harm.

### Better Regulatory Structures

While better corporate governance helps to better align incentives, Europe needs good regulatory structures to both improve those incentives and restrain behavior that is destructive to society. Thus, it is essential to regulate banks to prevent them from engaging in antisocial behavior. There are many aspects to this type of behavior. One example is devising and implementing tax avoidance and evasion schemes, the type that have robbed so many countries and the EU of badly needed revenue. European banks have played a big role in money laundering, including of ill-gotten gains from Russia and other countries of the former Soviet Union. Banks and private equity firms have also facilitated, and in many cases actually encouraged, mergers among firms that have helped create a less competitive economy. Indeed, this is a major part of an investment bank's business.

Most discussions of financial-sector reform focus on preventing the financial sector from harming the rest of society through reckless risk taking or exploitive behavior. But the reform discussion should have begun by asking how we can ensure that the financial sector actually serves the rest of society. There are critical roles for it to perform, such as providing credit to small- and medium-sized enterprises, especially important because these small firms cannot obtain money from capital markets.

With less energy devoted to antisocial activities, more of banks' energies will be devoted to doing what they should be doing. They will also encourage more efficient allocation of capital, such as through more lending to small businesses. Likewise, improved incentive structures that focus on long-term performance will discourage the short-term excesses of risk taking and exploitative behavior that have characterized the financial sector on both sides of the Atlantic.

We may not be able to regulate banks perfectly or prevent them from engaging in every antisocial activity. Banks have shown enormous ingenuity in circumventing the regulations that *do* exist. But, clearly, Europe can do a lot better than it has.

Dealing with the whole array of market failures—not only in which banks do terrible, headline-grabbing things, but also in which they are not doing the good things that ensure a well-functioning economy—again entails a better alignment of private incentives with societal goals, as well as the imposition of key constraints. The United States, for example, requires banks to assist underserved communities via the Community Reinvestment Act. Other measures could include ensuring a minimal level of credit to small business, or the restriction of the amount lent for real estate speculation.

## Capital requirements

Since the financial crisis, Europe has made important progress in improving the financial sector's regulatory structure. For example, capital requirements on banks have increased. One of the key problems before the crisis was that banks had an inadequate base of *capital*, which is defined as the bank's net worth or the difference between their assets and their liabilities. This meant that if there were an economic downturn and some of a bank's loans turned sour, the bank's net worth (the difference between its assets and its liabilities) could easily evaporate, thus necessitating a government bailout. If a bank's net worth is, say, only 3 percent of the value of its assets, a decrease in the value of its assets by 3 percent destroys its entire net worth.

Banks have strongly opposed the increase in capital requirements, arguing that requiring more capital will increase their costs, which will, in turn, require them to raise more expensive equity and charge more for loans. But a basic insight of modern economics is that this claim is largely false. A firm or bank with more *leverage* (a higher debt-to-equity ratio) pays for the leverage through a higher cost to *equity* (the funds it acquires through the sale of shares, for example) because of the greater risk that the equity has to bear. Could it be that our bankers, supposed experts in risk, do not understand how equity works? Or perhaps there's something else really going on here. More equity means a lower share price, which is a major benchmark for banker compensation. And with higher capital, the chances of a government bailout falls. Banks like these hidden subsidies; the public does not and for good reason.

Overall, the increase in capital requirements is a move in the right direction, but it is not enough.

### Too-big-to-fail and other bank maladies

The European Union, like the United States, nurtured the creation of large banks (whose collapse would one day threaten the financial system) for a variety of reasons including misplaced pride in having European mega-banks, and the political influence of large banks at the national and European level.

By the early 2000s, acquisitions such as the purchase of British bank Abbey National by Spain's Santander, or the decision by Italy's UniCredit to buy Germany's HypoVereinsbank, won praise as being future-oriented creators of European champions. Germany's Deutsche Bank, once a relationship lender with a focus on Germany, came to be dominated by London-oriented investment bankers, a mistake the bank has only recently begun to remedy. Sensible calls for European oversight were lost in the din of praise for these behemoths.

By 2010, as the worst of the banking crisis had passed, the top ten EU banks had about €15 trillion in assets, equivalent to 122 percent of GDP.[6] And Europe remains home to ten globally systemically important banks (G-SIBs), the designation that the international Financial Stability Board set up in response to the crisis, which highlights banks whose failure would have a significant effect on the world's economy.

Because the failure of any of these huge banks imposes such large collateral damage on the rest of the economy, governments typically will not allow them to fail—hence the moniker "too big to fail." Europe still has a serious too-big-to-fail dilemma on its hands. This is because too-big-to-fail banks represent a triple problem. First, they know that they are too big to fail so they take on inordinate risk since they will not pay the ultimate price of bankruptcy. They will be rescued, come what may—or at least with a high probability—thus, their incentives are distorted. Second, when these banks do fail, not only is the direct cost to the government and the economy large, but so are the indirect costs caused by their interlinkage with virtually all the other banks (even smaller banks can be too interlinked to fail). Third, because of the greater likelihood of a bailout, the too-big-to-fail banks can borrow at a lower rate. This hidden subsidy, granted because they are perceived as safer borrowers, allows them to grow still larger.

As the financial crisis unfolded, regulators, lawmakers, and eventually the public came to appreciate the consequences of letting banks grow to enormous size. Lending and trading activities across many countries translated into mind-boggling organizational complexity. Some banks even had more than 1,000 affiliates, and many were engaged in extremely complicated trading schemes hinged on their ability to access short-term credit markets. Because of the risks they had taken by creating complex derivatives and by financing their securities in short-term funding markets, the banks had become not only too big to fail, but also too big and too complex to manage.

If societal returns had been closely aligned with private returns, the growth would have avoided the problems of too-big-to-manage institutions. In contrast, bank executives claimed that there were large economies of scale and scope (in which it is more efficient to do many things than to specialize only in one or a few). But economists who have studied the matter have found no evidence of such economies of scale or scope, at least at the levels of scale and scope to which the mega-banks have grown; the problem of being too big to manage is a reflection of a large *diseconomy* of scale and scope. Banks grew in size partly because of the implicit bailout subsidy that lowered the cost of capital. They grew in size, too, partly because of the dysfunctions in corporate governance to which we have alluded—with CEO and other executive compensation increasing with the size of the bank—and also partly because banks can reduce competition and thereby increase profits through mergers and acquisitions.

Consider a merger between two banks. The merged bank focuses on its increased profits. Some of this may come from synergies between the two banks that can better be exploited when the two firms work together more closely. Much of the increased profits, however, may come from the reduction in competition. What really matters is not the number of banks in the country as a whole, but rather the level of local competition. Although there may be numerous banks in the country, if the only two operating in a given community merge, they form a monopoly. This monopoly may be somewhat fettered by the fact that if the banks charge too much for their loans or pay depositors too little, customers can go elsewhere. Still, there may be enough market power in the community to significantly increase bank profits. Small enterprises, well-known within the community but unknown elsewhere, may be particularly hard hit, as we have noted, and may face a significant increase in the interest rate charged (with all of the negative ramifications that were described earlier).

In short, what makes a market economy serve society well is competition. What makes for greater profits in banking, as elsewhere, is limiting competition. The consequences of inadequate competition in banking have particularly severe societal consequences because of finance's centrality to the economy. And the consequences of the resulting large banks are even worse because of the micro- and macro-distortions, compounded by the too-big-to-fail problem.

## MANAGING THE RISKS OF BIG BANKS

The implicit and explicit subsidies and systemic risks posed by the largest banks are out of proportion to their benefits. Indeed, as we have noted, much of the banks' seeming competitive advantages are artificial, arising from the hidden subsidies and their market power.

The Report of the European Commission's High-level Expert Group on Bank Structural Reform (usually referred to as the Liikanen Report of 2012 after its chairman, former governor of the Bank of Finland Erkki Liikanen) set out the official position for the Eurozone in detail: a structural separation of riskier activities from deposit-taking in order to protect European credit creation from volatile trading cycles. In fact, it resembled the separation between investment and commercial banking mandated under the Glass-Steagall Act of 1933, before its repeal in 1999. The Liikanen proposals went further than the new international rules, known as Basel III, and the Volcker rule in the United States,* in recognizing that to protect society from the reckless behavior of banks, both regulatory and structural reforms are needed.

In the wake of the Liikanen Report, the critical question of how to simplify finance, increase competition, and reduce perverse incentives remains. At one time, it was hoped that the creation of the Single Market would result in large numbers of banks in each community. But this naïve belief rested on a misunderstanding of the nature of banking. The chief responsibility of banks is to allocate capital, especially to small- and medium-sized enterprises, and this requires local information. Thus, the limited growth in cross-border banking, especially in providing finance to local small and medium enterprises, should not have come as a surprise.[7]

Moreover, the problem is not only too-big-to-fail banks, but also "too-interlinked-to-fail" banks and "too-correlated-to-fail" banks. The

---

* The main provisions of which restricted a bank's ability to engage in proprietary trading, i.e., trading on its own behalf, using the information that it gleans from serving others. The conflicts of interest were obvious, though banks pretended that they didn't exist.

Lehman Brothers collapse illustrated the risk of interlinkages. The collapse of one bank led quickly to the near collapse of the entire global financial system because Lehman was a counterparty to thousands of other banks. Banks, knowing that if they are closely interlinked they will be bailed out, have an incentive to develop these linkages. Regulations are required not only to separate the investment and commercial banks, but also to prevent excessive interlinkages, especially of systemically important banks.

Even if all banks were relatively small, if they all engaged in the same kinds of activities and took the same types of risks, there would be enormous pressure for a government bailout when things go badly. When so many banks held risky subprime mortgages, for example, it meant that when one was in trouble many others were also. The government could not simply look the other way. Again, because banks know this, they are incentivized to engage in similar kinds of risk taking. Designing policies to prevent too-correlated-to-fail investment strategies has proven exceedingly difficult.

The best that can be done in the financial sector is to ensure a diversity of financial institutions. With sufficient differences among financial institutions, they will pursue different investment strategies. Universal banks, which are all engaged in similar financial activities, thus can represent a threat to the stability of the financial system. Europe needs a rich ecology of financial institutions that focus on different lines of business. But this diversity of financial species will not arise on its own. As we have explained, there are market forces that promote excessive consolidation and correlation.

The separation of investment and commercial banks, as recommended by the Liikanen Report, is a move in the right direction, but it is not enough. And even limited reforms have found resistance. For example, a proposal by the European Commission on bank structural reform died in the European Parliament in October 2017, amid fierce industry opposition.[8] That failure put the burden on regulators and supervisors to ensure that large banks could be wound down without crashing the financial system, a subject we address in more detail below.

### Shadow banking trumps relationship banking

Some of the troubled institutions had once been straightforward financial intermediaries that simply took deposits and did the unglamorous work of assessing the creditworthiness of borrowers. Performing these tasks well required bank executives to have close, long-term relationships with their clients.

However, many banks turned from funding their activities through relatively stable retail depositors to borrowing from other financial institutions, in a process known as a wholesale approach to funding. By borrowing wholesale, banks could expand far more quickly than if they had to rely on convincing depositors to switch their allegiances. Wholesale funding was one of the pillars of what came to be called the *shadow banking system*. The other pillar was earning revenues from fees rather than from the spread between the rates at which they borrowed and those at which they lent. In the old system, banks earned money by finding borrowers who they thought were safe risks, and then by lending to them at a rate slightly higher than the one at which they themselves borrowed. Banks were penalized if they lent to a borrower who could not repay them.

In the new system, banks originated loans, but then would sell the loans to others. Loans were often bundled together, and the package was sold as a security. The idea was that even if one or two loans went bad, risk was diversified, so that the overall security was safe. The banks (and others originating loans and mortgages) did not bear the risk of a failure—the final investor did, a practice that weakened their incentives to be careful in whom they lent to.* The banks made money from fees on originating loans, packaging loans, and selling the resulting securities. Theoretically, this left the costs of default for others to pick up. There were fees all along the production process of securitization. Banks had an incentive to expand—even if it meant lending to less creditworthy individuals. Banking, as a result, became both evermore profitable and irresponsible.

On the eve of the financial crisis, European banks large and small had long since answered the siren call of this new form of banking in which returns were higher and came faster. They had relied on massive borrowing in depersonalized, fast-moving markets. The banks tapped into the inflated US housing bubble by borrowing wholesale to purchase the mortgage-backed securities described above.† This would become the trigger mechanism for the global financial crisis and the death knell for a number of banks.

These transformations of banking coincided with the explosion of the asset management sector, as citizens who used to rely on once-vibrant public pension systems tried to save money through the private sector. This new age of asset management saw the rapid rise of institutional investors such as pension funds and insurance companies. By 2009, the asset management industry grew to €12.8 trillion in assets, about one-third of the entire EU banking sector.

---

* There were provisions in the contracts that seemingly held the originators and investment banks partially accountable for losses. But after the financial crisis, both the originators and investment banks refused to honor those contracts. Only after long litigation were banks forced to pay amounts in the billions. The originators and investment banks also made representations about the quality of the mortgages in the securities they were selling. Investors relied on these, partially because they believed that no bank would risk its reputation. As it turned out, many of the originators engaged in massive fraud and the banks seemed resilient to the loss of reputation, perhaps because virtually all of them engaged in similar activities.

† The lenders to the banks often thought their loans were safe because they were collateralized. But in the midst of the crisis, the market value of the collateral often dropped rapidly, in some cases to zero.

With all that money to invest on behalf of savers, European asset managers—out to prove themselves better than their competitors in the easy, short-term metric of returns without adequate regard to risk—were only too happy to buy all manner of securities issued by banks. The credit rating agencies played a critical role in this scam, as they gave AAA ratings to securities that did not deserve them, engaging in massive fraud in a race to the bottom with other rating agencies.

Wholesale funding (versus the retail approach of wooing depositors) exploded in Europe even more than in the United States. In 2008, it amounted to 60 percent of total funding for the largest 16 banks in Europe. This was twice as high as for large US banks.[9]

Banks also saw an opportunity to increase their activities as so-called market makers, by holding inventories of securities, standing ready to buy and sell and making a profit from the buy-sell spreads. They had falsely claimed that the risk of the securities they were selling was far lower than it was, and during the crisis, they were bitten by their own deception. There was far more risk in holding these securities than banks had thought.

These structural changes in banking shaped the way that the Lehman Brothers collapse, in the fall of 2008, contaminated Europe. The first to suffer were European banks heavily involved in the US shadow banking system that turbocharged the housing bubble. Of the 23 banks that European governments had to bail out between 2008 and 2009, 18 got into trouble because of their trading activities.[10]

Europe's own crisis of shadow banking played out in periphery countries' government bond markets.[11] In 2010, as crisis-related pressures on public budgets and tighter ECB monetary policy raised doubts about the collateral value of periphery government bonds, these markets experienced fire sales. As a result of the subsequent fall in bond prices, systemically important European financial institutions such as LCH Clearnet, a major clearinghouse, and Eurex, a derivatives exchange, stopped accepting as collateral government bonds issued by crisis-prone member states. Prices of these bonds fell even further.

This vicious circle was especially diabolical because the banks themselves often held large amounts of their own government's debt, and because each country was supposed to bail out its own banks. As the banks became weaker, their lending contracted and national economies slowed. In many cases, markets anticipated a costly bailout, which the weaker periphery countries of the EU could ill afford, especially in light of the recessions and depressions into which they were plunging. The costs of the anticipated bailouts led to still-higher risks for government bonds and lower prices for those bonds, thus weakening banks' balance sheets still further.

## CURBING THE SHADOW BANKING SYSTEM

There is no magic bullet for curbing the shadow banking system. First, the reason for the growth of the shadow banking system needs to be recognized: it was largely an attempt to circumvent the regulations imposed on the commercial banking system. No government can or should allow such circumvention. For instance, the capital requirements imposed on shadow banks were much lower than on commercial banks, in the misguided belief that public money was not at risk because there was no systemic risk that would necessitate a public bailout. The government could easily let one of the investment banks collapse, went the theory, without the dire consequences that would follow from the failure of a large commercial bank.

The consequences of the collapse of Lehman Brothers put these beliefs to rest. The shadow banking system should operate under regulations as tough as those imposed on commercial banks, and indeed, the rules for banks that financed lending with wholesale funds should be far higher—such funding can, and did, disappear overnight. Moreover, mutual funds that pretend to be virtually a bank—promising

depositors (actually investors) a sure return plus a higher interest rate than commercial banks—need to make clear that there is no guaranteed return, there is no free lunch. These funds are not backed by deposit insurance, so if there were massive defaults in the commercial paper (short-term loans, mainly to large corporations) in which they invested their funds, investors will not be repaid.

European authorities have taken some measures to improve the regulation of shadow banking. For instance, in 2016 they introduced transparency and reporting requirements for complex repurchase and securities-lending transactions.[12] This change to the so-called "repo" market, an esoteric but essential part of the financial plumbing that allows banks to borrow cash with securities as collateral, was a welcome step. But the changes did not go far enough. The ECB has resisted deep reform of the repo market because it long championed these transactions for improving the transmission of monetary policy in the Eurozone and accelerating financial integration.

Similarly, the ECB, the Bank of England, and the European Commission together designed plans for simple, transparent, and standardized securitization. This plan would reduce the opacity, information asymmetries, conflicts of interest, and perverse incentives that made securitization the focal point of the global financial crisis. But these reforms do not adequately address the fundamental flaw of securitization, which is the separation of risk bearing from loan origination.

Thus, it is worrying that many in Europe are actively encouraging the revival of securitization markets without adequately taking into account their risks and limitations. What is needed is to strengthen the banking system (especially local, regional, and cooperative banks). Information, especially concerning small borrowers, is best acquired and processed through such institutions. Risk diversification can be achieved by those who wish to own a diversified portfolio of bank shares. There is little extra benefit in risk diversification that is achieved through securitization, while the evident costs are enormous. The EU's excessive focus on strengthening capital markets is very misguided. While improving capital markets is desirable, doing so will not solve the fundamental problems facing the financial sector.

## Capital Markets Union: A Move in the Wrong Direction

The crisis has also made clear the fundamental problems with capital markets. Information about the relative returns to particular assets is, in a sense, a public good of value to all holders of that asset. Inevitably, there will be an undersupply of quality information. The financial crisis exposed the basic flaw with the rating agencies, the institutional arrangement for providing information on securitizations. Being paid by the seller of the securitizations created an incentive to provide a good rating.

It might seem to make more sense for the buyer of the securities to pay for the information, but there is a free-rider problem in organizing markets in this way. If informed buyers (who have spent money to get their information) bid up the price of a security, uninformed buyers will infer that the informed investors know that the stock is worth more. Indeed, if capital markets were as informationally perfect as its advocates claim, the uninformed could get just as high returns on their investments without paying the cost of information. However, then no one would spend any money to get good information, and the capital market would fail in its essential role of allocating capital by judging risk and potential return.

Some in Europe think the solution to limited lending to small businesses is to promote securitization. The argument goes that if banks, under pressure from tighter regulation, could move loans to small- and medium-sized companies off their balance sheets by securitizing those loans, their willingness to lend would improve substantially. Europe has rightly identified the problem of a shortage of available credit for small firms, but securitization of small business loans is even more difficult than securitization of mortgages. There inevitably will be insufficient incentives to assess who is a good borrower, and a strong incentive to pass bad loans onto others.

Good underwriting of loans to small firms depends on localized information. As the financial crisis illustrates, it is dangerous to separate loan origination from risk bearing. There was an underlying logic to traditional banking. The correct solution to insufficient lending to small- and medium-sized enterprises is to strengthen well-regulated local banks, with assistance possibly provided through partial loan guarantees (see the discussion below). Alternatively, access to funds for these enterprises could be increased through the public option discussed earlier, for instance via a new development bank that is focused on small- and medium-sized enterprises.

## A European Banking Union

Many of the problems, like too-big-to-fail banks, complex and interconnected operations, opaque financial products, and myopic time horizons, are scarcely different on either side of the Atlantic. Where the European Union differs is in the absence of a European-wide banking system analogous to the national banking system that the United States created in 1863.

The creation of the euro, the common currency, combined with the Single Market, exacerbated the fragilities of European banking. Banks did not quickly forge new relationships with households and businesses across national borders: retail banking markets in the Eurozone remain stubbornly fragmented along national lines. In contrast, wholesale funding markets like the repo market integrated quickly.

Suddenly, money could easily and quickly flow out of the banking system of a country in trouble. And, as we have repeatedly noted, the ensuing reduction of credit deepened and prolonged the downturn.

There were other systemic problems with the financial architecture that evolved after the creation of the euro. Banks became the primary conduits by which money was recycled. Net exports kept flowing from Germany to the countries on the periphery, and through a variety of mechanisms, there was a corresponding flow of money into countries on the periphery, including Ireland, Spain, and Greece. Every party to this arrangement seemed to benefit, but as we now know, only temporarily. Ordinary citizens in the periphery countries would later be made to pay a high price when the money dried up.

The situation seemed to solve a key problem of the common currency. As long as a Greek bank, for example, could use its own government's debt as collateral to borrow in interbank markets from a German bank, all Eurozone sovereign bonds would be gilt-edged assets that were largely interchangeable. Since all those sovereign bonds could be used as collateral for borrowing from the ECB, the central bank effectively underwrote this system.

This setup was a highly technical and market-reliant way of providing a financial structure that seemed to work for a Europe that shared a common currency, even though some countries have large current account deficits and others have current account surpluses. It enabled northern Europe's surpluses to be recycled and used elsewhere in Europe. In fact, it seemed as if one could indeed have a common currency with only limited fiscal integration. But few people in finance, and even fewer in politics, understood the implications of this setup or its potential for disaster. With good reason, the resulting arrangement became known as the "deadly sovereign-bank embrace," and the euro crisis would show just how deadly it was.

Inherent in the creation of the euro was the fundamental problem that countries had to borrow in a currency that they did not control. Developing countries and emerging markets know this risk. They often can only borrow in dollars, but when hard times come along, they do not have the dollars they need to service their debt, thus facing a crisis that often leads them to the IMF. By contrast, the United States will never have such a problem because it borrows while promising to pay back dollars, and because it controls the figurative printing presses. It can always pay what it owes.

There was a second problem, however. As money flowed from Germany to the periphery, those countries experienced inflationary pressures, increasing the real exchange rate (say, relative to Germany). Their real exchange rates gradually got out of line. So long as money flowed into Spain, for example, and was based on perceived investment opportunities in, say, real estate, this overvalued exchange rate was not a problem. In this scenario, Spain could remain at full employment, even as large numbers of migrants entered the country. In short, the Eurozone was not really working well before the crisis. This poor performance facilitated the creation of the imbalances and misalignments that became manifest in the aftermath of the crisis.

In truth, Europe itself created a sovereign debt crisis because countries like Greece borrowed in euros but did not control the supply of euros. As in Spain, the inflow of euros into Greece before the crisis led to a noncompetitive real exchange rate before the crisis. In 2010, it seemed as if markets made a new discovery: while a common currency had eliminated exchange-rate risk, sovereign debt risk had actually increased. Before the euro, when Greece borrowed in drachmas, it could always have repaid what was owed; the only risk was what the drachmas might be worth. During the crisis, Greece simply didn't have the euros to pay its credits. With the realization of this sovereign debt risk, markets wrenched apart the system, which was based on supposedly interchangeable government bonds, at a frightening pace in 2012.

Debt markets lost faith in Greece's ability to refinance its debt, and its borrowing costs skyrocketed. In contrast to a few years prior, a Greek bond was suddenly worth far less than a German one.

Governments suddenly faced the costs of a bank bailout amid a searing recession that squeezed tax revenues. Borrowing costs soared to unaffordable levels for countries on Europe's periphery. Money flew out of Greek banks because the EU had smoothed the way, through the Single Market and the euro, for financial outflows without any way to restore the confidence needed to stem them (such as through common deposit insurance). As money streamed out of the weaker countries, those countries became shakier still. Their banks could not lend, which led to decreased investment, and in some cases even less production because of a shortage of working capital.

The European Union had failed to create the institutions necessary to make a common currency work. Among the key institutions that should have been created was a banking union, a European-wide banking system with a single supervisory body, a common and jointly financed system of resolution (to wind down troubled banks without upsetting the system), and a common deposit insurance scheme. While there has been an agreement to create a banking union, and some steps have been taken, even today a common deposit insurance system appears to be a distant hope.

Reforming Europe's financial system has to go hand in hand with reforming the dysfunctional macro-institutional architecture of the euro, as we discussed in Chapter 2. An unreformed shadow banking system both increases the risk of a crisis and undermines the ability of the ECB to respond. A lender of last resort that can address a bank run caused by retail deposit withdrawals faces a far greater challenge when market liquidity evaporates and falling securities prices prompt a run on wholesale funding. In this latter case, the scale of required intervention is greater and the mechanisms for preventing systemic collapse are less straightforward.

In the 2008 crisis, central banks bought up securities to keep markets stable, a more intrusive and massive intervention in markets than had traditionally been part of their work. While it may be the case that the ECB may have to be, from time to time, a market-maker as well as a lender of last resort, reforms in the financial system should be designed to make that unlikely.[13]

If an individual country like Greece cannot borrow, the EU could borrow instead through the ECB and then re-lend the money to Greece. European solidarity should mean that there is at least enough confidence across the EU to provide such lending, provided the country is undertaking reasonable actions to restore its fiscal position. Lending at a relatively low interest rate would free up resources that could be used to help stimulate the economy, thereby generating more tax revenues and reducing social protection expenditures.

EU borrowing would address another problem: it would create a single, safe European asset on which banks can rely. Unfortunately, Germany has strongly resisted proposals for a Eurozone bond, backed with collective resources of all members. The German mantra is, "Europe is not a transfer union." However, without this minimal level of solidarity, the euro may not be able to work, or at least as well as it should and could. In an efficient Eurozone, the probability of the feared transfers may actually be lower than under the current regime, in which they still occur, although less transparently, as was the case in Greece's repeated debt restructurings.

### Common deposit insurance
We have noted that one key reason for the depth of the euro crisis is that money flees the banking system of a country that appears weak

out of fear that the government will not have the resources to compensate insured depositors in the case of a bank failure. Only a system that replaces the current patchwork of national systems with a European deposit insurance scheme will prevent an outflow of funds from the banking systems of countries affected by negative shocks. Common deposit insurance will also help break the negative feedback loop between banks and sovereigns by reducing the incentives to pull money out of crisis-prone countries.

Germany and some other countries worry that common deposit insurance will be an invitation to reckless bank behavior in irresponsible countries. These countries believe that if they undertake risks, the other country and its banks will benefit, thus leaving Germany and the more responsible countries to pick up the pieces. This objection has an obvious answer: regulate the banks so they cannot engage in excessive risk, and then supervise them so they comply with the regulations.

But even prudent and well-regulated banks may go under when a country confronts a long period of economic recession. Common deposit insurance thus serves another function: it encourages and even incentivizes European solidarity. It guarantees that all countries work to ensure that none go through an extended period of recession like the one Greece experienced. By the same token, it disincentivizes imposing stringent austerity conditions without providing any basis of growth, a move that pushes all the costs of adjustment on the countries in the periphery (with current account deficits) and none on the surplus countries.

### Supervision

The creation of the Single Supervisory Mechanism, the label for the ECB's new authority to oversee the EU's largest banks, was viewed as an important institutional step forward in creating a real, single European financial market when it was created in 2014. (Although the

ECB has the authority to step in and supervise smaller banks, that task is ordinarily left to national authorities.)

But there is one unresolved problem confronting common supervision: Can it adequately reflect the differences in circumstances of different countries within the Eurozone? In other words, will it try to impose one-size-fits-all requirements on countries with vastly different circumstances? Bank regulators have long recognized that some judicious forbearance may be desirable in an economic downturn if the misdeeds of a bank are less to blame for its circumstances as much as an unanticipated macroeconomic situation. In fact, excessive zeal in shutting banks down may simply lead to further credit contraction that could exacerbate the economic downturn. Such forbearance may prove essential, especially in the absence of the maneuverability provided by flexible exchange rates and differential interest rates.

### Common resolution

When all else fails, Europe will need a mechanism for the resolution of troubled banks that winds them down without triggering a systemic crisis. When a single, isolated bank runs into a problem, resolution is straightforward: one wants to protect depositors, promote the continued flow of credit, and minimize the cost to taxpayers. The difficulty arises in a crisis, when many banks are in trouble at the same time. The United States created a new process for complex banks (Orderly Liquidation Authority) and a requirement that firms plan for their own demise (living wills) to supplement the previous system in which the Federal Deposit Insurance Corporation wound down banks while protecting depositors. This new approach has not been tested, and there is skepticism about the living wills. Each crisis is different, so specifying today how one will deal with the next crisis is next to impossible. A bank might say, for instance, that in the event of a crisis they will quickly liquidate their assets to pay back depositors. However, if carrying out that strategy results in large losses for influential individuals and large contractions in credit (if it is a large bank that collapses), it is unlikely that the terms of the living will would actually be fulfilled.*

European plans for the resolution of troubled cross-border banking groups remain embryonic and firmly in the hands of national authorities. While they may be more sensitive to the domestic consequences of different methods of resolving a bank in distress, they may be less sensitive to cross-border effects of such actions. But bank resolution often requires the government to put in additional funds. If that burden is imposed on national governments, it can set off the vicious cycle that we described earlier. A bank bailout leads to increased deficits and a lower price for government bonds (many of which are held by banks within the country). As the price of those bonds falls, other banks within the country become more fragile and then cut back lending. Moreover, often questions are raised about whether assistance a government provides to keep a bank alive violates European prohibitions against state aid, which might result in an unlevel playing field between enterprises in different countries.† But concerns about state aid have to be balanced by those over the macroeconomic consequences of the failure of a bank that is systemically important for a community or region, let alone a country. No bank gets into trouble in order to get state aid (though as we have noted, the fact that it might may affect the risks that it undertakes). The motive for state aid to save a bank is not to give the bank a leg up over its rivals, but to prevent macroeconomic harms to the community.

Financial responsibility for bank resolution must reside with Europe,

---

* Economists refer to this problem as one of "time consistency." What bankers intend to do in some future contingency may not be what is optimal to do when that future contingency actually arrives.

† Worries about state aid loomed large in the resolution of some of the troubled banks in Italy.

as it is an essential part of any banking union. But the resolution has to be sensitive to the consequences for the flow of credit in any country that might be affected. Shutting down a bank that plays an important role in a local or national economy has macroeconomic consequences that have to be taken into account.

## Partial Guarantees and Government Lending

But these interventions may not be enough to achieve fully the socially desirable flows of credit; Europe may need direct government support. One option to do so would be partial government guarantees for certain classes of loans, such as small-business loans. Another is government provision of finance (for instance, through the development banks discussed in Chapter 3). In some areas in which competition is lacking in the private sector, Europeans may need a public option, which would effectively be a national bank with a limited mandate to provide loans at competitive prices (at the benchmark government bond rate plus the appropriate risk premium, for example).

A public bank could prove an effective instrument, too, for providing subsidies to areas that the government wants to encourage—areas in which there are positive spillovers to others, such as in low-interest loans to businesses that prioritize research and development. Research shows that this sector provides spillover benefits to other firms, benefits that are not fully captured by the inventors.

Similarly, there is a public interest in retirees not living in poverty. To remedy this, a public bank might offer higher interest rates on deposits to promote retirement security. Furthermore, by providing ways of saving through national (public) social security accounts or public banks, governments can curb the conflicts of interest and the exploitation in private wealth management, especially of small accounts.

Another area where a public option might be beneficial is home mortgages. Studies show that there are societal benefits from home ownership, as it ties people to their communities, which in turn has ripple effects on the quality of local schools. In many European countries, mortgage rates are considerably higher than they should be, reflecting both market power and persistent inefficiencies in the banking system. A public option could provide long-term mortgages to those who have regularly paid their taxes, mortgages that would be limited in size to an amount the family could reasonably afford. Mortgage payments could be linked to a person's income (the length of the time over which the mortgage is paid back would simply increase if income fell too much) and could be based on housing valuations derived from records of sales of similar homes. Hopefully, competition from the government would encourage the private sector to offer mortgages that better served the interests of homeowners, and at lower prices.

## Cooperatives and Local Institutions

Cooperative and local banks provide an antidote to the unproductive activities of the large commercial banks and the shadow banking system and play an important role in ensuring the diversity in corporate organization that we discussed in Chapter 4. Cooperative banks are owned by their customers and depositors and are run in their interests and of the communities of which they are a part—the shareholders and the stakeholders are, in a sense, one and the same. Cooperative banks are already a major force in Europe. Across the EU, they serve more than 209 million customers—around half of the EU population—and account for more than 20 percent of the retail banking market.

There is a widespread view that the best financial system rests on privately owned banks, and even more, on capital markets in which firms issue bonds rather than borrow from banks. Both premises are wrong.

In both Europe and the United States, cooperatives and community-owned banks have performed far better in many ways than have private firms. This is understandable given the deficiencies in corporate governance within the private sector that we have noted.

Without the pressures of shareholder value, cooperative banks are able to have longer time horizons, which allow them to develop closer relationships with customers. They are an important source of stable funding for smaller enterprises. These attributes have led to a capital structure and risk profile of cooperative banks—more equity and smarter underwriting—that have made them more resilient. There is also convincing evidence that small banks can be more efficient and more growth-friendly than large ones. For example, small local German banks typically have better cost-income ratios than do big private banks. They also make higher relative contributions to the public purse.[14]

Since the beginning of the financial crisis, cooperatively owned banks have performed markedly better than their stock market–listed competitors, with an average return on equity ranging from 2 percent to 6 percent above the industry average. And they did not cut back their lending in the way that private banks did during the post-crisis recession.

Unfortunately, rather than encouraging institutional diversity, there are forces in the EU that seem to be pushing the other way. In recent years, for instance, Europe has tried to stifle at least some of the community-owned banks, especially in Italy. In spite of the fact that these banks have often played a pivotal role in their communities, they have been drawn into a debate about privatization.

Policymakers at the national and European levels should encourage cooperative banking by explicitly acknowledging the importance of a diversity of corporate organization models. Germany, for example, has improved the ability of cooperative banks to raise capital by allowing them to take on members who are not just depositors, but who invest more with the bank. These investor-members cannot outnumber or outvote regular members, thus preserving the integrity of the cooperative model.

Other countries have provided tax benefits to encourage cooperative banking. What is clear is that there are a variety of mechanisms by which Europe can and should encourage these institutions which see their mission as designing a financial system that serves their members and society more generally.

## CONCLUSION

Europe's financial system has not been serving Europe well—and certainly not as well as it could and must if Europe is to prosper. Under current arrangements, finance is a source of instability and divergence and not of growth and prosperity. This chapter has outlined a comprehensive agenda that would increase the prospects that the financial sector performs the essential functions that serve society, rather than allowing it to continue to reap returns from exploiting society. Patching the holes in Europe's financial regulatory system will be essential not only to the vibrancy of its economy, but to the European project itself.

Regulation, however, will not suffice. As we emphasized in Chapter 2, government needs to take an active role, in some cases through a development bank, in other cases through guarantees. There is a need for support for lending to small- and medium-sized businesses and for a public option in mortgages—to provide mortgages that make home ownership more affordable to European citizens of modest means. And there is a need for government to encourage greater diversity in financial institutions, especially through the support of cooperatives.

In the next chapter, we discuss another arena in which the EU needs more cooperation to ensure that the European project is a success: taxation.

*Chapter 6*

# Taxation to Promote Justice and Growth

**How governments raise** money profoundly shapes society and the economy. A good tax can increase economic efficiency and create a more shared prosperity; a bad tax can distort incentives and increase inequality. A poll tax—levied on anyone who wishes to vote—distorts democracy because only people with enough money can participate in the electoral process. A tax on inheritances can help prevent the creation and maintenance of an inherited plutocracy. A tax on savings or work may discourage both. A tax on carbon emissions may help save the planet by discouraging pollution.

The sheer magnitude of taxation in Europe, at an EU average tax ratio of over 35 percent of GDP, underscores the importance of the right tax framework. As economists have debated the effectiveness of various taxes, several principles have emerged. Good taxes do not discourage desirable behavior but discourage undesirable behavior, such as polluting or consuming alcohol and tobacco. Some taxes have no effect on behavior. These are called *non-distortionary* taxes. And to the extent possible, revenues should be raised from such taxes, which is why land taxes have traditionally been viewed as desirable since land will neither disappear nor move to another country when it is taxed.

In a society marked by rising inequality, taxation has to be sensitive to its impact on wealth and income distribution. We need progressive taxation—taxing those at the top at a higher rate than those with less income.* In the United States, regressive taxation, where the very rich actually pay a lower average tax rate than those less well off, has been an important reason why the country is the most unequal among the advanced industrial countries.

Often, ascertaining the total effects of a tax on society is difficult because there are direct and indirect effects. Much of the debate about taxation concerns the magnitude (and sometimes even direction) of these indirect effects. People who oppose inheritance taxes say that these taxes will discourage entrepreneurship and innovation, thus hurting ordinary citizens. Usually, however, these are simply self-serving arguments made by the rich with little, if any, evidence to support them. Even if they were partially true, the effect is sufficiently small to be overwhelmed by the benefits of progressive taxation.

Many critics of the European economic model point to the high taxes citizens pay in comparison to the United States. They say this discourages work and savings. They ignore the large benefits European citizens receive that the US population has to pay for.

Most European citizens, for instance, get access to free or nearly free health care. The United States spends almost 20 percent of its

---

* That is, the fraction of income that a high-income person pays in taxes should be higher than the fraction paid by someone with a lower income. Tax systems in which those at the top pay lower rates of taxation on average are called regressive. America's tax system, for instance, is notorious for its regressive nature, with Warren Buffett, one of that country's richest men, rightly pointing out that he was paying a lower tax rate than his secretary.

GDP in its private system, and its quality of health care is far lower. Public retirement benefits in the United States are typically lower than in Europe,[1] so Americans have to set aside large amounts of their paychecks (often 10 to 15 percent) to ensure that they have a decent retirement. And the transaction costs in America's private pension systems are typically very high, much higher than in public systems. If one adds these costs to the seemingly lower taxes Americans pay, it becomes clear they are not necessarily better off. An upper-middle-class New York City resident pays a combined state, local, and federal income tax of some 45 percent, but if one adds health care costs (conservatively) amounting to 15 percent and retirement benefits of 10 percent, the total is 70 percent, a calculation that ignores an approximately 7.65 percent social security tax and Medicare taxes (the former only on the first $132,900 of income), and an equal amount paid by employers for social security and Medicare.*

Ensuring that Europe maintains its high standards of living requires raising large amounts of revenue in ways that are efficient and fair. Good public transportation, schools, childcare facilities, parks, and public safety measures cost money, but they are important for creating a high standard of living. Europeans have traditionally realized the value of these investments, one reason why European cities like Vienna have long ranked among the world's most livable cities.

But Europe's tax system needs improvement. This chapter describes some of the problems and provides suggestions for how to address them.

---

* Economists debate the incidence of such charges imposed on employers, i.e., who really pays. The general consensus is that, in the long run, the effect of such taxes is no different from those imposed directly on individuals and therefore they should be added to the total taxes paid. There is a broader issue of tax incidence: as taxes get imposed, individuals may, for instance, reduce their supply of labor, and that will lead to higher wages, which would partially offset the initial adverse effect. Ascertaining these "general equilibrium" incidence effects is difficult and controversial. This is especially so for the corporate income tax, as we note below.

## CREATING A MORE PROGRESSIVE TAX SYSTEM

There has been an erosion in Europe's commitment to a progressive tax system.[2] Top income tax rates have gradually fallen across the EU. Between 1995 and 2018, the average top income tax rates in the 28 EU member states dropped by about 8 percentage points, to 39 percent.[3] One reason for this decrease is the introduction of flat tax regimes—a single rate on personal income that was implemented in eight EU nations.*

In practically all EU countries, capital is taxed more favorably than labor. And since capital is a more important source of income for the rich, this favorable tax treatment of capital results in more regressive taxation. This is especially true for *capital gains*, the increases in the value of assets, which in most countries are taxed at moderate flat rates and in some countries (Belgium, Cyprus, Croatia, Luxembourg, and Slovakia) are not taxed at all. The EU average income tax rate[†] on capital gains is 19 percent, and thus half the size of the regular top income tax rate and the overall tax rate on dividends distributed to shareholders, respectively. Interest income is taxed at 23 percent, on average.

Taxing some forms of capital income at lower rates than wages is not only inequitable; it also causes a distortion. There is an incentive to convert income into the category taxed at a lower rate. For instance, if capital gains are taxed at a lower rate than dividends, corporations can distribute their profits to their shareholders in the form of capital gains through share buybacks rather than in dividends.

Taxation of net wealth and of inheritances has also lost ground. In Europe, only Norway, Switzerland, and Spain impose a net wealth

---

\* Two countries (Slovakia and Latvia) subsequently replaced their flat taxes with progressive systems.

† The 28 EU member countries, including the UK.

tax—a recurring levy on a person's total assets. France's wealth tax, originally broadly based, captures only immovable assets as of 2019. Although 18 EU countries have an inheritance tax, its revenue potential is increasingly eroded by tax exemptions and rate reductions.[4]

The countries of the European Union must reverse these recent trends and recommit to progressivity. Making European tax systems more progressive would mitigate increasing income and wealth inequality. There are suggestions that it would also improve gender equality.[5] There is no evidence that these lower rates at the top (or lower inheritance and net wealth taxes) have led to more growth. Indeed, empirical studies suggest that there is no relationship between lowering tax rates at the top and economic growth.[6] But there is a persuasive argument that those lower taxes encourage rent-seeking, as it incentivizes attempts to increase profits by exploiting, for instance, market power or government relationships. Such behavior interferes with economic efficiency and undermines growth.[7]

Empirical studies also suggest that when heirs inherit a large sum they are not as motivated to work.[8] Taxing inheritances, therefore, might even have positive effects on growth and employment.

But those countries that have fought decreasing tax progressivity have encountered a problem: the threat of their citizens or their corporations to move should the government raise personal or corporate tax rates.

## Corporate Taxation and the Race to the Bottom

The EU made a fundamental mistake by failing to pay sufficient attention to tax harmonization when it created the Single Market, with its free migration and free mobility of capital. The underlying theory of an integrated market is that corporations will locate where costs are lowest and then ship the goods elsewhere in Europe. This would increase the demand for labor in low-wage countries, thus accelerating the process of convergence within Europe. But taxes can distort this seemingly harmonious process. Corporations care about their after-tax return, so they are sensitive not just to wages, the efficiency of labor, the overall business environment, transport costs, and other factors of production, but also to the taxes they have to pay. In the very short run, the one variable countries can change to attract businesses is the corporate income tax rate. Economists predicted that this would result in a race to the bottom, as companies could produce in a low-tax jurisdiction but enjoy access to the entire European Union and its markets.

We see evidence of this race to the bottom. Between 1995 and 2018, the average corporate income tax rates for the EU went down from 35 percent to 22 percent.[9] This trend can be expected to continue as France, Greece, the Netherlands, and Sweden have already announced further reductions of corporate income tax rates.[10]

By offering lower tax rates, countries gain jobs and some tax revenues, perhaps less than at higher tax rates, but the increased tax base, they hope, more than compensates. However, these gains are largely at the expense of others, including and especially other countries within the EU. This rob-thy-neighbor strategy is, of course, totally incompatible with the spirit of European solidarity.

There is an externality: lower tax rates in one country encourage investment to flow to that country, at least in the short run.

The EU, as we noted in Chapter 1, has focused on regulating cross-border externalities, but it has dwelled on the wrong problems. The drafters of the Maastricht Treaty thought that if a country had too high a deficit, it would induce EU-wide inflation, one of the reasons for the stringent limits on deficits. This externality turned out not to be important, or even to exist at all. But there is an opposite externality associated with austerity: running surpluses, or more generally, a country not doing what it can to sustain strong demand. In Chapter 1, for instance, we noted that Germany's trading partners end up bearing some of the cost of its failure to maintain rising wages or strong domestic demand.

The tax-competition externality is of first-order importance. The jobs and tax revenues that arrived in Ireland and Luxembourg, the two countries most aggressive in this tax competition, came largely at the expense of their erstwhile partners in the EU. But Ireland and Luxembourg never let these moral considerations interfere with their relentless pursuit of national self-interest. Remarkably, even after the European Commission caught Ireland out, having discovered their secret agreements with Apple that amounted to a $13 billion gift to the corporation, Ireland was not only unapologetic, it appealed the decision, effectively arguing it had the right to cheat its neighbors.

Companies, in fact, found myriad ways to pretend that they earned their profits in low-tax jurisdictions. They learned to shift where they recorded their profits without even changing where they did business. Starbucks could locate the ownership of its trademarks in Ireland, charging UK stores a fee for the use of the brand. The fee, it turned out, made UK operations a wash, with little profit (thus ensuring little tax would be paid) while putting money in its Irish subsidiary (where little tax need be paid). Curiously, Starbucks rapidly expanded in Britain, all the while claiming it was making no profits there.

Of course, when all countries lower their tax rates, they *collectively* do not really get more investment. Indeed, overall, investment is probably reduced. Lower tax rates mean lower tax revenues. This, in turn, means expenditures have to be cut, which includes spending on infrastructure and human capital that is complementary to private investment. Reduced investments lower national output.

It was foolish to expect that lower taxes on corporations would lead to higher incomes for Europeans. The corporate lobby put forth the self-serving argument that lower taxes will encourage them to invest more. At first blush, it might seem obvious that taxes lower the returns on investment. But a closer look suggests that the magnitude of the effect may be small, that details matter, and that it is even possible that raising tax rates encourages investment.

Most firms borrow from banks and capital markets for any investment beyond their retained earnings. All EU countries make interest expenses tax deductible.[11] The marginal cost of finance for these firms is reduced by the tax deduction by exactly the same amount that the return to capital is reduced.* Thus, there is no effect on investment. Things get more complicated once one introduces accelerated depreciation allowances. The whole point of accelerated depreciation is to reduce the cost of capital to below what it would be with the actual depreciation of assets. The value of these accelerated depreciation allowances increases as the tax rate increases. Therefore, the higher the tax rate, the higher the level of investment.[12] On the other hand, for firms that invest their retained earnings but no more, an increase in their tax adversely affects investment rate by diminishing the amount they have to reinvest.† And for the few firms that turn to equity markets to finance their marginal investments, higher corporate taxation is also likely to discourage investment.‡

Empirically, the net effect of an increase in the corporation tax on investment seems to be at most small, particularly if one takes into

---

* For example, if a firm borrows at an interest rate of 6 percent and the tax rate is 33 percent, the after-tax cost of capital is just 4 percent.

† For firms that invest all of their retained earnings and no more, what is relevant is the average tax rate, not the marginal tax rate. Firms still have discretion in deciding how much to retain.

‡ A full analysis requires integrating the impacts of the personal and corporate income tax. Equity financing leads to dilution, which lowers stock market values and leads to a capital loss or at least a capital gain that is lower than it otherwise would be. If there is a capital gains tax, the savings on that tax, plus the benefits of accelerated depreciation, partially offset the burden of the corporation tax and diminish the adverse effect of the tax on investment.

account the benefits that the corporation may receive from public expenditures, such as improved infrastructure and education.

Lowering the overall level of corporate taxes to attract new businesses means lower revenues from all existing businesses. This revenue decrease restrains the extent of tax competition for most countries within Europe. But countries with a small corporate sector face no such restraint, and that is why Luxembourg and Ireland have been among the most aggressive in tax competition.

Offering firms entering a market special tax exemptions that are not given to firms already in the country is another way to engage in less-costly tax competition. Of course, the companies already in the country view this as grossly unfair since entrants then have a competitive advantage. The EU was sensitive to this kind of unfair competition and outlawed it under the banner of state aid.

In spite of this prohibition, Ireland and Luxembourg made low taxes and special deals an integral part of their development strategies—and they were able to attract many businesses. In some cases, they garnered only a few jobs and limited tax revenues, but from their perspective, something was better than nothing. It was, of course, a negative-sum game: Ireland gained tax revenues that were a fraction of those lost by others, and the jobs that it acquired were those that would have been created elsewhere in Europe.

Apple became the quintessential example of the behavior of a tax avoider. It demonstrated the same creativity in tax avoidance that it did in product design and marketing. With the connivance of Ireland, Apple set up a scheme for avoiding essentially all of its taxes on profits earned in Europe by claiming that they were attributable to the management services of an Irish subsidiary with only a few hundred employees. According to the European Commission, its reported tax rate for European profits was as low as 0.005 percent in 2014.

More broadly, according to the European Commission,[13] the EU effective tax rate for digital businesses, such as online retailing or social media, which derive much or all of their value from the intangible assets of information and data, is 8.5 percent, or less than half the effective tax rate for traditional businesses (which are between 20.9 percent and 23.2 percent). This lower rate occurs because digital businesses are based on intangible assets that benefit both from specific tax incentives and the ease of shifting the recorded source of profits to low-tax jurisdictions. With aggressive tax planning, corporations can winnow down their effective taxation to essentially zero.

This kind of tax avoidance and tax evasion* is, of course, a global phenomenon, and it moved toward the top of the international community's agenda after the 2008 crisis revealed an acute need for government revenue. During this time, countries realized that they were losing massive amounts of money from evasion and avoidance through tax havens and profit shifting. A recent study puts the global extent of international profit shifting at more than 5 percent of total corporate profits, or about $620 billion.[14] Estimates of tax losses due to profit shifting vary between 4 percent and 10 percent of corporate income tax revenues for the advanced OECD industrial economies.[15] A recent simulation study finds corporate tax losses of 7.7 percent of total corporate tax revenues in the EU.[16]

Investigations reported in the "Panama Papers" and "Paradise Papers" uncovered the extent of this tax evasion and avoidance. As a result, the G-20 put increased pressure on the offshore financial centers to increase their transparency, and to participate in systems of automatic exchange of tax information. Unfortunately, some of the most important secrecy havens are not offshore, in places like Panama and the Cay-

---

* Tax evasion is not paying taxes that are legally due. Tax avoidance is taking advantage of existing loopholes and creating new ones to lower one's taxes, all in ways that are within the law. The distinction, however, can be blurry, as Apple illustrates.

man Islands, but onshore, in countries such as the United States and the UK. Many in the advanced countries looked the other way when these on- and offshore secrecy havens hid the ill-gotten gains coming out of developing countries. They paid attention, however, when they realized that their own treasuries were also being robbed.

The OECD instituted a process, known as the BEPS initiative, to attack what has come to be called "base erosion and profit shifting." These schemes shift profits from high-tax jurisdictions to low-tax jurisdictions, resulting in lower corporate profit taxes paid in many countries than should be the case. Such tactics include using accounting tricks to pretend that the real source of the corporation's profits was in a low-tax jurisdiction (exemplified by Apple's claims about its profits originating in Ireland). But the BEPS initiative, while successful in attacking some of the egregious ways of shifting profits, has failed to address some of the key methods corporations used, such as shifting intellectual property rights to low-tax jurisdictions.*

The EU has a framework for addressing some of these egregious practices, including what Apple did in Ireland. The favorable tax treatment to Apple was found to violate the provisions on state aid. Were similar terms to have been made available to all foreign corporations operating in the EU, corporate tax revenues from non-EU entities would have been almost entirely drained from the rest of Europe. The kinds of tax deals, like that with Apple, are simply not viable in the long run; Europe has to do something about them.

But Ireland's offering of across-the-board low tax rates (only 12.25

---

* This failure was, not surprisingly, because the United States (and perhaps some other powerful countries) put pressure not to go into these areas—ironic because the United States itself was a major loser of tax revenue as a result of profit shifting. The US position was the result of the power of special corporate interests in the United States that benefited largely from the ability to shift profits to low-taxed jurisdictions. Interestingly, the 2017 US tax bill directly attacked this issue with several provisions designed to limit base erosion resulting from profit shifting associated with intangibles.

percent) is not a violation of current rules, and these rates could be even lower. To prevent this race to the bottom, there needs to be harmonization of tax rates. At the very least, the EU needs an agreement on a minimum tax rate to prevent the current situation from growing even worse.

Importantly, the Ireland-Apple case highlighted a broader reality of the global economy: multinational corporations operate within many countries, which raises the questions of how their profits should be apportioned among those countries. The traditional method of such allocation is called *transfer pricing*, a process in which companies are supposed to value the inputs they obtain from international parts of the company and the goods and services they deliver to other parts of the company at fair market prices (what are called arms-length prices, what prices would be if they were set by competitive, unrelated entities). The problem is that there is no way to ascertain the fair market value of most inputs. For example, what is the value of an unfinished car without an engine or wheels, or a shirt without buttons, sleeves, and a collar? Moreover, how do we value the contribution of intellectual property? Companies have found that the transfer price system gives them an almost entirely free hand to shift their profits to low-taxed jurisdictions. Occasionally, tax authorities dispute the transfer prices, but this process is long and expensive.

Within the United States, where goods in the process of production move frequently across state borders, the transfer price system has long been abandoned. Instead, US states use what is called a *formulaic system*, in which the total profits of the firm are allocated based on the proportion of the capital, sales, and employment within the state.

Europe has been moving toward change since the beginning of the 1990s.[17] Without an adequate resolution, the location of production will be distorted, and the race to the bottom, in one form or another, will continue. The self-serving argument put forward by corporations, that low corporate tax rates result in higher growth that benefits all, is disputed in theory as well as in empirical research.[18] Indeed, we have already explained why the corporate tax should not be expected to have any significant effect on investment. Far more important for most firms is the availability of well-trained labor and good infrastructure, but these elements can only be provided through adequate tax revenues.

## Harmonizing Individual Income Taxes and a Progressive Tax for the EU

Harmonization of the corporate income tax has received the most extensive discussion among reforms, but there is also a need for harmonization of individual rates, for instance. A strongly progressive income tax at the EU level would eliminate the incentive for high-wealth residents to move to a low-tax jurisdiction.[19] If the EU wants to preserve the freedom of movement its residents so value, it needs to grapple with the consequences of taxation.[20]

This major step, though, is unlikely to occur any time soon, and further inaction will impose strong limits on progressive taxation. These limits will undermine the European social model and move Europe more in the direction of the United States, with its high level of economic and social inequality.

There is another path forward: Europe can impose a surtax of 15 percent on all people with incomes in excess of, say, €100,000, wherever they reside. The revenues would be used to finance EU activities. The common budget of the EU is abysmally small, amounting to only 1 percent of EU GDP. The budget of the US federal government, by contrast, in 2018 amounted to 21 percent of GDP, and the budgets of the EU member states reach over 40 percent of GDP. An expansion of the EU budget would provide the steady revenue needed for Europe's common undertakings and European public goods, including a common defense force, an expanded student-exchange program, an expanded research program, solidarity funds for the new entrants, foreign aid and programs to integrate refugees and migrants, or a solidarity fund for stabilization.

Another option would be to introduce an EU-wide net wealth tax on a harmonized basis. A progressive net wealth tax with a rate per household of 1 percent on net wealth above €1 million and 1.5 percent on net wealth above €5 million could raise revenues of more than €150 billion. Such a tax could finance the total current EU budget.[21]

## FIGHTING EXTERNALITIES AND INTERNALITIES THROUGH TAXATION

One of the principles of taxation, as we've said, is to tax bad things because taxes discourage behavior that generates costs for others (negative externalities) or for the people themselves (negative internalities). There are three important categories of such taxes: sin taxes, environmental levies, and taxes on the financial sector.

### Sin Taxes

Drinking alcohol and smoking cigarettes have significant health consequences and generate negative externalities, especially in Europe, where the financial costs are largely borne by the public. At the same time, there is mounting evidence that taxes on alcohol and tobacco have a significant potential to reduce consumption.[22] Yet, Europe has not instituted sin taxes to the degree it should. Overall, the effective tax burden on cigarettes has increased steadily, and there is a tendency of converging tax rates.[23] For alcohol, the tax picture is more scattered, with a number of member states taxing alcohol consumption rather leniently.[24] There is, therefore, ample room for tax increases that could contribute to better public health.

Empirical studies also suggest that concerns about regressive effects are unfounded, particularly for tobacco products, which appear to place a higher burden on the wealthier population.[25]

## Environmental Taxes

Pollution is perhaps the most important negative externality. Because firms are not charged for the pollution they create, they have no incentive to reduce it. In the EU, the share of environmental taxes in overall tax revenues has been stagnating since the mid-1990s, when it went down in the 15 countries that joined the EU before 2004.[26] Environmental charges for carbon emissions, for instance, is an efficient way to discourage carbon emissions. Indeed, the recent Stiglitz-Stern Report[27] highlights the important role a moderate carbon tax (in the range of €60 to €100 per ton) can play in reaching the goals set in the Copenhagen and Paris agreements, to not allow an increase in temperature of more than 2 degrees Celsius. There are many other environmental taxes that can or should be imposed, such as a carbon-based plane ticket tax,[28] or a tax on jet fuel.[29]

Harmonization of environmental taxes is as or more important than the harmonization of corporation taxes discussed earlier. Without harmonization, polluting companies have an incentive to relocate, which results in what is called *carbon leakage*. Lower carbon emissions in one country may be more than offset by more carbon emissions in locations with weaker regulations and lower carbon charges. A border carbon adjustment for the EU Emissions Trading System may mitigate carbon leakage toward countries outside the EU.[30]

If full harmonization is not achievable, there should at least be an agreement about a minimum rate and an arrangement to impose cross-border carbon-adjustment taxes within Europe.*

## Time for a Financial Transaction Tax

We have noted the significant externalities that financial sector misdeeds have imposed on society. This industry has the power to, and does, take advantage of the poor and rich alike, and its excessive risk-taking led to the financial crisis. Moreover, financial sector short-term thinking has not only resulted in costs for the rest of society but has also infected the rest of the corporate sector with a similar kind of short-term thinking.

Taxes on the financial sector can help address these and other distortions, thus complementing the strong regulatory framework that was discussed in the previous chapter. We have noted how too-big-to-fail banks have an incentive to take excessive risks and to profit from implicit bailout guarantees. They have an advantage over smaller banks, not because of their greater efficiency, better services, or higher level of innovation, but simply because of the large implicit subsidy.

This big bank advantage needs to be reversed by a tax. The banking system as a whole has received large subsidies, sometimes hidden, through repeated bailouts, and this has resulted in a larger-than-optimal banking system. Again, to offset this implicit subsidy, there must be a tax on the banking system as a whole.

---

* The current minimum rates for energy taxes in the EU are, however, well below the rates required to reach the agreed goals of Paris and Copenhagen.

A tax on financial transactions themselves, if well designed, can discourage the short-termism that characterizes much of today's financial system. Stable, long-term growth has to be based on long-term thinking and long-term investments. Short-term holdings only encourage short-term thinking, and the resulting volatility in financial markets has both direct and indirect costs that weaken long-term growth. In Chapter 4, we showed how changes in corporate governance could encourage more long-term thinking, but a financial transactions tax can play an important role, too. A small tax on the purchase or sale of an asset has a negligible effect on an asset held for years but can significantly lower the returns of an asset held for a day or less. A levy would discourage this kind of socially unproductive, short-term investing.[31]

Since 2008, there have been extensive discussions of a European financial transaction tax (FTT) to address short-termism in finance.[32] In 2011, the European Commission adopted a comprehensive approach that encompassed all markets, institutions, and instruments. It carved out basic lending and debt issuance while targeting derivatives, repo markets, and secondary trading in sovereign and private securities.

Even the debate over the tax has proved to be a tonic for a Europe that has long shunted discussions of financial matters off to experts. A broad range of civil society, including trade unions, antipoverty groups, and consumer advocates, has supported the FTT concept.

This type of tax would raise money that EU countries need for fiscal stimulus (Chapter 1), public investment (Chapter 3), vital social policies (Chapters 7 and 8), and active labor market policies (Chapter 9). Applying the tax might also help clarify who owns what financial assets, thus advancing the public agenda to stop tax evasion and avoidance and bring many transactions out of the shadows.[33]

More ambitious than the tax originally advocated by the American economist James Tobin,[34] the FTT explicitly targets short-term (or "impatient") finance of all kinds. European regulators would set the FTT at a low enough level to prevent disruption to financial markets but high enough to generate revenue from business models associated with impatient finance. The FTT would encourage long-term, buy-to-hold strategies and patient investment.

Estimates from Goldman Sachs show that banks with capital market activities would pay the bulk of this tax, and that these banks would pay most of the taxes based on their wholesale funding and derivative market activities.[35] The FTT also directly targets the flow of funds from asset managers to investment banks based on short-term financial instruments that underpin shadow banking. It might even render unprofitable the funding strategies of global banks that use short-term borrowing to fund speculation.

There are a few standard objections to FTTs that are now widely discredited. These typically invoke the impact on volume and market liquidity that would render prices more volatile. Yet, the marked lowering of transactions costs in recent years or even decades—acting exactly as would a reduction in an FTT—has not resulted in markedly more stable financial markets. Indeed, if anything, lower transactions costs are associated with just the opposite—for example, with the sudden, computer-driven crashes of the computerized age.[36] Indeed, Tobin's original argument (in line with a similar one put forward earlier by Keynes) was that sand in the wheels can actually help stabilize the economy. The tax would help bend finance to the needs of the European economy and not the other way around. Against this background, European leaders should reconsider their decision, made in late 2018, not to further pursue the introduction of a broad-based European financial transaction tax (see Box 6.1).

# Box 6.1: The Financial Transaction Tax

Politically, the financial transaction tax (FTT) gained popularity after the financial crisis destroyed the reputation of the financial services sector, and by extension, reduced its lobbying muscle. In September 2011, the European Commission officially presented its proposal for a transaction tax for the 27 member states as a way to (1) avoid a fragmentation of the internal market; (2) ensure that the financial sector makes a fair contribution to recover the costs of the financial crisis, as well as to compensate for the "under-taxation" of the financial sector owing to the value-added tax exemption; (3) create disincentives for high-frequency trading; and (4) enable the development of an FTT at the global level.

After an EU-wide introduction of an FTT, as advocated by civil society groups, was rejected by a majority of member states (including the UK), a subgroup of 11 members (spearheaded by France and Germany) decided in January 2013 to move ahead by introducing the FTT with enhanced cooperation that would only bind participating member states. Following an "all institutions, all markets, all instruments" approach, the proposed tax had a wide scope, which encompassed derivatives and pension funds and included only a few exemptions. The commission estimated that the tax would raise around €57 billion per year.

In the end, the participating 11 members made little progress toward implementation, and negotiations were subject to massive lobbying by the financial services sector, which led to political gridlock. The initially ambitious reform proposal, which included a broad-based tax with very few exemptions, was subsequently watered down to a narrow tax with many exemptions for various financial instruments. Then, in May 2014, 10 participating Eurozone countries announced in a joint declaration the progressive introduction of a scaled-back version of the original FTT proposal. Despite the official pro-tax rhetoric of the participating member states, the fact that the issue remained at a standstill in the European Council, and council working group meetings throughout 2016, revealed significant differences among the remaining participants.

In light of Brexit negotiations and the imminent loss of the UK's contribution to the EU budget, the finance ministers of Germany and France again revived the idea of using a transaction tax to bolster the EU budget in late 2018, proposing to include the tax in the EU financial framework agreement for 2021 to 2027. The proposed tax would be modeled after the system currently in place in France. It would therefore not be levied on all financial transactions, but would only tax transactions with shares, and thus not cover derivatives and bonds.

Industry groups are mobilizing against this proposal, which represents a massively watered-down version compared to the original FTT proposal. They argue that the planned transaction tax would harm the plan to take trading away from the City of London, and make Paris and Frankfurt into the new European financial centers.

However, a reformulation of the FTT might easily answer this objection by imposing the tax on the party engaging in the transaction, regardless of where the transaction occurs. If this were the case, there would be no advantage for anyone to trade in London or New York rather than in Paris.*

# CONCLUSION

Part I outlined how we could restore full employment and growth to a Europe that has been suffering from near stagnation and unacceptably high unemployment (especially among youth). In the first two chapters of Part II, we examined the rules and regulations that govern the corporate and financial sector to try to better understand why Europe is not working as well as it should. To improve the outlook, we have suggested how to reform rules on competition policy, corporate governance, intellectual property, and the financial sector.

A new, more dynamic EU must raise funds for the public activities that a well-functioning society requires and has to do so in ways that are consonant with basic principles of efficient and equitable taxation. The impact on the distribution of income is particularly important today, given the clear increase in inequality that marks most countries within Europe.

Tax competition has made it difficult to impose progressive income

---

* A relatively few individuals might choose to change their citizenship to avoid the tax. This tax-motivated change in citizenship, in turn, can be curbed by imposing exit taxes on individuals giving up their citizenship, as the United States effectively does.

taxes, and the race to the bottom in corporation taxation has shifted the burden of taxation toward individuals. This chapter has shown how Europe, working together, can end this destructive competition and restore progressivity to the tax system. We have also shown how, by taxing negative externality–generating activities, such as pollution and short-term financial trading, we can actually improve economic performance. The reforms discussed here would thus not only increase equity and efficiency but would provide the EU with more funds to carry out the broadened agenda suggested elsewhere in the book.

We now turn to what has historically distinguished European capitalism from variants elsewhere. The difference is in the way Europe treats those in need, and in the system of social protection and public services it provides for all, which is sometimes called the "European social model." The system was sometimes wrongly blamed for the crisis, even though it ensured that the consequences of the crisis were far less severe than they otherwise would have been. It was the excesses of the financial sector, described in Part II, not the welfare state that brought on the crisis. But since the crisis, governments have weakened the welfare systems in many European countries exactly when they need to strengthen them.

Part III outlines a progressive approach to strengthening Europe's social model.

# Inequality and a Twenty-First-Century European Social Model

*Chapter 7*

# Poverty, Inequality, and the Welfare State

**To Europeans who** grew up as the EU took shape and the pace of integration increased, the more recent rise in poverty and inequality has come as a terrible shock. The level of social solidarity that most European countries managed to achieve in the years after World War II reflected a broad compact, shared across the political spectrum, of mutual responsibility for fellow citizens. The European welfare state that emerged embodied this consensus.

The EU, the euro, globalization, and all the other economic changes that have occurred over the past half century—combined with advances in technology—should have led to a new era of prosperity from which all would benefit. It has not played out that way. Instead, the divides appear greater than ever before, with large fractions of the population seeing incomes stagnate or decline, especially after the euro crisis.

Inequality is a big, abstract word that can have economic, racial, and gender dimensions. In the words of former US President Barack

Obama, the issue of wealth and income inequality is the "defining challenge of our time." It is also one we cannot avoid, which is why so much of this book deals with the subject, sometimes obliquely, sometimes directly.

We are calling here for a new approach to the welfare state. The European social model that ensured broadly shared prosperity has been eroded because of numerous misguided changes, especially in the crisis countries, where external powers imposed spending cuts under the banner of austerity.

Today, we should conceive of the welfare state as more than a safety net that provides for subsistence through social insurance and redistribution. The new social welfare model that we are suggesting here also demands a state that invests in its future and especially its youth, to ensure that there is full equality of opportunity. It recognizes that private markets, when left on their own, will underinvest and will not provide the instruments that will enable those of limited resources to invest in themselves. The model we propose also includes measures of consumer, investor, and worker protections, as well as systems to make markets fair, transparent, and competitive so that they improve the welfare of society as a whole and allow everyone to compete on equal terms in the economic game.

In this sense, the modern welfare state consists of all those programs that "put people first," to use a common slogan. Three propositions are at its core: the economy is not an end in itself but a means; a country's economic growth, on its own, will not necessarily translate into the well-being of all (or even most) of its citizens; and finally, the government can make a difference both in enhancing sustainable growth and ensuring that the fruits of that growth are equitably shared.

A variant of the theory of trickle-down economics holds that high growth will redound to the benefit of all and therefore that economic policy should be directed at maximizing growth. The evidence of the past 40 years has thoroughly discredited this idea. A high rate of GDP growth does not necessarily mean that most within the country see an increase in their living standards. Poverty can increase even when output rises, which is happening in large parts of Europe. A well-functioning society has to have some mechanisms for ensuring that the fruits of the economy are appropriately shared. In our rich, twenty-first-century economy, no one should suffer major deprivations.

In Chapter 8, we take up a particularly important aspect of individual well-being, an area in which there have been massive market failures. Whether it is the loss of a job, the consequences of an illness, or some other adverse event, markets do not provide adequate insurance—at least not at affordable prices—against many of the key risks that individuals confront. However, through the welfare state's provision of social insurance, society as a whole provides a measure of security to individuals.

While the main justification of this broadly conceived welfare state is moral, economics *alone* would provide ample reason for these policies. Societies that are more equal produce more sustainable economic growth and demonstrate greater political stability, something that Europe and the United States should not take for granted.[1] Citizens who enjoy greater security will be more willing to take risks and create the kind of innovative society that Europe needs. Not giving all citizens full opportunity to achieve the education level that would enable them to live up to their potential is a waste of a country's most valuable resources, its people.

Economic insecurity had been increasing even before the financial crisis and ensuing recession. However, those events worsened matters immeasurably, as unemployment grew in all European countries. Europe, however, was fortunate to have a strong welfare state that not only did a reasonably good job of protecting a large portion of the population but prevented the downturn from becoming worse, thanks to the "automatic stabilizer" of increased welfare expenditures. These increased public expenditures came precisely when they were needed.

Remarkably, the welfare state has often been scapegoated as the source of Europe's economic problems. Mario Draghi, president of the European Central Bank, reflexively criticized the welfare state as a major cause of the crisis, seemingly suggesting that it was something that needed dismantling.[2] His views perhaps reflected the financial sector's bias against the welfare state, but it was also an attempt to shift blame away from policymakers who should have done a better job of preventing and mitigating the crisis.

But the fundamental problem facing Europe has never been an over-mighty welfare state, which is why efforts to chip away at it after the crisis were so misguided. In truth, excessive private-sector leverage and financialization caused the crisis, not the welfare state. The countries with the largest welfare states, including Sweden and Norway, fared well. Germany's model, which Germans call the Social Market Economy, helped a highly industrialized country to equitably share the burden of the slowdown and prevented the unemployment rate from soaring, as it did in countries without similar social protections, like the United States.*

Moreover, it is extremely important not to confuse ends and means. Even if it were true that GDP might be increased by scaling back on the welfare state, it is not necessarily desirable. Economic output is

---

* Another criticism of the welfare state is that, to put it bluntly, it leads to laziness and thus destroys productivity. This is nonsense. Well-designed welfare states actually increase economic efficiency, as they remedy key market failures such as the absence of risk and capital markets. Again, the countries with the strongest welfare states are among Europe's most productive economies.

not an end in itself; it is a means for Europeans to live more fulfilling lives. As the international Commission on the Measurement of Economic Performance and Social Progress has emphasized, GDP is not a good measure of societal performance.[3] People care about insecurity, and cutbacks in the welfare state increase insecurity. Even if growth increased slightly as a result of such cutbacks, people would still be worse off.

To only criticize the cost of today's welfare state is to ignore its benefits. As we have already noted, its benefits enhance the economy's macroeconomic stability. Most importantly, it tempers the intolerable economic and social outcomes of an unfettered market in ways that build a shared prosperity.

## GROWING INEQUALITIES

After World War II and until the mid-1970s, most countries in Western Europe experienced sustained economic growth, falling poverty, and decreasing inequality. A European social model emerged that guaranteed stable employment, growing incomes, and upward social mobility. Governments extended pensions and other forms of social welfare for all people—including people outside of the labor force. Other initiatives promoted well-being, including better health, education, and housing.

At the same time, improved education led to a more educated, skilled, and productive labor force, and collective bargaining defended workers' claims to a share of their growing productivity.

But starting in the mid-1970s, a policy shift toward deregulation and liberalization led to strong pressure to cut social protections and spending. The advocates of this shift argued that, even if labor's income share declined, a faster-growing economy would ensure increasing incomes for all. Unfortunately, these reforms did not lead to faster economic growth. Instead, growth slowed relative to what it had been in the decades immediately after World War II.*

However, the prediction that these reforms would lead to lower labor income shares was accurate. Figure 7.1 shows a steep decline in labor's share of total income since the 1980s, with a 12 percentage-point decline in Italy, 10 percentage-point decline in France, and a 5 percentage-point decline in Germany, with these amounts in effect transferred from workers to profit earners and rentiers.†

The fall of labor's share indicates that since the mid-1970s, real wages have increased at a lower rate than average labor productivity. In other words, workers have been able to appropriate only a fraction of their increased efficiency at producing goods or providing services for themselves. This is in marked contrast to the past, where workers' compensation and productivity moved in tandem. As we discuss below, the reasons for this include workers' weaker bargaining power, globalization, weakened unions, and changes in labor legislation. Unfortunately, in too many European countries policies seem directed at making matters worse by weakening workers' rights even further.

The burden that the welfare state needed to carry to correct skewed market outcomes rose dramatically, beginning in the late 1970s. But

---

* The failure was not a surprise. Europe's experience corresponded to that of the United States in which Reagan's supply-side politics were no more successful. Lowering taxes, especially on the rich, did not lead to the predicted supply responses. It did lead to the anticipated increases in inequality. Also predictably, it led to more rent-seeking, which became more profitable. Liberalization increased gaps between social and private returns, which led to a diversion of resources from wealth creation to exploitation of market power and dominant positions.

† The change may be even greater than these numbers suggest. National labor income includes the incomes of bankers, CEOs, and other highly paid professionals. To the extent that these incomes have not declined, the decline depicted in Figure 7.1 implies a steeper loss for all other workers.

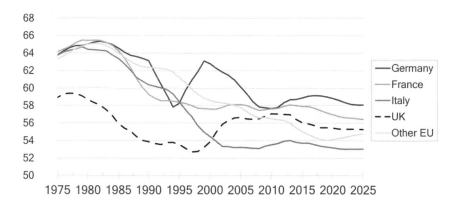

**FIGURE 7.1: DECLINE IN LABOR SHARE OF INCOME (% OF GDP)**

*Note:* Labor share defined as compensation of employees and mixed income as percentage of GDP. Five-year moving averages are depicted to smooth out trends. Compensation of employees includes salaries and employers' social security contributions. Data after 2016 are projections.

*Source: United Nations Global Policy Model.*

rather than addressing the economic causes, many European governments only focused on the effects on public spending. Just when there was a need for a stronger welfare state and more redistribution, many countries weakened the welfare state, cut back on redistributive payments, and reduced the progressivity of taxation.

The unfavorable trends at work before the crisis have continued, and in some cases worsened in the aftermath, as illustrated by a wide variety of statistics showing increasing inequality and growing poverty. In 2016, the richest 10 percent of Europeans received 38 percent of pretax national income, while the bottom 50 percent received 19 percent, or half as much.[4]

As Figure 7.2 shows, over the past 40 years, the steepest rise in income inequalities has occurred in the UK, Germany, and Ireland. By contrast, some of the Nordic countries seem, on the whole, to have succeeded in containing the trend. Spain and a few of the southern EU

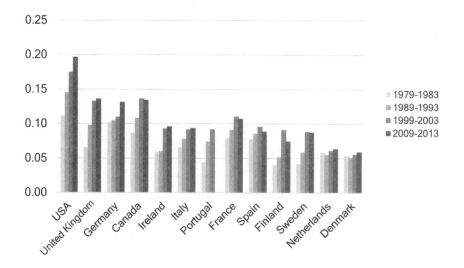

**FIGURE 7.2: INCOME SHARE OF THE TOP 1 PERCENT IN EUROPE: RISING SINCE THE 1980S**

*Note:* Since data for some countries and periods are not available, five-year averages have been considered (periods are indicated in the legend) for the figure above. Figures reflect income before tax but after social transfers.

*Source: Authors' calculations based on the World Inequality Database (https://wid.world/).*

member states even contained the rise of inequality as the post-2008 recession in these countries affected higher- and lower-income earners alike.

Alongside the increase in both income and wealth inequality, Europe has witnessed a steep increase in the number of people in poverty and facing the risk of poverty. As seen in Figure 7.3, in 2016, 7 million more people were at risk of poverty than were a decade earlier. Nearly 87 million people in the then-28 member states of the European Union were poor in 2016,* which represented more than 17 percent of the EU's entire population.

---

* The "at risk of poverty" threshold is set at 60 percent of the national median equivalized disposable income after social transfers.

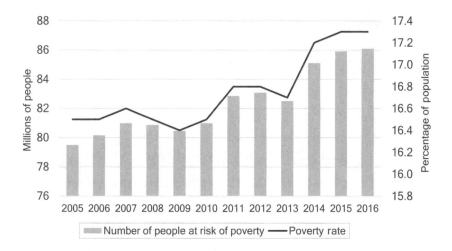

**FIGURE 7.3: POVERTY IN EUROPE**

The number of Europeans living in poverty, or facing the threat of it, has edged upward over the last decade.

*Source: Eurostat.*

Poverty has especially increased since the 2010 euro crisis, caused by a rise in unemployment and heavy cuts to social protection systems and other public expenditures that were imposed as conditions for receiving financial support. People in Greece, Spain, Portugal, Ireland, and Italy were particularly affected by these trends.

There were several factors that contributed to this growth in inequality:

- *Globalization.* The expansion of trade with developing countries and emerging markets meant that Europe increasingly imported labor-intensive goods, thus decreasing the demand for labor (and especially unskilled labor) and lowering wages from what they would have otherwise been.
- *Technological change.* Technology was biased toward skilled labor, which meant the demand for unskilled labor decreased,

especially relative to skilled labor, and this increased wage inequality. Though this trend helps explain the decrease in unskilled wages relative to skilled, it does not explain the decreased share of labor overall.*

- ■ *Changes in the structure of the economy.* Changes in the economy may lead to more market power and thus a growth of rents associated with monopolies and oligopolies. Other changes in economic structure have led to increased rents going to land and intellectual property. Urbanization, for example, is associated with a growth in land rents. The financialization of the economy has led to significant rents for that sector. The move from a manufacturing-based economy to a service economy may itself contribute to an increase in inequality. In the manufacturing economy of the postwar era, there was wage compression within large firms. Differences in productivity among workers was not necessarily reflected fully in wage differences. In the service-sector economy, with its smaller units of production, this may no longer be possible. If so, there will be more instances of winner-take-all outcomes in which the disparity in incomes (in any sector) between the top and those below is huge.†

- ■ *Increased intergenerational transmission of advantages and disadvantages.* Lower effective capital taxes and inheritance taxes have helped create inherited plutocracies. Privatization of education, where it has occurred, has further perpetuated divides.

- ■ *The management of globalization and its effects.* Lack of inter-

---

* To the extent that it was biased against labor, technology lowered the income that accrued to labor. While there is considerable evidence that technology evolved toward higher employment of skilled workers (compared to unskilled ones), there is little evidence that it evolved toward higher use of capital (compared to labor).

† For instance, the best singers or athletes are enormously well paid but others receive low incomes.

national tax policy cooperation to combat tax evasion, stronger intellectual property laws in trade agreements, lax global enforcement of competition rules, and cross-border financial market liberalization all led to greater rents.

■ *Weaker unions and adverse changes in labor laws.* Weaker unions are one of the most significant causes of rising inequality. In countries where unions have remained strong, even if inequality has increased, it has remained relatively low. Changes to labor laws, part of an ill-advised standard package of structural reforms, compounded the effects of globalization by eroding worker bargaining power.

Many of the changes in Europe's economy and society bring together several of the elements just described.[5] Unions have become weaker because globalization has made it more difficult for unions to achieve wage gains without employment losses. Unions have also been weakened by the shift in the economy away from large manufacturing enterprises, and because the rules of the economic game have been rewritten in ways to disadvantage them. But weaker unions mean that the voice of workers is weakened, which in turn has made it easier for governments to rewrite the rules in ways that favor businesses. Ultimately, the combination of weaker bargaining power of workers and more market (and political) power of firms has shifted income away from workers, thus increasing inequality.

## An Aside on Globalization

The politics of globalization, as well as the economics, played a role in how globalization affected inequality. The strong emphasis on international competitiveness that became especially intense in the 1990s brought on efforts to cut labor costs, and that (the corporations contended) required curbing job protections. Ideologues argued, too, that for countries to be competitive, they had to have macroeconomic policies built around low or no inflation, but also a low fiscal deficit and low taxes. What government spending there was, in this view, should be directed at investment to make the economy more competitive. An immediate corollary of this approach was a squeeze on the welfare state.

These ideas were problematic in many ways, including the obvious one that there was little correlation between countries that followed these dictums and countries that had strong and stable growth. But, more fundamentally, marrying this pro-business political agenda (fewer labor protections, lower taxes, less welfare spending) with the economics of globalization (lower wages, especially for the unskilled) had the immediate effect of workers becoming worse off. Globalization had been sold as a path to higher standards of living. However, workers were then told that to be competitive, they must accept lower wages and worse working conditions and that government had to cut back on the basic programs on which they depended. How, workers argued, can this be the basis of an increase in standards of living? If growth had soared, one might have assumed that eventually the economic pie would become so large that at least those in the middle would receive a substantial increase in living standards. But that has not happened, and disillusionment with globalization and politicians who advocate it has only grown.

The problem was not so much with globalization itself, but in how it was managed. A few countries, such as Sweden, managed it well so that unemployment remained low and growth high. While there were some adjustments to the welfare state in these countries, there was no massive downsizing. In other words, even though globalization, technological advancement, and changes in the structure of the economy happened everywhere, some countries have been able to maintain a high level of equality and social cohesion in the face of it. Government policy is crucial in countering inequality.

The analytic framework we have provided lays out the basis of a reform agenda. But whatever the underlying forces, and whatever else we do to combat growing inequality and poverty, an essential part of the response entails strengthening the European welfare state and the broader social model, and reforming them where necessary.

In short, a central thesis of this book is that one of the key factors contributing to increasing inequality and poverty in Europe is that the rules of the game have been rewritten over the past 30 years. One of the central objectives of the welfare state is to promote equality of outcomes and equality of opportunity. To achieve those goals, the rules must be rewritten again, this time to increase equality and reduce poverty.

## SOLUTIONS

We can think of the agenda for achieving a more equitable society as consisting of two parts: (a) improving the distribution of market incomes (what is sometimes called "pre-distribution") and (b) strengthening redistribution.

Pre-distribution includes rewriting many of the key rules of the market economy. It includes strengthening worker bargaining power, limiting concentrated market power, weakening the intergenerational transmission of advantages and disadvantages through better public education and inheritance laws, and redirecting research budgets away from saving labor to research on green technologies. A key in limiting inequality is that all those who want jobs can get them, which is why the macroeconomic policies that we discussed in Part I of this book are so important.

Redistribution entails more progressive taxation (as discussed in Chapter 6), but also public programs to ensure that all individuals have access to the means for a decent life. It starts with having a good job, but also includes having access to appropriate health care, quality education for one's children, secure retirement, and decent housing. Here, we discuss education and housing. The next chapter will focus on retirement and health.

The two parts of achieving a more equitable society—pre-distribution and redistribution—are linked in many ways. For instance, access to decent health care increases an individual's productivity, and hence his or her ability to work (whether he or she can actually work more depends on whether jobs are available). So, too, does better education. Likewise, good public transportation systems that connect underprivileged areas to city centers and industrial parks can increase economic opportunity and reduce inequalities in market income.

## INVESTMENT IN EDUCATION

Among the most important differences between the rich and the poor are their assets, such as the capital that they inherit from their parents and their human capital from investments in education and experience. Inheritance taxes attempt, in a limited manner, to reduce disparities in inherited financial capital. And government policies have been successful in helping equalize human capital in the past. Good public education for all children, regardless of their parents' education and income, can be a powerful equalizing force in society.

Overall, public educational expenditures have suffered as countries have faced fiscal constraints. This development is as shortsighted as it is pervasive. And with free migration throughout Europe, the provision of good education is no longer a local or national issue; it is a European issue. If those who receive a less than adequate education migrate to richer countries, the adverse effects on productivity—with all the attendant consequences—are effectively shipped elsewhere.

Today some of the poorest countries in Europe are effectively sub-sidizing some of the richer ones, as young, well-educated people from the crisis countries migrate in search of jobs. Their education was paid for by the citizens of the country they left, but the rewards accrue to the rich country they moved to. One public official described this brain drain as the theft of his country's intellectual property, though within the European rule of law.[6]

Repeatedly in this book, we have emphasized that the success of the European project rests on addressing key cross-border externalities; what one country does has effects on other members of the EU. But the EU has focused its energies on the wrong effects. The cross-border effects of deficits turned out to be imaginary. Those associated with taxation (Chapter 6) and education are real.

The welfare state begins with the premise that, at a minimum, every child should have the opportunity to achieve his or her poten-tial. This entails access to affordable quality education. Europe needs to invest more in education, with more support from the EU budget to help equalize educational opportunities throughout the EU. What is required is a comprehensive European agenda from prekindergarten through university.

## From Preschool to University Education

The imperative of education starts with Europe's youngest citizens. Research shows that by the time children enter first grade, there already are large disparities among them that are unlikely to be overcome. This is one reason why expenditures on early childhood education in many OECD countries are increasing rapidly.[7] Some countries in Europe have led the way in implementing these programs and have gathered valuable data establishing their efficacy. But many countries, especially the poor and crisis-afflicted, do not have adequate early childhood education for all children.

Children growing up in poverty present one of the greatest challenges in Europe, for malnourishment and other forms of deprivation impede learning. In 2016, more than one in four children were identified as at risk of poverty or social exclusion. However, this statistic hides significant disparities among European countries. The worst rates are in peripheral countries that experienced significant austerity cuts (over 30 percent of children, and sometimes nearing 50). This list includes Romania, Bulgaria, Greece, Hungary, Spain, Italy, and Lithuania. Although child and family benefits exist in all countries, their coverage and levels have been reduced in recent years in the name of austerity. This has contributed to the large numbers of children today growing up in poverty. Benefits need to be increased to bring children out of poverty.

In addition to raising the amount and coverage of child benefits, members of the European Parliament have called for a European Child Guarantee,[8] which would ensure that all children, including those growing up in deprived circumstances, get an adequate education (see Box 7.1).[9]

## Box 7.1: A European Child Guarantee

Such a guarantee could include free school meals and uniforms for low-income children, compensatory investments in public education in deprived areas, and other policies such as family income support. A key aspect would be a financing mechanism in which those countries with larger child poverty rates would receive more funds. (It should be noted that the United States has a program intended to equalize educational opportunity across states, which also differ significantly in the incidence of poverty and quality of education.) Though there is generally resistance from higher-income European countries to supporting lower-income peripheral European countries, doing so should be seen as an investment in Europe's future—its human capital—a natural concomitant of the principle of free migration.

Ensuring that all have access to higher education is also a challenge. The two different systems in the United Kingdom illustrate alternative approaches. In England, tuition was raised in recent years, but to ensure access, students have been given income-contingent loans whose repayment depends on the income of the students after they enter the labor force. In Scotland, however, tuition has been reduced, with current workers paying for the education of the next generation.

These policies have different intergenerational impacts and must be seen within the broader framework of social security, housing, and other programs that affect the intergenerational distribution of wealth.* Both, however, are markedly superior to the US system, which forces many young Americans from families of modest backgrounds to take on large debts to pay for their education; they face an ugly choice—either forgo the education that they need to live up to their potential or borrow and be saddled with debt for decades. Whatever approach Europe takes, it will need constant monitoring to ensure that the children of the poor avail themselves of opportunities for advanced schooling.

## A Commitment to Public Education

Equal opportunity will depend on Europe's commitment to public education. However, in keeping with recent fads about privatization more generally, some countries have increasingly turned to private education in the belief that it might be more efficient, more effective, or more responsive to the needs of students and the desires of their parents.

The evidence for this is ambiguous at best. The large majority of

---

* Shifting old-age retirement programs from pay-as-you-go pensions to fully funded retirement accounts breaks intergenerational solidarity and leaves individuals to save for their own retirement, undermining economic stability.

the best universities in Europe are public.[10] In the United States, Trump University has become the poster child for the for-profit universities, which excel in only one thing—fleecing their students, especially those who are poor and vulnerable. All the great American universities are state universities or not-for-profit organizations.

At the elementary and secondary school level in the United States, however, independent, not-for-profit charter schools have become fashionable and intensely studied. The evidence reveals that they have not performed any better than public schools, especially when taking selection bias into account (namely, that private schools can choose who attends and turn down any student who might not perform well).[11]

The interests of private, for-profit schools are aligned neither with those of their students nor with those of society. Instead, they prioritize profit. Parents, especially those who have less formal education themselves, have a hard time judging what makes for a good school. At best, they can judge whether their children are happy, working hard, getting good grades, and doing well on standardized tests. But typically, they have no notion of a school's impact on creativity or long-run performance. Moreover, parents know little about how much teachers are getting paid, how much money is going to school administrators, and other similar factors that contribute to their child's education.

Moreover, there are social consequences from the way the private education system works. For example, public schools play an important role in creating a civic community through social integration. Of course, it's challenging when there are significant economic, racial, and ethnic divides. But still, public schools can do a better job at promoting social integration and implementing other societal objectives than do private schools, whose objective is simply to make money. Regulations that force some degree of diversity or constrain the amount of profits that can be taken out of the school can help, but typically only a little.

And once the door is opened for private schools, they become a lobby, a special interest of their own. This scenario is evidenced in Sweden, where attempts to impose mild regulations—to ensure that a minimal fraction of expenditure goes to direct educational costs—were beaten back. In the United States, with great efforts, limited regulations on for-profit schools were implemented over the fierce opposition of the industry; they are now being torn down by the Trump administration.

## Moving from School to Work

A final important role of the education system is to help graduates move from school to work. This has been a significant problem in many European countries that have experienced high levels of youth unemployment. Europe has recently adopted a *Youth Guarantee*, "a commitment by all Member States to ensure that all young people under the age of 25 years receive a good quality offer of employment, continued education, apprenticeship, and/or traineeship within a period of four months of becoming unemployed or leaving formal education."[12] It is too soon to judge its success, but so far, youth unemployment rates in some countries remain stubbornly high.

## DECENT HOUSING

The post-crisis recession had huge consequences on housing for many Europeans. High unemployment and cuts in salaries and state support meant many could not afford to pay their rent or mortgage. Between 2008 and 2013, more than four million Europeans were estimated to have faced evictions.[13] The recession brought to a head a housing crisis that had been festering for years.

Europe has become increasingly urbanized, and the availability and affordability of housing, especially for those with limited income, have become major problems in most large cities. In many urban areas, the price of residential housing has risen sharply since the 1980s. Likewise, the average fraction of income spent on housing has also increased significantly, especially for those whose incomes have fallen or stagnated, and for those at the bottom of the income distribution. In Greece, households in the bottom quintile of the income distribution face housing rental costs up to half or more of their income, while in the majority of European countries, low-income households face median housing rental costs of between 20 and 45 percent of their incomes.[14]

Mortgages and household debt have also risen markedly in most European countries since the turn of the century. In countries such as France and Ireland, the median household in the bottom quintile of the income distribution faces mortgage costs between 40 and 55 percent of their income. Because of the high costs of housing in city centers, many people are forced to live in suburbs, thus creating a system of economic segregation, and confronting them with high transportation costs. These problems cry out for government intervention.

There are numerous reasons that markets do not guide private actors in making efficient locational choices. For example, there are large externalities, including congestion costs; when individuals move into a crowded city, they seldom take account of costs they impose on others, including more crowded roads and public transport. In the close quarters of the city, what one person does affects others, which is why most communities engage in at least a minimum form of zoning.* There can also be positive externalities associated with agglomeration

---

* Zoning is used because designing a price mechanism is essentially far too complex.

economies, and there can be social benefits from large numbers of people living in close proximity.

Moreover, financial markets, which are responsible for providing mortgages in Europe's market-oriented economy, are themselves rife with market failures, as discussed extensively in Chapter 5. Today in the United States, even a decade after the crisis, the government still underwrites a large majority of home loans. In Europe, market failure is evident in a lack of well-designed housing mortgages that help individuals manage the risk of home ownership at affordable rates where the spread between government and consumer rates are small.

The challenge facing Europe is to provide more affordable housing, with more economic integration, located with access to jobs and public transportation. There are three pieces of this puzzle: land use, housing finance, and the provision of housing.

## Land Use and Property Taxes

The most important determinant of housing availability of various types is *zoning*, or the rules that specify land use. Increasingly, as Europe becomes more urbanized, zoning will need to focus on mixed-income, high-density housing—the construction of multifamily apartment complexes that make housing available for those in different income categories. In the design of these programs, there may have to be some implicit subsidy from high-income housing to low-income housing if everyone is to have decent, affordable housing.

Modern zoning focuses on creating communities, with a range of public (schools, clinics) and private (retail, entertainment) services, with good public transportation that links housing to employment opportunities and with recreational facilities.

Given the importance of housing, general government revenues should be used for supporting housing programs with the characteristics described above. But there are several specific taxes that are naturally tied to the support of housing.

Property taxes are a natural and efficient source of revenues, especially for local public services, including housing for people of limited means. Ironically, in many communities, such taxes are not progressive; they are levied as a fixed percentage of the value of the property. However, there is a natural way of imposing a progressive tax. Since having a large apartment or house is one of the most important signals of wealth, taxing large apartments and houses at a significantly higher rate than smaller domiciles is a straightforward way to infuse progressivity into our tax system. Moreover, large apartments in the city center impose a high cost, since many more individuals have to commute long distances from suburbs to get to the city center. Thus, it especially makes sense to impose higher tax rates on large apartments and houses near the city center.

In some urban centers, there are many centrally located buildings with empty apartments being held for speculation or by foreigners for what they perceive as an option to migrate, should conditions in their own countries deteriorate. It is not just that space in a city is scarce—presumably, the prices they have paid for the apartments reflect that scarcity—but that cities are living communities and empty apartments detract from the vibrancy of the community. There is a social cost to these empty apartments. Besides, the holders of these apartments are typically wealthy, and thus a tax on them is a progressive way to reduce wealth inequality.

Governments should impose higher taxes on uninhabited homes and on capital gains from high-priced real estate, higher than on capital gains from other sources. Additionally, there is a value to housing price stability, which can be adversely affected by excessive speculation.

Particularly, higher taxes on large capital gains could also be imposed in the case of short-term real estate speculation.

## Mortgages

Affordability is largely a question of financing. We noted earlier the multiple market failures in mortgage markets. The market has not provided the kinds of mortgages that would help individuals manage the risk of ownership of the most important asset that families have, their homes, in the presence of vicissitudes in interest rates and labor markets. Managing these risks is especially critical because housing is often a family's most important savings vehicle, in many cases providing important funds for retirement.

Private markets have, at least in some countries, focused more on enhancing the fees they collect and the risks confronting the bank, than on the risks confronting borrowers, and they have engaged in predatory and sometimes discriminatory lending. Interest rates typically are far higher than they would be in fully competitive markets. Regulation is necessary, but in many countries, regulations in this realm have been inadequate. Moreover, the financial sector has demonstrated an unparalleled expertise in circumventing regulations.

There is an alternative, however, that could have a direct competitive effect by driving down private interest rates and improving lending practices, such as offering better mortgages for managing owner risk: the government itself should offer mortgages.

This *public option* entails governments directly supplying mortgages. Under this scheme, any individual who has paid taxes for, say, five years, would have the right to a conventional 30-year mortgage at a rate slightly above the government bond rate of that duration, with the usual restrictions on loan-to-value ratios and debt-service-to-income ratios. Even better, the loans could be made income-contingent, that is, the amount repaid in any year could be made contingent on the income (reported on tax returns) of the individual.[15]

When the borrower is going through a bad patch, such as an illness or temporary unemployment, rather than putting the stress of possible home loss on the owner (as is the case with conventional mortgages), payments would automatically be reduced to an affordable level and the duration of the mortgage would be extended. This is an example of the kind of financial product that helps people manage the risk of home ownership, but which the private sector has been slow to provide. In fact, as we saw in the United States, private financial markets invented financial products that were designed to explode in the face of untoward events.

Banks originating mortgages currently evaluate loan applications based on two pieces of information: the client's income (and possibly their income history) and the market value of the property (based on the price of similar properties). The key pieces of this information are already in the public domain. A government agency with access to tax records and property sales can process this information at low cost. Moreover, technology would make it easy to incorporate mortgage payments with tax withholdings so that the costs of collection would be lower than under current arrangements. Furthermore, this option would provide an incentive to correctly report taxable income, because a higher reported income would qualify an applicant for a larger mortgage.

Citizens often wonder what they get from the government. Direct mortgages (and the many other benefits of the welfare state) are tangible benefits that should lead to more support for government and the essential collective action functions that it serves.

A complementary approach would involve encouraging more private sector lending, with better practices and more competitive interest rates. Keeping within its mandate, the European Central Bank can set and enforce targets for commercial banks for the expansion of mortgages, especially for first-time buyers, and simultaneously impose rules that discourage speculative real estate transactions, such as mortgages for those who simply want to buy and sell properties quickly.*

The American program of requiring a minimal amount of lending to underserved groups, the Community Reinvestment Act, has proven an effective way to get funds to minorities and limit the most egregious discriminatory practices, though this law is now also under adverse pressure from Trump-appointed regulators. The banks have learned how to identify good borrowers within these groups, so that default rates are little different from similar lending rates to nonminorities. Those European countries that do not have such a program should consider adopting one, which could also be designed at the level of the EU.

## Adequate Housing for Low-Income Families

But even with all of these initiatives, it may be the case that in some places the supply of rental homes for low-income families will be inadequate. In these situations, families are forced to live in crowded spaces for which they pay exorbitant rents, especially once one takes into account the quality of housing and its location. The record of public housing has been mixed. These often-large housing complexes have sometimes been called "warehouses of the poor." The poor are segregated from the rest of the community, and in the absence of adequate

---

* Again, the ECB, national central banks, and European governments can use both carrots and sticks. The ECB, for instance, could restrict access to refinancing to banks that satisfied these targets. Alternatively, governments could make available the information described earlier (for issuing public option mortgages) at no cost to private lenders.

public services and community organization, public housing has sometimes become a center for gangs and crime.

The alternative, though still somewhat controversial, is to pick up part of housing costs (through, for instance, a housing voucher), so citizens can live in communities of their choosing. Also part of this plan would be to encourage builders to build mixed-income housing, either by making it a requirement for getting a building permit or a needed zoning variance, or by providing some financial assistance (construction loans at more favorable terms) to builders who are engaged in constructing mixed-income homes. The social benefits of creating more economically integrated communities far outweigh the mild costs of these programs.

Good housing is essential for maintaining a reasonable sense of well-being and for a decent standard of living. Europe's high population density means that for a modern urban economy, city land rents will be high, and thus housing will be expensive. The positive side of high land rents is that government can impose high, nondistortionary taxes on land, which in turn can be used to make sure that cities are livable for everyone, and not just for the rich.

How we structure our cities—from zoning to public transport and public amenities—has a large effect on standards of living and differences in well-being, inequalities that go well beyond income. It also has a major effect on the environment. More dense cities mean less commuting and lower greenhouse gas emissions. But a side effect of designing such cities is that rents in the center may be higher, thus making the need for government assistance to avoid economic segregation.

Overall, the lack of affordable housing for the poor means that the deprivations they face may be far greater than is suggested only by their income. Indeed, many are at near subsistence level once they pay for rent. Addressing housing is necessary, then, if we are to have a just society. Ensuring access to decent housing through the various mechanisms described in this chapter is an essential pillar of a modern welfare state.

## CONCLUSION

In this chapter, we made the case for the welfare state as broadly understood and updated for the twenty-first century, with a particular emphasis on the centrality of children and families. We have argued that the welfare state is about more than absorbing risks to health or old age that citizens bear, but about helping them through key stages and challenges of life. In this chapter, we have focused on education and housing.

A key rationale for this twenty-first-century welfare state is a commitment to social justice. Economists might debate why individuals face the specific deprivations they confront—whether they result from market failures, poor individual decision making, or the failure of the political process to do what it should. But the fact remains that the deprivations exist, are pervasive, and will remain so unless there is government intervention. Most importantly, access to quality education, health care, social security, and housing, as well as jobs with fair wages, are basic human rights under the UN's 1948 Universal Declaration of Human Rights, rights that are still unrealized for many Europeans.

But in this chapter we have also shown that there is a strong economic efficiency argument for the welfare state. The idea is about both increasing well-being and tapping into the full potential of a society's resources so people who want to can participate fully. We have argued against leaving this task to the market, and for good reason. In many of the areas, such as in the provision of well-designed and affordable mortgages, markets have simply failed. Many of the problems with which the welfare state must contend are created by the market, such as growing inequality and insecurity.

In some of the areas, like the provision of pensions (discussed in the next chapter), the government has proven to be far more efficient than the private sector. In other areas, if the state does not take action, important social needs will simply not be addressed. Only the state can undertake some of the roles of the modern welfare state. Only it has the resources and the reach to do so. Markets have neither the capacity nor the incentives to provide certain essential services. Markets by themselves, for instance, will not ensure that the children of poor workers get the education they need to achieve their potential.

Research over the last 40 years has helped us understand the magnitude and sources of market failures—instances in which the market fails to deliver on its promise of efficient outcomes with stable growth. Some of those failures—associated with the absence of good risk markets, for example—have direct bearing on well-being. As we have noted, markets impose high levels of insecurity but then fail to deliver products or services that would enable individuals to cope with these risks. The next chapter will discuss, at greater length, the role of the welfare state in providing social protection in helping individuals and families manage the multiple risks that they face as they move through life.

# Chapter 8

# A European Social Security System for the Twenty-First Century

**The social insurance** systems that Europe—notably Germany—pioneered in the late nineteenth century have served its people well. They have provided a cushion against risks Europeans may face in life. Seen as good politics when Otto von Bismarck did it to dampen the social conflict sown by the Industrial Revolution, social insurance is now a vital mechanism of economic stabilization and a building block of European living standards. Social insurance—state insurance programs that guard against major risks facing citizens—must remain central to the welfare state.

For many years now, these critical achievements have been under attack. An ill-informed debate has propagated the notion that various forms of social protection (and the welfare state more generally) are impediments to the efficient functioning of a market economy and, as such, must be cut down to size. Moreover, some market fundamentalists have argued that shifting as much social protection to the private sector as possible, including by privatizing public retirement programs, would enhance economic efficiency. Neoliberals contend, moreover, that many European societies live beyond their means with a system of social protection beyond their capacities to support, and with programs for the elderly that come at the expense of future generations and economic growth. Unfortunately, the euro crisis in 2010 provided an opportunity for those arguing for a cutback in welfare programs. In many countries, austerity cuts have seriously imperiled the ability of these programs to deliver the basic guarantees of income security, health care, and comfort in old age.

In fact, the traditional welfare state addresses the absence of affordable private-sector services that are critical to human well-being, such as health care, unemployment support, disability, and old-age pensions. During the post–World War II era, governments around the world stepped up their efforts to provide public pension programs or health insurance because the private market simply was not meeting those needs.

As we have noted, a vibrant welfare state also has important implications for macroeconomic policy during economic downturns. Unemployment insurance systems, which we take up in Chapter 9, help to automatically stabilize the economy. The origins of the social protection and risk-sharing aspects of the welfare state are, however, also ethical, based on solidarity and social justice and built around a shared responsibility for fellow human beings.

This chapter discusses three key social protection programs: health, pensions, and disability and long-term care. We then explain why governments should provide universal coverage and discuss the pros and cons of a universal basic income program.

# HEALTH CARE

European countries have universal health care systems, which they should not take for granted, that offer treatment and preventive care, often of excellent quality. European governments often provide health care directly. In other cases, the services are provided through private establishments but are paid for by the government. In all cases, contributions to national health care systems are compulsory. Private insurance is available as a voluntary (often supplementary) option almost everywhere, the use of which does not exempt people from contributions to the national system.

The United States provides a model of what Europe should avoid. A look at the American health care system, which is run mainly by private, for-profit companies, makes the advantages of Europe's system of public provision clear. Health care costs in the United States are the highest in the world, yet outcomes are far poorer than in many countries that spend significantly less.* Without adequate health insurance, people face high levels of insecurity; an illness can easily lead to bankruptcy and destitution. The deficiencies in the health care system are a major contributor to that country's inequalities. The situation is so bad that life expectancies, already low in comparison to other advanced countries, have declined in recent years.

Above all, it is important that European countries resist pressure to privatize health insurance. Private markets will tend to insure only

---

* One of the reasons for the high costs in the United States is the large amount of monopoly rents garnered by a health care sector marked by high levels of market power, for instance in the provision of health insurance and pharmaceuticals. Europe needs to guard against importing these problems. A stronger competition agenda along the lines of the one detailed in Chapter 4 would reduce costs. Costs are also high because private insurance firms try to "cream skim," insuring only the healthiest people.

the healthy and/or will charge unaffordable prices to those with pre-existing conditions because they are at a high risk for needing medical services. Private companies will work hard, often successfully, to circumvent regulations designed to ensure access at affordable prices to insurance for all, including those with pre-existing conditions.

In recent years, European health care provision has been weakened by austerity measures. The worst case is Greece, where the public health care budget was cut approximately in half in less than a decade. Roughly seven in ten Greek adults in 2017 could not afford medications, and preventive care plummeted.[1] Not surprisingly, the situation also led to deteriorating mental health outcomes. The prevalence of depressive episodes for Greeks increased from 3.3 percent in 2008, to 12.3 percent in 2013.[2] There was a shocking 40 percent rise in suicides in Greece between 2010 and 2011.[3]

Other countries facing austerity also saw cutbacks in health care services. In some countries, copayments for basic services were introduced or raised, thereby increasing out-of-pocket payments for many households. Furthermore, hiring freezes or job cuts that were imposed on public health professionals sometimes led to long wait times for surgery and treatment. According to the World Health Organization, the full effects of the recession on health may not be apparent for years.[4] Experience from past economic crises tells us there are likely to be further adverse medium- and long-term health effects due, for instance, to falling household incomes and inadequate or delayed access to health services.

The EU should continue working to ensure full portability of health insurance across the bloc by allowing people to access care in all EU countries regardless of their citizenship or residence. A lack of portability undermines the principle of free mobility of people within Europe. Policies should encourage an upward convergence of European health systems toward the quality of the best health care systems.

That said, given the large disparities in incomes across Europe, convergence will be hard to achieve without EU budgetary support.

## PENSIONS

The distinction between the precepts of market fundamentalism (or neoliberalism) and a welfare state is perhaps clearest in the context of the treatment of older adults. If retirees have insufficient income to live a decent life, the neoliberal response is that they should have saved more for their retirement, and that the "nanny state" undermines incentives for individuals to take care of themselves. Yet, this neoliberal perspective ignores multiple market failures, including a failure to ensure full employment at decent wages, and a failure to provide annuities and other retirement products designed to meet the needs of retirees on reasonable terms.

Markets have been slow to provide adequate annuities. Before Bismarck undertook *public* provision, the private sector simply didn't make such financial products widely available. Where and when they have provided annuities, premiums have been high as a result of administrative costs that exceed those of government programs. Markets also do not provide insurance against inflation and, without adequate government regulation, force pensioners to face other risks, including that the insurance provider goes bankrupt and/or does not deliver the retirement benefits they promised.

In many quarters, however, public pension programs are under attack.

With more longevity, and lower birth rates, Europe is experiencing a significant demographic change. This change, together with the slowdown of economic growth, has raised questions as to whether existing public programs are economically viable.

Around the world, ideology and budget pressures have led to many misguided changes to public pension programs—responses to the ideology of market fundamentalism. Most notable in this case was what happened in eastern Europe over the last 20 years. Many eastern European countries, advised by the World Bank, privatized their pension systems.* Privatization did not deliver the expected results. Some countries have started to reverse the privatizations by partially or fully re-nationalizing their pension systems (Box 8.1).

## Box 8.1: Reversing Pension Privatizations

In the 1990s–2000s, many eastern European countries privatized their pension systems: Hungary (1998), Croatia and Poland (1999), Latvia (2001), Bulgaria and Estonia (2002), Lithuania and Romania (2004), Slovakia (2005), Macedonia (2006), and Czech Republic (2013). The objective was to avert a crisis in which social expenditures would drive up government spending; to promote individual savings; to avoid government mismanagement of pension funds; and to encourage the development of the private financial sector that would manage people's savings.

However, such pension reforms did not yield the expected results:

**Negative social impacts.** With the introduction of individual savings accounts, privatizations broke the social contract enshrined in government-run social security in which current workers support retired workers. The privatizations led to increasing inequalities, especially when Europe entered a phase of higher unemployment; those with low incomes had very small savings and ended up with small pensions. Furthermore, gender inequalities were exacerbated because many women paused their careers for long periods to take care of children or parents (or they worked part-time or in lesser-paid jobs). Pension benefits for women and low-income workers decreased in all countries.

---

* Privatization entails a shift from public pay-as-you-go systems, where contributions by employed workers pay for retirees' pensions, to capitalization systems, where everyone pays for themselves. This shift undermines intergenerational solidarity; at the very least, such changes penalize the generation caught in the middle, as that generation pays both for its own retirement and for that of its parents.

*High fiscal costs of transition.* Countries seriously underestimated the costs of moving from a public to a privately funded system. Governments had to transfer to private pension funds all the accumulated contributions that were paid by workers. But in pay-as-you-go systems, the main asset is the obligation by workers to pay contributions. Thus, governments had to borrow to obtain those prospective funds. In Hungary, the transition costs of the reform put a fiscal burden on the government that increased from 0.3 percent of GDP in 1998 to 1.2 percent by 2010. In Poland during the period between 1999 and 2012, the accumulated transition costs were estimated to be 14.4 percent of GDP.

*High administrative costs.* Much of the interest in privatization of social security arose from the desire of the financial sector to increase its profits by collecting fees from pensioners. The administrative costs of insurance/pension fund companies are much higher than those of public administration, thus making returns and, ultimately, pensions lower. Adding administration charges, investment management fees, custodian fees, guarantees fees, audit fees, marketing fees, and legal fees, among others, can reduce accumulated assets (or pensions) over a 40-year working life by as much as 39 percent in Latvia, 31 percent in Estonia, or 20 percent in Bulgaria.

*Greater pensioner risk burden.* The costs of financial market fluctuations were transferred to pensioners, who risk losing all their life savings if financial markets collapse, as happened during the global crisis; in some countries, the government (meaning the taxpayer) had to act as a guarantor of last resort in having to supplement pensions for citizens during the financial downturn.

*Reversals.* In 2010, Hungary officially re-nationalized private pension assets and eliminated the mandatory private individual accounts savings scheme. It returned to its pre-1998 mandatory pay-as-you-go public pension system. In 2013, the government of Poland allowed workers to transfer their contributions from the private to the public pension plan and eliminated mandatory contributions to the private system, with the result that in 2014, only 100,000 members remained in the private individual accounts system, leaving the private pension fund administrators with very small portfolios. Other countries such as Slovakia (2008–12), Estonia, Latvia, and Lithuania (all 2009) have reduced the size of their individual account private schemes by lowering their contribution rates and redirecting the financing to the public pension programs.

The privatizations of pensions, which were justified by the alleged need to avert an aging crisis and reduce public spending on pensions, ironically generated higher fiscal costs, lower retirement incomes, and more inequality. Because private pension systems have very high administrative costs, more money went to the pension fund managers and less was available for pensioners.[5]

European countries can defuse pressure for full or partial privatization by making minor adjustments to their pension systems regarding contributions, benefits, and eligibility. Some governments have done so. When benefits (in the aggregate) are not commensurate with contributions, these reforms made sense since such programs are not sustainable without general government subsidies, which may be hard to come by. Moreover, the early retirement ages in many government schemes are not consistent with the increases in health and longevity in recent decades. These adjustments should guarantee sustainable systems that deliver adequate pensions to all Europeans.

The focus on employment that we outlined in Chapter 1 is relevant here. Increasing job creation—including for older Europeans—can doubly benefit the public pension programs by increasing revenues and reducing expenditures. It is a waste of valuable human capital not to provide meaningful jobs for older people who want to work. Moreover, this increased labor supply will be important in the future to offset the reduced labor supply from lower population growth. However, even if on average people are living longer and can work longer, this is not true for everyone. Of particular concern, for instance, are workers who have led a life of hard physical labor. If there are upward adjustments to the normal retirement age, then there have to be special adjustments for these individuals.

However, in the austerity period from 2010 onward, a number of European governments have undertaken too many cost-cutting adjustments without paying sufficient attention to the negative impacts of reducing pension benefits and restricting eligibility.* In Spain, for instance, pensions have been de-linked from inflation since 2013. In other cases, pension reserves have been used for purposes other than pensions, threatening the future viability of the system.†

Additionally, some governments, such as Britain's, are weakening public pensions, as they try to encourage increasing reliance on private pensions. In particular, middle- and upper-income groups are expected to rely more heavily on individual savings to supplement decreased public pensions. Some governments started to subsidize private voluntary pension plans with hefty tax incentives, a change which is justified as encouraging higher self-reliance. On average, these incentives may simply give extra benefits to those who are better off, making inequality in old age worse.

Overall, these changes have resulted in lower total retirement incomes and an increase in the number of older people living in poverty, so much so that the United Nations Office of the High Commissioner for Human Rights has warned that "austerity measures endanger social protection schemes, including pensions, thereby dramatically affecting the enjoyment of the rights to social security and to an adequate standard of living."[6] For example, between 2005 and 2012, poverty rates for older people increased by 80 percent in Sweden (from 10 to 18 percent) and have doubled in Poland (from 7 to 14 percent).[7]

A key, persistent issue is the fight against informality, or workers

---

* In several cases (most famously, Portugal), moreover, there was insufficient attention to the legality of the cuts. The reforms proposed by the Troika (the European Central Bank, the European Commission, and the IMF) have been questioned in national courts, and were found unconstitutional in Portugal, Latvia, and Romania, thus leading to their reversals. *World Social Protection Report 2014–15* (Geneva: International Labour Organization, 2014), p. 138.

† The Irish National Pension Reserve Fund—a sovereign wealth fund established to finance civil service pensions—was tapped to participate in the IMF-led bailout of private banks, jeopardizing its future financial viability.

employed off the books. Of course, this shadow labor is illegal, but it can seem a convenient arrangement to both the employer, who does not have to pay payroll taxes or social security contributions, and the employee, who also can evade taxes. But it is shortsighted: such workers will likely find themselves in poverty once they reach old age. In Italy, for example, around 60 percent of domestic workers are not integrated into the social security system. This number is around 30 percent in Spain and France.

Social insurance can and must be adapted to respond to specific categories of workers, such as domestic workers, to make it more likely that they and their employers both contribute. Reducing transaction costs and making it easier for employers/employees to make their contributions can be an important step. A number of governments have tried to extend coverage to vulnerable workers, including those with multiple employers, those with irregular jobs, and those who are self-employed. In Austria and Spain, part-timers and the self-employed are allowed a more favorable way of calculating benefits for any given level of contributions. In Indonesia and Uruguay, taxi and motorcycle taxi drivers, including those working through gig economy platforms, are covered by social insurance through payments via an online application.[8] *Formalization*, or bringing workers onto the books, would have further benefits, including the improvement of working conditions of those in the informal economy. What these examples illustrate is that public pensions can be provided even to those in the informal economy.

Several additional reforms of existing pension systems could also provide more security in old age. First, with increased job mobility, pension portability—as is the case with health care—is important, and legislation has to ensure such portability. Common standards among national social security systems would facilitate economic convergence among member countries and help align labor costs across countries.

Second, just as many governments have been cutting back on public pensions, private-sector retirement programs have shifted risk from corporations to individuals as they have moved from defined-benefit programs (where retired workers receive for the remainder of their lives a monthly payment, often indexed to inflation and, therefore, fixed in terms of purchasing power) to defined-contribution systems (where the employer contributes a fixed amount to a retirement account, which is invested in traded financial assets whose value fluctuates on the market, effectively making retirement income a gamble). In some countries, governments have even encouraged these defined-contribution systems by giving them tax preferences. Employers are in a far better position to manage and bear the risks associated with pensions, and governments should accordingly find ways of encouraging them to do so.

Third, many people want to supplement their public and corporate pensions with more savings. Currently, they must turn to funds that are managed by the financial sector. In some cases, these funds have shown themselves to be better at rewarding *themselves* than pensioners. For example, fees are often high and there are sometimes large, undisclosed conflicts of interest.

Creating a voluntary *public pension option* would allow individuals who want to secure a higher pension to do so without the risk of being preyed upon by the private financial sector. So far, voluntary complementary pensions are private, are managed by the financial sector, and are vulnerable to the problems explained above. But a public voluntary pension scheme is feasible—even easy to implement. To determine the individual's retirement benefits, the voluntary contributions would simply be added to the mandated contributions. This public option would create greater security with lower administrative costs.* Additionally,

---

* There are many details associated with the public option that each country would have to work out. For instance, for these supplementary programs, early withdrawals could be allowed and pension savings could be used as collateral for housing mortgages.

the funds contributed to a voluntary public pension pillar could be part of the capital base for public investment.

## DISABILITY AND LONG-TERM CARE

People with disabilities are exposed to multiple risks throughout their lives and face higher poverty rates. Children with disabilities are often excluded from society, including from mainstream education, due to stigma, institutionalization, or a lack of support services. As adults, people with disabilities often find it extremely difficult to land a job, which results in higher levels of unemployment, unstable earnings, and a reduced capacity to live independently.[9] Public programs need to be complemented with regulations over the private sector, ensuring that people with disabilities are not discriminated against and have adequate access to buildings, public transportation, and public spaces.*

Europe has done relatively well in addressing the issues of disability, but one area it has overlooked is the need for long-term care. In European countries, people who are frail or who have severe disabilities are taken care of predominately by relatives, mainly women who are typically not paid for their work.[10] The fact that there are now smaller families, more mobility, and two-earner families makes this solution increasingly untenable. At present, long-term care through the market is mainly accessible to patients who can afford to hire a private nurse. On average, OECD countries spend only 0.8 percent of GDP on long-

---

* There are many obvious elements to such programs: ensuring greater income security, promoting employment, and facilitating access to social services, including social work and the provision of assistive devices. Many countries provide a combined package of social insurance (disability pensions) and social assistance, which includes cash and in-kind benefits, such as free and adapted public transport, access to other public services free of charge, and free or subsidized wheelchairs, scooters, crutches, or prosthetic devices.

term care, but this figure will need to increase substantially with the aging of the population.[11]

While caring for older Europeans imposes large costs on society, it also creates jobs. The number of long-term care workers per 100 people who are 65 and older varies significantly by country, ranging from only 0.4 in Portugal to 17.1 in Norway. The International Labour Organization estimates that the deficit of long-term care workers in Europe is 2.3 million.[12] These employment opportunities may be particularly important as machines and artificial intelligence replace workers in manufacturing and other jobs. But care workers will have to receive higher pay to avoid furthering inequality. Currently, wages in this sector are low, which in part reflects pervasive gender discrimination.

More generally, how much government pays those who teach children and take care of the elderly and the sick reflects our values: if we value our children, our aged, and our sick, we should pay those who care for them well. If taxation is reformed, which we have advocated in this book, the necessary funds will be available.

## FROM SOCIAL ASSISTANCE TO A UNIVERSAL BASIC INCOME?

Social protection systems should be universal and designed to protect all citizens in Europe. While social insurance covers the majority of people, social assistance programs (that is, transfers unrelated to any prior contributions) support, for instance, those without formal employment and therefore the ability to contribute, as well as those with special needs or disabilities.

Unfortunately, driven by an austerity mindset that prioritizes budget savings, European governments have been reducing and narrowly targeting social assistance programs. Many important social assistance benefits such as child allowances, disability benefits, and social support programs (aid to victims of domestic violence, for example) have been reduced or dismantled, leaving many without adequate support.

There has long been a debate within the economics profession over the desirability of broad-based (or universal) versus narrowly targeted programs. The latter, some people argue, can use money more efficiently by channeling it to the poorest, those who really need it.

But such targeting is expensive, excludes many vulnerable people, and introduces distortions into the economy (since some people change behavior to achieve eligibility). Moreover, it has long been a maxim that "means-tested programs are mean." There is a tendency to starve programs that are extended only to a small part of the population.

Recently, proposals for a universal basic income (UBI) have achieved considerable attention. Their advocates hold that a single program could replace the multiplicity of programs aimed at different groups and at different needs, such as social assistance, unemployment support, and housing. Proponents champion the simplicity of the scheme and the "dignity that it confers, an income that one receives simply as a right of citizenship."[13]

The net redistributive impacts of UBI vary depending on the benefit level and financing source. For instance, a benefit at 25 percent of the median income would decrease inequality substantially, if financed progressively.[14] There are also indirect distributional benefits: a UBI would increase the bargaining power of workers, as they may not be forced to accept employment under poor working conditions.

Pilot UBI experiences in India and Namibia show positive developmental impacts; when individuals received the UBI benefit, nutrition, health, and school enrollment improved. There was also a marked reduction in child labor.[15] In the United States, an earlier predecessor of this idea is Alaska's Permanent Fund, which distributes part of the state's oil revenues to all residents, though the amount redistributed is too low to have significant social impacts. Also, in the United States, the negative income tax, under which those whose income fell below a certain threshold received a payment from the government, was shown to enable workers to continue to search to get better jobs and provided particular benefits to the well-being of women, who became less economically dependent on their husbands.[16]

Currently, there are UBI pilots being developed in Finland, Canada (Ontario), the Netherlands (Utrecht), and other countries, all with different benefit levels and sources of funding. These should deliver interesting lessons. Ultimately, the impact of basic income on poverty and inequality depends on the level of benefits as well as the source of funding, which should be progressive and sustainable over time.

One of the main controversies around a UBI centers on its effect on work incentives. On the one hand, some worry that an unconditional income could cause people to stop looking for paid work. The counter argument is that UBI allows people to search for jobs better matched to their abilities and interests, and that this will increase national productivity. It also holds that UBI will enhance workers' bargaining power—a good thing in an era in which wages, especially at the bottom, are so depressed. The pilot experiences conducted in Canada, India, and Namibia do not reveal significant adverse effects on employment; in Iran, some UBI recipients actually increased their working hours.

A more serious concern involves the danger that UBI may lessen pressure on governments to ensure that there are jobs for everyone who wants to work. The problem today is not on the side of the supply of workers but on the supply of jobs. Most people believe that work is part of what gives them dignity. We noted earlier that there is considerable evidence that having a job is important to well-being. If the EU and national governments make sure that economy and society function so that everyone who wants a job gets one, then the task of ensuring that everyone in Europe has a decent living standard is far more manageable. The UBI may play a role, but the need for all to have a minimum income may be better addressed through programs ensuring that there are jobs for all and that the jobs pay decently.

The real challenge for UBI is money. To provide a UBI at what most people in Europe would view as a sufficient level would require significant increases in taxation. That said, there are feasible intermediate options that should be considered, such as universal benefits for people with disabilities or parents of young children.

## CONCLUSION

Changes over the past decade have weakened one of Europe's strongest features, its system of social protection for taking care of the aged, the sick, the disabled, and the unemployed. Europe should reverse this trend, and it can be done even within strict budgetary constraints. These programs enhance individual and societal well-being and make household spending more stable. Healthier people, for example, are more likely to participate in the labor force, and a healthier labor force is a more productive labor force. It is neither good for families nor society if people are grappling with financial insecurity in retirement. There are innovative ways to improve Europe's systems of social protection, such as a public option for voluntary pensions, increasing choice and enhancing competition in the market.

Still, we should not lose sight of the goal of well-compensated, meaningful jobs for all Europeans who wish to work. Ensuring that everyone who wants to work has a job with decent pay may be the most important thing that government can do to reduce inequality and for social protection. This will require macroeconomic policies of the kind discussed in Part I, as well as microeconomic policies, especially if work is to pay a livable wage. We consider this challenge in Chapter 9.

*Chapter 9*

# Labor Markets, Good Wages, and Working Conditions

**The European social** model that developed in the post–World War II period committed countries to high growth with high living standards and shared prosperity. A cause and effect of this was improved industrial relations between management and employees, between the corporate sector and labor unions, and between governments and the private sector. A clear sign of this commitment was the deployment of a wide array of labor-protection measures that supported incomes and well-being regardless of economic fluctuations over the decades.

In recent decades, however, this commitment to some version of the European social model has weakened. In most countries, this trend has resulted in stagnant incomes for large portions of the population and poorer and less secure working conditions for many people. For example, a growing number of low-skilled people have become long-term unemployed, and the numbers of young people who are not in some form of education, employment, or training has risen to alarming levels. These youths have lost out on the benefits of globalization and of advances in technology. After the global crisis, employment creation was anemic, and in recent years it has been unsustainably uneven, with some countries such as Greece, Spain, and Italy having large unemployment rates and even higher youth unemployment rates. Not surprisingly, citizens are becoming disenchanted with European governments and their policies that seem unable to ensure jobs for all who are able and willing to work.

If jobs are hard to find in many countries, well-paying ones are even more so. Most real wages throughout Europe have grown less than 1 percent since 2008, and they have actually fallen in Greece, Italy, Spain, and the UK.[1] Meanwhile, labor has continued to become more productive in all EU countries (with the exception of Greece, where productivity has remained at 2007 levels). As a result, employees in many countries today receive a lower share of total income than they did a decade ago, while profit earners and rentiers have seen their shares grow.* As wages have weakened, so too have working conditions. Workers are now asked to bear more risk with fewer job protections.

Changes in technology, the structure of demand, institutions, and rules have all interacted in ways that put workers at a disadvantage. Some of the key forces, such as globalization and changes in technology, have a worldwide reach. However, the fact that workers fare better in some countries than in others at a similar level of development suggests that, as we have argued repeatedly, the rules and policies adopted by each country matter.

At least part of the reason for many workers' poor situation is their

---

* The labor share is the ratio of compensation of employees to GDP. Increases in real wages have not kept up with increases in productivity. For data on productivity (as measured by GDP per hour worked) and labor income shares (measured by real unit labor costs), see the European Commission's AMECO database.

weaker bargaining power, and at least part of the reason for that is how the rules of the game have changed—including rules governing labor bargaining, worker protections, economic security, and globalization. (We discuss globalization in Chapter 10.) One of the most important changes has been in the rules governing collective bargaining, in ways which reduce the effectiveness of unions in negotiations. It is no accident that in those countries where these changes have been less drastic, workers have done better.

Several interrelated changes in national economic structures have affected workers in all advanced countries. First, large corporations—where the management often collaborated with unions (syndicates)—used to be major providers of social protection. However, firms have been shedding that responsibility. In many places, the change has focused on risk-shifting, such as the move from defined-benefit to defined-contribution systems, even though, as we noted in the last chapter, firms are obviously in a better position than workers to manage risks. In a globalized economy, companies in those countries in which retirement or other social protection costs are assumed by the state are at an advantage; it is an accepted form of worker subsidization. But if companies cut back on the benefits and protections they provide, workers in those countries in which government does not respond will be left unprotected.

Second, there has been a shift from manufacturing to the service sector. In the service sector, firms are typically smaller and have less opportunity for *wage compression*; that is, differences in wages are smaller than differences in productivity. The smaller establishment size itself makes unionization more difficult.

These and other changes have, in turn, led to weaker unions in many countries. A smaller fraction of the labor force belongs to unions and is represented by collective bargaining agreements. The weaker bargaining position of workers has undermined what unions can deliver, which in turn has discouraged union membership. With unions weaker from decreasing membership, they are delivering even less. The large variation in patterns of unionization and wage differentials among the advanced countries shows that the adverse outcomes are far from inevitable. There may be underlying forces, but they are shaped by economic and social policies.

A couple of decades ago, some argued that increased earnings differentials (and especially the plight of unskilled workers) had more to do with changes in technology. Much technological progress is skills-biased, they argued, thus driving down the relative demand for less-skilled labor and driving up the relative demand for skilled workers. This explanation had some persuasive power 20 years ago. Today it is less convincing, as even *skilled* workers have seen their wages fall. Skills-biased technical change may be able to explain some of the changes in *relative* wages, but not the overall decline in the share of labor.

Bad policy has also contributed to unskilled workers' distress. It is not necessary to detail the relative role of the different forces that contribute to this dire situation to begin formulating remedies.

It is clear that these adverse conditions for workers are not required for economic efficiency—indeed, they are harmful to the overall prosperity of Europe. Obviously, Europe cannot prosper if its workers do not prosper. Europe has had some good experiences in building more equitable labor markets, generating jobs with adequate wages, balancing employer demands for flexible cost structures and workers' needs for employment security, providing training, and in encouraging new industries and firms. All European countries need to learn from these experiences, adapting the policies that were so effective elsewhere to the specifics of their own situations.

The most important policy for workers is for the government to maintain full employment. The gross insufficiency of aggregate demand that has long been part of much of Europe's policy framework contributes directly and indirectly to the problems of workers. Directly, because those without jobs suffer now, and their future job prospects diminish the longer they remain unemployed. Indirectly, because high levels of unemployment weaken the bargaining power of workers, which drives down wages. Chapters 1, 2, and 3 focused on the kinds of macro-policies and European rules that are most likely to lead to full employment. However, structural policies matter as well, and in this chapter we discuss the role of what are known as active labor market and industrial policies.

Even with full employment, European workers might not have done well because of weakened bargaining power. A significant change is globalization, which forces European workers to compete with low-wage workers in developing countries and emerging markets. Standard economic theory predicted that this would be the case. For instance, as Europe imports labor-intensive goods from China and other developing and emerging countries, the demand for labor (especially unskilled labor) diminishes, and this alone would drive down wages, and would do so even in perfectly competitive markets. But markets are not fully competitive. In Europe's economy, firms have significant market power over workers, which globalization amplified. Firms can threaten to move out of the country, say to China, where labor is so much cheaper, and then ship the goods they produce back to Europe, if European workers refuse to accept lower wages and worse working conditions. Matters have been made still worse by trade agreements that have given more secure property rights to firms investing abroad than those investing at home, making the threat to move abroad unless wages are restrained all the more credible. Workers feel powerless against such threats and accept what the employer demands. It is better to have a low-wage job than no job.

The agenda to ensure that everyone in Europe who wants a job can get one, with living wages and good working conditions, is long but entirely realistic. It includes at least eight items:

- The first priority, beyond ensuring full employment, is to enhance employee bargaining power. That will require changing many rules governing corporate governance, labor relations, globalization, and competition to curb the market power of large firms.
- Wages at the bottom of the income scale in many countries are simply too low. In many countries, it will be important to raise minimum wages and/or to supplement the incomes of low-wage earners.
- A new problem that Europe has to confront is the emergence of precarious jobs, like those involved in the so-called gig economy.
- In many countries, there has been an erosion of labor standards. Standards have to be raised and programs designed to bring the informal economy onto the books.
- Europe has suffered from excesses of long-term unemployment and high rates of youth unemployment. Active labor market policies can help move these individuals into jobs, provided enough jobs are available.
- More broadly, the state may have to actively intervene in labor markets to provide employment. It may need to consider an employment guarantee program.
- A dynamic economy constantly requires adjustment, but ordinary workers should not bear all the costs. Countries can combine flexibility for employers with income security for workers, such as along the lines of Denmark's flexicurity system.

■ Finally, Europe needs an EU-wide program for unemployment compensation, not as a means to transfer money from richer to poorer members, but as a mutual insurance plan.

These ideas are overdue changes to labor market policies that reflect the movement from a twentieth-century manufacturing economy to a twenty-first-century service and innovation economy. As economies and societies change, the efficient and fair division of sharing economic risks will of necessity change as well. Evolutions in family structure mean that many people of modest means are less able to assume risk; this is especially the case with one-earner households. Globalization, too, means that arrangements that worked in the past may now fail. Firms grappling with competitors whose governments relieve them of certain risks will face disadvantages—or so it may appear. Many very small, undercapitalized firms were always at a disadvantage in managing risks compared to large firms, and the move to a service-sector economy may be associated with a shift in the size distribution of firms. While large firms are in a better position to manage risks than ordinary individuals, these shifts in economic structure help explain the shift of responsibility of social protection away from employers toward the state. The state, which can spread risk among the entire population, has a natural advantage here.

As society and the economy evolves, the best way of allocating risk will, too. And what works well in one country and in one sector may not work well in others. Two principles should guide this process of rethinking systems of social protection. First, ordinary individuals on their own are not in a good position to bear these risks, as we know from data showing many individuals have insufficient savings to handle an emergency they might confront. Second, we cannot let social protection fall between the cracks, with corporations saying that it should be the government's responsibility, and government saying that it should be the corporation's. We should be especially wary of a corporate agenda that puts the onus on the state, but at the same time seeks to limit the capacity of the state to fulfill these responsibilities, especially by limiting taxation.

## RAISING INCOMES

### Restore Workers' Bargaining Power

In the decades after World War II, collective bargaining helped sustain growth and fairer income distribution. However, since the 1990s, most countries have taken steps to erode the bargaining power of workers. Above, we described several aspects of this erosion associated with globalization. There are still other contributing factors. For example, many workers in some countries (notably the United States) are sometimes forced to sign agreements dictating that any disputes with employers are resolved by arbitration, without the option of recourse to the legal system. This kind of system means management effectively runs the dispute settlement process.

In this section, we focus on one aspect of the erosion of workers' bargaining power, the attack on unionization. In different countries, the strategy of weakening unions has taken different forms. In some cases, it has entailed taking away some of the social roles that unions have played, for instance in the governance of pension boards. It has also included making it easier for workers who do not want to support unions to free ride on those who do. In the United States, this is called the "right to work," or in other words, the right to work without joining a union. It would more aptly be called the "right to be a free rider."

Game theory is a branch of economics that has made rapid advances in recent years. It recognizes that there is imperfect competition in all markets, and this is especially true in labor markets. But standard economic theory holds that a worker who loses a job can easily get another job that is just as good. This is simply not true. For example, the loss of a job can be especially traumatic in a small town where there may be few other jobs that require a worker's particular skill.

Another important if perhaps equally obvious insight is that the structure of bargaining makes a big difference. Decentralized bargaining weakens the bargaining power of workers, but in many countries throughout Europe, collective bargaining processes have become increasingly decentralized and cover fewer workers. If bargaining is done on a national level, as was traditional in some European countries, there can be more of a macroeconomic perspective that focuses on how the national income pie is to be grown and divided so that the firms in the country can, sometimes with government assistance, remain competitive.

The pace of these changes and the level of decentralization are both relevant. The decentralization of bargaining took place gradually in Germany and some Nordic countries. But key bargaining was still done at the industry/sector level. On the other hand, decentralization happened abruptly in Ireland and eastern and southern Europe, and it went further down to the company level, largely as a result of changes governments accepted during the financial crises of 2008–2011. The Troika's economic strategy for recovery, as we noted, was one of internal devaluation, an approach that required wages to fall. Companies and governments came under pressure to weaken unions. Unfortunately, while these abrupt changes generally lowered labor incomes, they did not lead to the promised improvements in dynamic competitiveness, growth, and employment.[2]

The magnitude and pace of the changes across Europe—and especially in the crisis-stricken countries—has been dramatic. In the first decade of the twenty-first century alone, the coverage of collective agreements in Europe fell from 68 percent to 61 percent of workers.[3] In some countries, the decline was precipitous. For example, collective bargaining coverage in Greece fell from around 82 percent of workers before the crisis to 18 percent afterward. In Romania, the decrease was from 85 percent to 35 percent.[4]

### More effective collective bargaining

More effective collective bargaining can be reintroduced by adopting several changes:

- Encourage (rather than discourage) more bargaining at the national and sectoral levels, with flexibility provisions that allow limited deviations in response to special circumstances, but within a framework that is sensitive to how abuse of such flexibility can undermine efforts of workers to bargain collectively. National negotiations, for instance, should set the minimum conditions for sector-, local-, and firm-level negotiations. They should set the general parameters for pay increases. The process should be similar for sectoral negotiations. Worker representatives in each firm might be able to propose higher productivity targets and request proportional pay increases. Negotiations should recognize that labor should not be asked to bear risk that might force remuneration to fall below the minimum necessary for maintaining a decent living standard.
- Increase union strength by delegating more responsibilities to unions to implement policies that advance workers' interests, such as the governance of pension boards, the running of cooperative banks, and offering of job training programs (subject to appropriate oversight). Strength can also be achieved by lim-

iting the ability of workers to free ride on those who support the union, and also (where relevant) by limiting the scope for management-dictated arbitration systems for dispute resolution.

■ Increase coverage of collective bargaining by making it easier for unions to organize, gain recognition, and collect dues.

■ Reduce the likelihood of a race to the bottom by mandating that basic minimum conditions apply to all workers not covered by more favorable contractual terms.

■ Support collective bargaining for all categories of workers. Sector agreements may help to extend collective bargaining where unionization is low.

## Raise Minimum Wages

The purpose of minimum wages is to protect workers from unduly low pay. A traditional criticism against minimum wages has been that raising the cost of labor might lead to lower employment. However, a series of empirical studies has dispelled fears that minimum wages, at least at moderate levels, may undermine employment. David Card and Alan Krueger's 1994 paper on the fast food industry in the United States[5] and a host of follow-up studies show that the effects of minimum wages on employment are usually insignificant or positive.[6] Studies in countries such as New Zealand and South Africa have led to similar results.[7]

There are three theoretical reasons for the differences between these empirical findings and standard predictions.[8] First, many economists simply assumed that labor markets are fully competitive, which they are not. Firms often have large market (monopsony) power, so that a minimum wage can result in both more employment and higher wages. In noncompetitive markets, firms worry that if they hire more workers, the wage they will have to pay will increase; hiring is limited by the *marginal cost* of hiring an additional worker, which is the wage plus the increase that others may have to be paid. This marginal cost may, in fact, be greater than the higher minimum wage.

Moreover, we now recognize that paying workers higher wages leads to a more productive labor force, a phenomenon called "efficiency wage effects." Shorter hours and better working conditions have played important roles in increasing worker productivity.

Finally, payments to labor support household spending, an important part of aggregate demand. Hence, higher wages stimulate income and employment growth when there is a deficiency in private spending, as was the case in so much of Europe in the years following the 2008 crisis.

Because of different national economic conditions, minimum wages vary markedly across Europe. While almost all EU countries have national minimum wages, in 2017 these ranged from less than €235 per month in Bulgaria to almost €2,000 in Luxembourg. Pronounced economic differences between European countries require that minimum wage levels remain different. Of course, the minimum wage tends to be lower in countries in which the cost of living is lower and, not surprisingly, when workers (unions) have less political power. The decline in workers' political power has meant that in many countries minimum wage levels have not kept pace with the cost of living, thus resulting in minimum wages that today fail to qualify as living wages.

In order to guarantee decent living standards for all workers, all countries should adopt a national minimum wage, and minimum wage levels in all countries should at least keep pace with the cost of living.* Increasing minimum wages would particularly improve prospects for women and disadvantaged groups that have weak bargaining power.

Efforts should be made toward more convergence among EU

---

* It may be appropriate to set a higher minimum wage in locations where there is a higher cost of living, such as major urban centers.

member states. The absence of national pay floors in Austria, Denmark, Finland, Italy, and Sweden is usually explained by pointing out that strong collective bargaining in these countries has succeeded in promoting workers' interests. While setting a national minimum wage should, accordingly, pose few problems in these countries, it could also even facilitate the process of European convergence. Setting a national minimum wage can play a role in establishing norms for what is meant by decent compensation.

Still, the large differences in per capita incomes across the EU will limit the extent of convergence. There should, however, be an ongoing review of real wages that identifies in which countries increases in the average and minimum real wage have lagged behind productivity increases and that outlines the reasons why that is the case.

Unfortunately, minimum wages are currently typically only set for full-time employment, thus muting their impact, especially because workers are increasingly engaged in part-time or atypical work arrangements. Moreover, the fact that part-time work sometimes offers more flexibility to employers encourages its spread. Minimum wages need to be extended to all workers.

A complementary policy that could guarantee a minimum income for workers is a wage subsidy, such as the earned income tax credit (EITC) in the United States. In this system, households are supported with a refundable tax credit that is paid to them annually.* The minimum wage is particularly effective when there are imperfections in competition, and possibly results in both more employment and higher wages. Different labor markets may vary both in the elasticity of labor

---

* Advocates of the EITC argue that it is preferable to a minimum wage because it does not interfere with the workings of the market but still ensures that workers get a living wage. Critics point out that if there is any supply elasticity to labor, it results in before-tax wages falling; hence, if the elasticity of labor supply is large, much of the benefit actually goes to employers.

supply and in the degree of imperfection in the market. The optimal policy may accordingly entail using both instruments, as the United States does, though its minimum wage is far below a living wage, and its wage subsidy via tax credit is too small to bring it up to a living wage.

## IMPROVING WORKER CONFIDENCE

### Regulate Precarious Jobs

Scarcity of good jobs in Europe has forced many to enter precarious work arrangements, which includes part-time jobs, mini-jobs, and on-call and zero-hours contracts,* to mention some of the new forms of employment (Box 9.1). In some cases, changes in technology have facilitated these new arrangements; whatever the efficiency benefits of the technological changes, they all have distributive consequences of which we must be mindful.

These job arrangements are underregulated, generally offer poor working conditions, and often come with no social security benefits. While some take these jobs to supplement household income, others must rely on them as their primary sources of income. The paradox is that, in some respects, we seem to be reversing a long-term trend associated with development, which is the move from informal jobs to formal jobs with better protections. In some cases, firms like Uber have tried to take advantage of legalistic arguments by claiming that their workers are independent contractors—even as the company controls many details of what they do. In some countries, courts have ruled against these obvious ruses.

---

* Zero-hours contracts allow employers to hire staff without a guarantee of a minimum number of work hours. Employees work on an as-needed basis, often on short notice, and are paid only for the time they work.

# Box 9.1: The Gig Economy in Europe, Its Problems, and Possible Solutions

Uber, Airbnb, and TaskRabbit are examples of internet-based companies that connect clients with service providers (mini-cab drivers, owners of accommodation, and domestic work, respectively) through easy-to-use mobile apps. They often operate in a legal vacuum. While owners and shareholders reap large profits from low labor costs, workers–contractors pay for fuel, maintenance, insurance, and other direct costs. Additionally, risk is transferred from the employer to the service provider—if there is no demand, there is no work. Furthermore, no regulation exists on working time and there is no provision of paid leave for childbirth, illness, or other contingencies.

Low prices have made these companies very popular with customers but have led to protests by licensed taxi drivers and hospitality workers who pay taxes and comply with specific regulations.

There are a number of solutions for addressing the challenges posed by these companies, their unfair practices, and the problems they have created for workers:

*Regulation.* Companies like Uber are not competing on equal grounds, as they avoid labor and other regulations; this must be redressed through EU guidelines that keep pace with digital technologies. Part of the response is to recognize that workers in these areas are in fact employees, and that the platforms should accordingly have to satisfy regulations concerning hours, working conditions, and wage standards that apply to comparable workers in regular employment, such as taxi drivers. Some aspects of the new technologies should enable better enforcement of at least minimum wage and hourly conditions.* Platforms that fail to comply with regulations or engage in other illegal activities should be dealt with harshly. Importantly, claiming to be a "technology company," a common dodge, should not be seen as a free pass for exploitation.

*Taxation.* A value-added tax has been applied to Airbnb; other taxes could be applied automatically to other internet transactions. In Uruguay, the government requires mandatory social security coverage for all taxi drivers who operate through Uber and other platforms. This is done through a customized

---

* New York City, for instance, has imposed a minimum wage on ride-service drivers, one that includes time waiting for a job. The new technologies allow one to implement such a regulation.

electronic application—again showing that the new technologies can actually be used to implement better policies.

**Ownership.** These internet platforms could function as cooperatives that facilitate profit- and cost-sharing among service providers, ensuring that more of the value created by the service providers would accrue to them. Cooperatives are also less likely to engage in one form of worker exploitation or another than are the private platforms. Government could encourage such cooperatives, for instance, through preferential tax treatment.

## Enforce Labor Standards and Bring All Workers into Formal Employment

Low-wage workers and those working in precarious conditions are often powerless and lack the capacity to seek legal protection. Europe must strengthen labor inspection and make sure that any violation of labor standards is redressed.

Labor inspection plays a fundamental role in protecting worker rights. It ensures occupational safety and health and decent working conditions, reduces informal employment, and ensures that wages and social security contributions are actually paid. It can help prevent the increasing practice of wage theft, whereby workers are not compensated for work they have actually performed. Thus, it increases tax revenues and ensures that all employees are covered for unemployment, sickness, workplace accidents, and pensions.

Nevertheless, labor inspection has largely fallen off the radar of policymakers. The number of labor inspectors varies greatly across the EU. Eurostat reports that in some countries, such as Denmark, there was one inspector per 5,000 workers before the crisis.* Other

---

* Of course, in countries where there are generally high levels of compliance with the law, the necessity of inspection will be low.

countries, including Poland and Spain, had one inspector per 10,000 workers, while Belgium and the UK had one inspector per 20,000 workers. While some countries have increased the number of labor inspectors, as is the case with France, Poland, and Spain, recent surveys show that the majority of European countries have reduced their number of labor inspectors because of budget cuts and austerity measures.[9] The result is that enforcement has been uneven, which has resulted in a growing informal economy with precarious working conditions.

Labor standards will not be consistently respected unless there is effective enforcement. Several reforms are needed:

■ Strengthen labor inspection mechanisms, increase funding for enforcement, carry out unannounced on-site inspections, raise penalties for violations of labor standards, and increase numbers of inspection staff, at least to meet the target recommended by the International Labour Organization (one inspector for every 10,000 workers).

■ Create a more homogeneous set of penalties across Europe to reduce the scope of social dumping, or the moving of jobs to countries where worker protections are weaker, and to ensure fair competition. The size of the penalties must be large enough to discourage violations. (To really avoid social dumping, there will have to be more harmonization of labor standards.)

■ Make the public sector an example of a good employer. Public procurement provides an opportunity to promote decent work. Contracts awarded by European governments, at national, regional, and municipal levels, could be granted on the condition that contractors meet higher labor standards than the minimums set in labor codes. This practice would set an example of how firms should operate and would raise the bar for compliance with labor standards.

## Promote Flexible Working Times

We have already noted many of the ways in which the world of work is changing. Some of these, such as those associated with the gig economy, pose real challenges for ensuring decent work for all. But some of the changes also offer new opportunities for designing jobs more attuned to individuals' circumstances. Factories with assembly lines have a certain rigidity to them, requiring fixed shifts with everyone showing up in time to work. Other jobs offer more flexibility.

Flexibility provides an opportunity to better integrate often-marginalized groups into the labor market. Many of these individuals find difficulty in adapting to the standard work-week. Flexibility can allow more women (especially those with young children) and older citizens to participate in the labor market.

Bringing these segments of the population into the labor force will be especially important given Europe's low birthrates and aging workforce. Doing so will be good not only for Europe's economy, but also for the well-being of older citizens and their families. Better health and longer lives mean that workers can remain in the labor force long after the traditional retirement age of 60 or 65. Indeed, for those who can, remaining active in the labor market actually contributes to health. We should be able to improve the labor market in ways that can accommodate the many women and older citizens who want to work.

It is important to note that flexible jobs can have decent working conditions that are protected by government regulations. Some European governments have done particularly well in this regard for these more flexible jobs by requiring family leave, paternity and maternity leave, and by providing child day care facilities.*

# IMPROVING EMPLOYMENT OPPORTUNITY AND SECURITY

## *Active Labor Market Programs, Industrial Policies, and Place-Based Assistance*

Current EU active labor market programs place a strong emphasis on *activation*, which focuses on increasing labor-force participation rates. There are two sides of activation: a demand side, ensuring that there is not an insufficiency of demand, and a supply side, ensuring that workers have the skills required by the labor market.

Modern economies are very dynamic, with jobs being created and destroyed all the time. Unfortunately, the new jobs are often not in the same places as the old jobs and often require different skills than the old ones. Active labor market policies aim to match unemployed workers with existing jobs, and generally provide training to acquire necessary skills.

Industrial policies aim to help develop critical industries, aiding the economy to make the difficult structural transformations. The move from carbon-intensive to low-carbon manufacturing, or from a lingering overdependence on manufacturing to a more robust service sector, are two examples.

---

* Corporate governance reforms, discussed in Chapter 4, may reinforce these government initiatives. With more women on boards, corporations may become increasingly sensitive to the needs and desires of this large segment of the labor force.

Part of industrial policy is place-based policies, recognizing that there is often considerable social and physical capital in places where individuals are already living, and accordingly, that it makes sense to create jobs where people are located.

Markets on their own have proven unable to accomplish structural transformations, or make efficient locational decisions, especially from a social perspective. Too often, there is excessive concentration in only a few locations (often in the capital city). Place-based policies represent a significant departure from the traditional argument that people should move to where private firms choose to locate.

## An Employment Guarantee Program

None of these recommendations will work, of course, if there are not enough jobs. The true problem in many places in Europe today is the lack of jobs, which means that there will be insufficient employment regardless of whether the workforce is better trained. For long periods of time, the labor supply has exceeded demand virtually without regard to qualification, and the situation is particularly stark for those with low qualifications.

Matters may well get worse. Recent estimates suggest that between 2015 and 2025, low-skilled jobs in Europe will decline by more than seven million.[10] An insufficient demand for labor also affects those with higher qualifications, which can have ripple effects throughout the economy as workers take jobs below their qualifications or skill levels.

Europe must tackle this jobs deficit by focusing efforts on creating jobs by stimulating demand for goods and services, as was discussed in earlier chapters. Traditionally it has been argued that government should do this indirectly through fiscal and monetary policy. But this policy approach may not work (or perhaps not fast enough), or it may not create the jobs that demand the skill sets of workers in the locations where employment is needed most. Pervasive discrimination in the labor market has meant that the unemployment rate among minorities is far higher than that of the national average. In short, these indirect mechanisms may not create full employment for everyone. And unemployment has both a direct cost on well-being, as most individuals value being productive members of the community, and indirect costs on the families and communities of the unemployed, as well as the economy as a whole. It is a major contributing factor to inequality, as we have noted.

Europe should consider more direct actions to tackle the unemployment problem. Government employment programs may take many forms, ranging from public works to subsidies that share labor costs and social security contributions, particularly for new employees (with subsidies ranging from 30 to 90 percent of total contributions). Policies like these directly favor job creation and may be targeted to where the failures in the markets are most evident. They may facilitate transitions into the labor market and be fine-tuned toward job creation for people with fewer opportunities, such as minorities or those located in the deindustrialized parts of Europe.*

India has created an employment guarantee scheme for the hundreds of millions of people living in rural areas that ensures at least 100 days of work per person each year. If a country like India, with its low per capita income, can guarantee jobs, then Europe can, too. Designing a jobs program entails many complexities, such as ensuring that work is meaningful, that workers can transition to standard jobs that

---

* Of course, they have to be designed carefully to ensure that employers do not fire older workers in order to tap into the subsidies that are earmarked for new employees.

pay decent wages, and that the program itself will not undermine work elsewhere in the economy.

Supporting self-employment and small/micro enterprises is also important, especially given the relatively large number of smaller businesses in most EU member countries. These enterprises often lack access to credit and some of the management skills that are necessary for success. Government programs can provide the financing or encourage lending institutions to do so, but these kinds of programs have to be designed while recognizing that even with such assistance, business survival rates may remain low.

## Employment Programs for the Long-Term Unemployed and Youth

EU-level employment programs have only just begun, so there is insufficient data to fully assess the extent to which they have been successful. The programs include the European Employment Services program and the EU Programme for Employment and Social Innovation, both of which focus on providing placement services, disseminating information about job vacancies, providing job counseling, and supporting geographical mobility.[11]

Only a few such programs, however, target job creation. One is the European Progress Microfinance Facility, which provides loans below €25,000 for small businesses. The Youth Guarantee program is focused on ensuring that all young people under age 25 receive an employment offer, continued education, apprenticeship, or traineeship within four months of completing their formal education. This program has provided direct support to more than 1.7 million young people.

An expanded European Employment Services program could include the following components:

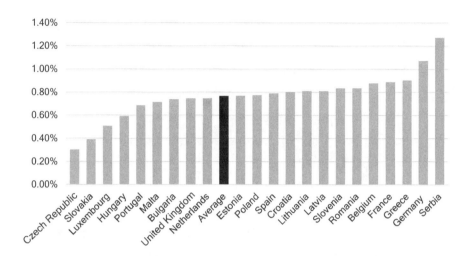

**FIGURE 9.1: EUROPEAN EMPLOYMENT GUARANTEE PROGRAM FOR THE LONG-TERM UNEMPLOYED**

*Note:* Costs are calculated as percentage of GDP for an employment guarantee program. The calculation includes 10 percent administrative costs. Estimates are based on one person per vulnerable household at minimum wage for 100 days per year. A total of 26.2 million households would receive benefits.

*Source: Calculations by Isabel Ortiz based on data from Eurostat, ILO, and UN Population Prospects.*

**1.** *A public employment program for the long-term unemployed to support 100 days of guaranteed work per household* in areas such as environmental services, public works, and long-term care.* Cost estimates can be found in Figure 9.1.

**2.** *Further support of self-employment and small enterprises* through loans to micro/small businesses and cooperatives. The United States

---

\* If set at national minimum wages, implementing such a program in Europe would cost an estimated average of 0.77 percent of GDP per country per year, including administrative costs, and would benefit 26 million vulnerable households.

requires banks to lend a certain fraction of their funds to minorities and other underserved groups through the Community Reinvestment Act, a law we have discussed in other contexts. Europe could enact a similar program that focuses lending on employment and job creation. The ECB could support this program by requiring commercial banks to dedicate a portion of their lending for these purposes as a condition for access to ECB funds.

**3. *Expand the Youth (Employment) Guarantee:*** Youth unemployment and NEET rates (young people not in employment, education, or training) are at alarming levels for the EU as a whole, 17 and 13.4 percent as of 2017, respectively.* Reflecting the slow recovery from the 2008 crisis, the pace of youth employment gains has not been fast enough. The NEET cohort represents a wasted resource. Not only are they not contributing to the economy today, but the fact that they are not receiving education and training will also limit the contributions they can make in the future. These young workers are at risk of becoming alienated from society, a phenomenon with untoward political and social consequences.

In 2017, the unemployment rate for youths between 15 and 24 years old was 17 percent for the EU as a whole. The highest *employment* rates for young people between ages 15 and 24 were recorded in the Netherlands (60.8 percent), followed by Denmark (58.2 percent), Austria (51 percent), and the United Kingdom (50.8 percent). All of the remaining countries recorded rates below 50 percent, with Bulgaria, Spain, Italy, and Greece at rates below 20 percent.

The current program could greatly benefit from expansion by

---

* More recent data show that matters are little better.

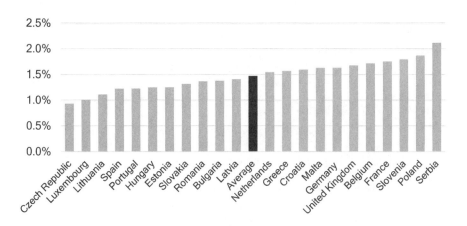

**FIGURE 9.2: EXTENSION OF EUROPEAN YOUTH GUARANTEE**

*Note:* Costs are calculated as a percentage of GDP for a wage subsidy provided to all young people 25–29 years old at 50 percent of the national minimum salary. Includes 10 percent administrative costs. A total of five million people would benefit.

*Source: Calculations by Isabel Ortiz, based on data from ILO and Eurostat.*

extending the eligibility age to 30 years old (since more people are staying in formal education for longer) and by providing either wage subsidies or partial temporary exemption from payroll taxes to firms that hire young workers.* Cost estimates can be found in Figure 9.2.

These should be pan-European programs that ideally entail transfers between countries and regions. Only with this kind of pan-European program with cost-sharing can there be the convergence between the

---

* If the program were limited to young workers between 25 and 29 years old and the subsidy were set to 50 percent of the national minimum wage, it would cost an estimated average of 1.5 percent of GDP and would benefit more than five million youths in Europe. The long-term benefits for Europe, in terms of increased growth based on the skills acquired and reduced alienation, would almost surely outweigh these costs.

rich and poor countries that was promised, rather than the divergence that has been observed.*

## Flexicurity: Combining Employment Flexibility with Economic Security

We explained why flexible work times are crucial. But there's another side of flexibility that has played an important role in policy debates during the last three decades: employers want more flexibility to restructure their labor force, which may entail dismissing workers. Employers emphasize the advantages this flexibility has in terms of the allocation of labor. For an economy to be dynamic, it is important to make sure that all resources, including labor, are employed in ways that maximize their productivity. Employers also point out that difficulties in dismissing workers are an impediment to hiring. However, employees rightly point out that this power to dismiss also increases employers' bargaining power and thus will almost inevitably lead to lower wages. It also shifts more of the burden of adjustment onto workers. Moreover, as we have previously noted, labor productivity also depends on how labor is compensated and treated. There is some truth in all of these arguments. It should thus be clear that the regulations that govern labor markets can have significant effects on a sector's dynamism.[12]

The Danish "flexicurity" model (see Box 9.2) provides a way to balance these concerns. Most importantly, before employers are given greater rights to dismiss, Europe needs active labor market policies to

---

* Planning and overall coordination of these programs should be at the European level, and implementation should be national, in order to make the programs more aligned with local conditions.

enhance the probability of workers finding another job, as well as good systems of unemployment insurance and social protection (for use if the worker does not get reemployed quickly). It is especially important to provide these protections when there is high unemployment.

## Box 9.2: Employment Security: The Danish Model

Nordic countries have performed much better in ensuring employment security. The Danish model, for example, has traditionally consisted of four major components:

- Macroeconomic policies that ensure full employment
- Flexicurity: The combination of flexibility for companies to hire and fire with income security for workers through robust systems of social protection*
- Collective bargaining processes that ensure extensive worker protection while taking into account changing production and market conditions for companies†
- Employment subsidies and active labor market programs that help workers in transition and promote full employment

## A European Unemployment Compensation Program

Europe today does not have an EU-level unemployment scheme, but there are strong arguments for creating the program. As it is now, when countries go into a recession and revenues decline, they then have to meet the additional financial obligations presented by unemployment. Especially in the context of the budgetary constraints imposed by the

---

* A European employment guarantee program, as described earlier, could be an important component in providing this income security.

† Unions can play an important role in protecting workers against capricious and wrongful dismissal, and in identifying when the job dismissals are a part of an important labor restructuring necessary to address issues of competitiveness.

EU, the obligations caused by unemployment mean cutbacks in some other programs (and it is often investments that suffer the most). Effectively in this case, the country's future is put in jeopardy as it tries to ensure that today's unemployed receive income support.

A European-wide unemployment scheme is one way in which Europe can pool risks, given that not all EU economies experience unemployment to the same degree and at the same time. In an EU-wide system, workers in countries where unemployment is low could be funding payments to workers in countries where unemployment is high. This is the same principle underlying health insurance, in which the healthy pay for the sick.

The one difficulty is that structural unemployment (the number of people unemployed for reasons other than a temporarily weak economy) differs across countries. Therefore, the program should be focused on sharing the burden of unemployment above the usual levels that arise from cyclical fluctuations. With these provisions, a Europe-wide unemployment system would clearly not be a move toward what Germany has criticized as a "transfer union." It would be, instead, a true Europe-wide insurance program, enabling Europe, as a whole, to provide more security for all its citizens. A further advantage of such a scheme is that it would enhance counter-cyclical spending, which would strengthen the automatic stabilizers and lead to greater economic stability. Moreover, by avoiding the cutbacks in investment that would otherwise occur, an EU-wide unemployment system would help promote convergence within Europe.

One concern raised about unemployment support is that it weakens incentives to search for another job, but this is not supported by actual experience. A number of measures have been put in place to correct possible abuse of the system, such as promoting activation and job-placement policies, or shortening income-replacement periods that are covered by social insurance, after which the unemployed fall into social assistance with lower benefits. Sanctions against abuses are also possible, though recent evaluations of social security sanctions show that these are expensive and deliver mixed results.[13] Ultimately, sustainable labor market policy is about generating jobs with good working conditions—not focusing on sanctions and the weakening of the welfare state.

## CONCLUSION

It is possible to restore prosperity in Europe by creating a Europe rich in jobs with decent wages and working conditions, and by lifting Europe out of its low-growth and low-employment trap. Macroeconomic policies focused on full employment and long-term growth are essential, but not sufficient.

In the last three chapters, we argued for a broad approach to the welfare state. We stated that policy must strengthen the bargaining power of workers and ensure that those at the bottom receive a livable wage. We also made the case that social insurance must address risks in a progressive manner where the markets have failed to do so.

But even more may be required, such as active intervention in the economy to facilitate labor market entry for new entrants, to address the challenges posed by the long-term unemployed, and to ensure that everyone who is willing and able to work can have meaningful work at decent wages. Decisive policies like these, and not a continued erosion of the European social model, would promote solidarity and strengthen the European project and economy.

# PART IV

# Managing Globalization for Europe and the World

*Chapter 10*

# The Future of Europe in a Globalized World

**Globalization is being** rapidly redefined, both by the rise of China and the about-face of the United States under President Donald Trump. Once the champion of globalization, the United States (or at least, Trump) is now among its harshest critics. Within Europe, too, there is disillusionment that the promised benefits of globalization did not materialize for large swaths of the population, leaving them bereft of jobs and, for some, even bereft of hope. Nationalist figures like Marine Le Pen in France, President Andrzej Duda in Poland, and Italian Deputy Prime Minister and Minister of the Interior Matteo Salvini have exploited the discontent with globalization by advocating nativist, anti-immigrant policies.

Their economic premises are the opposite of those that define Europe. The EU was founded partially on the premise that closer integration—more movement of goods, services, and people—would strengthen the continent. Europe has had a decades-long, abiding faith that open economies grow better.

The key messages of this chapter are different from what we might have written before the rise of Trump. But we should understand that the grievances to which he gave voice will not go away when he leaves office. These feelings are deep-seated and reflect a failure to manage globalization in a way that benefits most citizens. We must work to understand the reasons that nativist sentiments have gained such purchase, and work to address them.

While globalization did bring benefits to Europe as a whole, it brought more to some countries than to others, and within the countries themselves the distribution of benefits was uneven. The advocates of globalization exaggerated the benefits to growth and underestimated the distributive effects, including the crippling impacts on industries that employed millions. While advances in technology would have, on their own, led to large losses in lower-skilled jobs in manufacturing, globalization exacerbated this process. The way that globalization was managed—including the constraints that were put on the members of the Eurozone—made its effects even worse.

We have to understand better why it was that globalization, which seemed to hold out such promise for all, has come to be viewed through dark lenses by so many. Part of the reason was globalization-euphoria—the very belief that it would *automatically* bring such benefits—meant that too little attention was paid to the downside risks. Relatedly, trickle-down dogma held that everyone would share in the benefits, even if the benefits mostly accrue to high earners. There was no basis for this belief either in theory or in the empirical or historical evidence. But almost surely, part of the reason for the disappointing results was that the globalization agenda has been driven by corporate interests; the adverse effects on workers were not always accidents.

For example, corporations benefited as they found cheaper labor abroad and received stronger protections for investment. They bene-fited again as the weaker bargaining position of workers suppressed wages at home. Trade between advanced countries like those in the EU and developing countries and emerging markets results in Europe importing goods that are labor intensive, especially unskilled-labor intensive. It was a long-established notion that, as a result, trade between advanced and less-developed countries lowers wages, espe-cially unskilled wages, in the advanced country. Remarkably, politi-cians (and even some economists) ignored this basic economic insight. Any economist who believes in the law of supply and demand has to believe that wages, especially of unskilled labor, will decline as a result of trade integration with developing countries and emerging markets.

This chapter calls for a massive rewriting of the rules of interna-tional engagement and a rethinking of Europe's role in the world. Two aspects bear close scrutiny: the international rules themselves, and the way Europe responds to the stresses and opportunities posed by globalization.

The rules of the international system cannot, of course, be rewrit-ten by Europe alone. However, Europe will have to take the lead. There is simply no other plausible candidate, at least not until a period of reactionary politics eases in the United States.

Today, we are experiencing a situation with some parallels to the end of World War II, as the Allies stood atop Europe's rubble. On an almost daily basis, we come face-to-face with vivid evidence of a global interdependence that must be managed anew by each generation, if the world is to be peaceful and prosperous.

Europe has to rise to the challenge of promoting global progressive norms. There must be an international rule of law, but it must be bal-anced and fair. Globalization will not survive politically if the rules are not fair to workers in developed and developing countries alike. This is partly a matter of solidarity, but it is also more than that. It is a matter of political and economic sustainability. The new global architecture that we are calling for is a big departure from the model that corporate interests have been advancing for more than a half century.

There are ten key messages in this chapter, some of which we will cover only briefly:

1. *Global cooperation.* What one country or group of countries does often has large effects on others. When all countries work together, all can benefit; when they do not, all can suffer.

2. *Global macroeconomics and finance.* We have to work toward more global coordination in this sphere. In the aftermath of the 2008 crisis, such cooperation prevented the global downturn from being even deeper. And we also have to prevent the kind of global race to the bottom that marked financial regulation in the years before the crisis.

3. *Rule of law.* An international rule of law is important—as important for the global economy, in fact, as for any national economy. In the area of trade, the World Trade Organization (WTO), created in 1995, provided the rudiments of such an international rule of law.* Rather than attacking this arrangement, we should be improving the rules and working to sustain and extend them in areas in which cooperation is vital.

4. *Democratic governance, including transparency.* The rules cannot be imposed by one country or group of countries

---

* The WTO built on GATT, the General Agreement on Tariffs and Trade, which went into effect in 1948. It covers goods, as well as (under separate agreements) services, intellectual property, government procurement, and other facets of international commerce. Not all countries have signed up to every WTO agreement.

on the others, a global order that was the hallmark of the colonial era, the vestiges of which we still deal with today. Instead, we have evolved toward a system of global governance without global government. A major failure in the past was the process by which agreements were reached— that is, without democratic transparency.

5. *Trade.* We now know that the benefits of trade agreements were exaggerated, and the costs underestimated. The benefits of further trade agreements, beyond those already in existence, such as the WTO, are likely to be smaller than those of the past, and in some cases, even questionable. At the very least, we need to be attentive to the resulting consequences for workers, the environment, and health.

6. *Taxation.* Managing globalization requires that we eliminate tax havens and create a fair system of multinational taxation.

7. *Investment agreements.* Current investment agreements are particularly problematic, and Europe should work with other countries to revise these agreements. It should not sign any further agreements until there is a broader consensus on what they should entail.

8. *Intellectual property rights.* The governance of global knowledge is an important part of the governance of international economic relations in our modern, knowledge-based economy. But here, the rules of the game have largely been written by and for the advanced countries, and especially the large corporations within them.

9. *Competition policy.* The globalization of production has resulted in the globalization of problems of competition. The competition policies that Europe pursues have global consequences.

10. ***Climate change.*** Climate change is a global issue and can only be addressed through global coordination. It is an existential issue for the world that demands strong punishments against any country not doing its part.

Before we dive into these key messages, however, it is useful to review the key problems facing the world today, which give urgency to the project of developing an international economic policy for the future.

## THE TWIN CHALLENGES OF THE UNITED STATES AND CHINA

### *The Challenge Posed by Trump*

The election of Donald Trump to the US presidency has threatened such a large number of the foundations of the liberal global order that it can be hard to keep track of them all. In the United States, hanging over his bigotry and ruinous environmental and economic policies is the shadow of his broader threat to American democracy and its institutions. Trump and his movement, such as it is, have even frayed the Enlightenment consensus on the value of facts and science.

All of these aspects of Trump's presidency are cause for worry not just for the United States but also for the rest of the world, simply because of continuing American influence and power. This chapter, however, will limit its consideration of the problems Trump poses to issues of trade and global cooperation and their implications for the future of Europe's economic policy.

The root of Trump's toxic economic policies is his misapprehension of the ways globalization has gone wrong. He was elected, in large part, by Americans who saw their quality of life decline and/or faced growing insecurity. It was easier to blame outsiders for America's problems than to look inward, and Trump exploited that natural tendency. He blamed globalization, and especially unfair trade agreements, for these Americans' plight, though most economists would also assign an important role to technological change that reduces the demand for labor, especially unskilled workers. However, as we shall explain in more detail, we assign the real failure to our economic and social policies in how we responded to the challenges posed by globalization and technological change. European nations are lucky to have had a better system of social protection than many other countries, so it better managed the effects of globalization, in some cases reasonably well.

We can, however, all agree that globalization has played *some* role in the plight of the disaffected Americans. From this point of agreement, though, Trump's beliefs and assertions quickly veer into the absurd and the dangerous. For example, Trump seems to believe that we can easily roll globalization back, that the clock can somehow be reset to a time before the world was so closely integrated, and before China and other emerging markets had the economic power they have today. He blames the trade agreements for his country's own failures, argues for bilateral agreements, and threatens that without an ill-defined "better deal," he will hit the biggest American trading partners with high tariffs. Rather than trying to help workers who have been left behind by globalization, Trump has promoted protectionism.

Trump's policies will ultimately fail miserably at restoring American economic vitality and dynamism. Further, they are dangerous to the world. It is important for Europe to understand why these policies will not work, especially because there are many Europeans who would follow in Trump's footsteps down the path of protectionism.

For one, manufacturing jobs are simply not returning to advanced countries. All over the world, employment in manufacturing is declining because gains in productivity have exceeded increases in demand. Even if the output of the manufacturing sector were not shrinking, the number of manufacturing jobs would still be decreasing. Moreover, emerging markets can now compete effectively, even in complex manufacturing. There is no way to go back to an earlier era in which the United States and Europe dominated manufacturing, just as there is no way to undo the technological improvements that have led to productivity gains.

But Trump is trying anyway. Among his methods is the renegotiation of trade agreements. It is not that such pacts have no room for improvement; some tweaks could make them better. The problem for Trump is that most of these agreements, contrary to his (admittedly vague) assertions, are already highly favorable to US corporations and, more broadly, to advanced countries in general. It will be hard to get others to join agreements that are even more unbalanced.

Trump's approach to trade is misguided in several other ways, which hold important lessons for Europe's policy makers. He focuses on bilateral trade deficits; yet what really matters is the multilateral trade deficit, and the multilateral trade deficit is determined by the underlying macroeconomics, the disparity between domestic investment and domestic savings, not by trade agreements. Some in Europe also focus excessively on trade surpluses—Germany tells others that they should follow its example in achieving a large trade surplus. But by definition, for every trade surplus there has to be a deficit. Germany's surplus imposes an externality on others. Problems of global instability are created as much by those with trade surpluses as by those with trade deficits. Indeed, Keynes argued persuasively that the surpluses resulted in weak global aggregate demand, and that large surpluses should be discouraged, even taxed.

Much would be lost by the abrogation of trade agreements—most importantly, American withdrawal from the WTO. But that is unlikely, as there is not enough political support, including from Trump's own party, for these steps. Perhaps that is why the renegotiated NAFTA is little different from the old NAFTA, though Trump tried to spin it otherwise. But the most immediate threat from Trump's hostility toward trade agreements has more to do with the uncertainty he has sowed. Firms cannot make plans for the future when there is a threat that rules will be upended.

Further, Trump's administration has caused pain in other ways that fall short of canceling agreements. For example, he has blocked the appointment of WTO appellate judges, which may bring its dispute settlement system to a standstill. Trump's penchant for trade wars (and trade skirmishes) is another example. These foolish gambits seem to be based on a premodern-era perception of commerce as a zero-sum game, which holds that one country's gains in trade must be another's losses.

The entire edifice of markets, including trade, is based on the premise that voluntary exchanges are mutually beneficial. The most basic economics tell us that by taking advantage of comparative advantage and of specialization, both countries gain from trade.* The critical mistake of globalization advocates was to ignore its effects on different groups within the country. A country's GDP could have increased, enabling all to be better off. But still, some groups—lesser-skilled laborers in advanced countries, for example—can actually be worse off unless government takes preventive actions. Today's crisis in globalization is the result of governments not taking those actions.

In the twenty-first century, trade wars would have especially adverse effects. It is true that the United States could harm China's economy in a full-out trade war, though just how much is quite uncertain, since China has many other trading partners and the capacity to create domestic demand to offset the loss of exports. But the United

---

* The analysis is somewhat more complicated, especially when markets are not working well, as evidenced, for instance, by high levels of unemployment. So too, if financial markets are not working well, job losses from imports may occur faster than the job gains from the new export opportunities.

States would only be hurting itself, in this case, since the economies of the two countries are so closely linked. Consumers are already facing markedly higher prices for many of the goods they buy, thanks to Trump's trade wars, and American producers will lose some of their competitiveness as they were forced to use higher-priced inputs. Even as talk of a trade war began, some firms producing in the United States but selling elsewhere discussed moving their factories.

More broadly, Trump's disdain for multilateral settings runs across policy areas. A concerted diplomatic effort by European nations to dissuade Trump from pulling out of the Paris climate accord failed. Trump shows no sign of making human rights a priority in US foreign policy—in fact, quite the contrary. Furthermore, international development work is on the chopping block and Trump left the Iran agreement, which was intended to reduce the threat of Iran acquiring nuclear weapons.

We live in a highly integrated global world. Peace, a stable climate, and a rules-based international trading system within which commerce can flourish are all *global* public goods from which everyone in the world can benefit. There need to be concerted, multilateral efforts in all of these arenas. Europe must guard itself against the specific threats posed by Trump's unilateralism, and also more generally against the chaos threatened by the US withdrawal from positive leadership in the world. It will now fall to Europeans to champion international cooperation. Europe will have to formulate contingency plans. Europe must articulate its commitment to the WTO—with or without the United States. Many of the proposals of this chapter are similarly designed, in part, to respond to the new threats that US economic and trade policies pose.

As Europe contemplates a post-Trump world, it will have to recognize one important fact: Just as Trump was wrong in thinking one could go back in time to an era when America's hegemony was unchallenged, so too are those who think that once Trump is gone, the world can return to the way it was. Trump has shown that borders matter, and he has brought to the surface fears that were always present. Would the United States, in spite of all the agreements, ever do anything that was not in its own interests, even its own *short-run* interests? Trump has answered with a resounding "No!" Indeed, since Trump lives in a zero-sum world, making Europe weaker makes the United States stronger, which is one reason he attempts to undermine the EU at every available opportunity.

Europe has to become as strategic about using the United States to advance its own interests as the United States has been in using Europe. The full implications of these ideas for Europe's security posture would take us well beyond the parameters of this book.

## The Challenge Posed by China

Nearly 20 years after the Cold War wound down, the 2008 global financial crisis demonstrated that all was not well with twenty-first-century capitalism, a view that has been reinforced by data showing that most of the benefits of growth over the past third of a century have gone to a relatively few at the top. Then, as if in echo of these economic maladies, Trump was elected president of the United States, and the UK voted to exit the EU.

China skillfully navigated the global financial crisis, continuing on its path of soaring growth to the point where, in 2015, it became the largest economy in the world (measured by purchasing power parity). Evidently, its distinctive economic system—what it calls a socialist market economy with Chinese characteristics, and what others refer to as state capitalism, Chinese style—has been working well. In fact, it has done so for more than four decades.

But with the ascendancy of President Xi Jinping in 2012, and especially with his elimination of term limits in 2018, two things changed: First, the hope was dashed that China would quickly become, if not a liberal democracy, at least *more* liberal. Second, while China previously had focused on its own growth, it now sought to restore itself to its rightful place on the global stage, including through its One Belt, One Road initiative.

These changes cast a new light on the dramatic shift in geopolitical power that was happening. When China began its economic transformation, its income levels were so low that no one in the West could have imagined it would become an economic or strategic threat. But that has changed. In some areas of crucial importance, like artificial intelligence (AI) and cyber warfare, China is now at the very forefront.

China's system of state capitalism stands a good chance of ensuring that its economy will grow far faster than the United States' and the EU's for years to come, and that the gap in technology and knowledge between the East and West will narrow. US demands for China to abandon its state-led initiative to close the technological gap will almost surely be rebuffed. The United States might have been able to block China's growth a quarter century ago, but not now. Attempts to do so are only hardening China's resolve to rise.

But competition in AI is helping to crystallize the fundamental problem of designing a global trading system among countries with fundamentally different values and different economic and political systems. In a world in which access to vast amounts of data matters, the lack of privacy concerns in China may give China an advantage over Europe and the United States. Indeed, China's political system requires surveillance of a kind that most in the West find unacceptable. This surveillance, however, generates huge amounts of data that may have commercial value. Because Europeans seem so much more focused on privacy than Americans, Europe may find itself at a disadvantage to both China and the United States.

The controversy over genetically modified organisms (GMOs) between the United States and the EU also illustrates the challenges of trade between countries with different values. Europe (correctly) argues that if Europeans care about whether food is genetically modified, they have the right to reflect that in their regulations on labeling even if disclosing that information discourages Europeans from buying American food products. The United States views these disclosure requirements as an unfair trade practice. In short, the two different policies reflect differences in deeply held political values.

Given that these political differences can have large economic consequences, the challenge is to create a reasonably level playing field with fair competition. The hope at the founding of the WTO was that convergence to a shared set of values would lead to less friction over economic policy. Although problems would remain—the GMO example tells us that—they would be small and isolated. But if differences in underlying economic, political, and social models persist, as appears to be the case, how will the global economic system be able to work?

The principle that trade is desirable is still valid, though not necessarily the kind of trade liberalization that was imagined a quarter century ago when the WTO began. The world will have to work toward a set of fewer rules, with more discretion, than if all countries subscribed to the same economic and value system. Europe will have to take the lead in forging these new rules.

China, it seems, is also attempting to create or expand rifts within the EU. A relatively new Chinese diplomatic initiative, aimed at central and eastern Europe, is based on the idea that Brussels—and the United States—can no longer boost the economic dynamism in this part of Europe. EU member states continue to jostle, as always, for Chinese investment, which creates leverage for Beijing. As Europe focuses on Trump's relationship with Russia, China is quietly expanding the reach and depth of its influence in Europe.

Some of China's success in this arena is a reflection of Europe's failure, as detailed in earlier chapters. If the EU imposes constraints that limit growth, and if it fails to provide the assistance that is needed, one should expect those countries most adversely affected to be receptive to investments from China. And given the EU's legal framework, it will be well-nigh impossible to proscribe member states from availing themselves of these investments, even if the result is a weaker European Union. Europe's response must thus be a positive one, where countries do not feel that the only lifeline they are being given is from China. The challenges provided by China, though, extend even to those countries that have seemingly done well against Chinese competition, notably Germany. As we discussed in Chapter 1, Germany will eventually face competition from China in capital goods and will also face the challenge of restructuring that the countries of the European periphery have had to deal with for a quarter of a century.

## Responding to the Twin Challenges of the United States and China

The election of Trump and the decision of Britain to abandon the EU have at least had the positive effect of focusing minds in the rest of Europe, particularly on the consequences of not having a united stance in the face of such international turbulence. The reaction of EU authorities to Trump's steel and aluminum tariff announcement showed a willingness to stand up to the US president. The next step will be to push Trump as far away from this and other acts of protectionism as possible.

The EU will need to assemble a broad coalition to challenge him in multilateral institutions like the WTO. As long as Trump is in office, this lesson is an important one for Europe: the globe's multilateral institutions require active cultivation and support because Trump will relentlessly undermine them. Only the EU is capable of keeping the WTO's rules-based trade regime alive.

Europe should also consider how it can best support civil society and human rights in the United States. Americans who were horrified by Trump's election took notice of German chancellor Angela Merkel's insistence that cooperation must come on the basis of "common values" that Trump and some of his supporters may not share. This position was the right stance to take. It also has strategic value for the struggle to salvage the international order.

Trump's election has also forced European governments and the European Union to look toward alternative centers of political power in the United States, a strategy that will pay dividends down the line. With cities like New York and states like California taking the lead on climate change, Europe has credible interlocutors on the subject—no matter what Trump does—and policy would benefit by taking greater account of the complexity of the United States. Europe ought to pay attention to the massive political mobilization of the center-left in the United States; from it will come future leaders with whom they will have to deal.

Finding the right European approach will be tricky, as areas of common interests fluctuate or become overshadowed by areas of conflict. China has made clear its interest in fighting climate change, a European priority. But the EU and China will continue to clash over an area at the core of the European Commission's work: whether China should shed its "non-market economy" status, a change that would loosen some trade rules that are a legacy of its accession to the WTO. Those rules were designed for another era in which there was no functioning price system in China. They were protectionist in nature; their objective was to give countries the power to keep out goods made in Communist countries.

We are in a different era now. China's economic system is far different than it was 40 years ago. In reality, it is not a market economy, but neither is it a Communist one. We may not be able to use the same rules in judging whether a country is dumping (selling goods below costs) when the country is a "normal" market economy, as when in it is a "socialist market economy with Chinese characteristics." But the current rules for judging whether China is dumping make no sense either. If we accept the premise that trade can be mutually beneficial with the right rules, then it is imperative to seek new rules against dumping.

The investment that has come about as a result of China's One Belt, One Road initiative has had a positive influence in some countries, by helping to round out transportation infrastructure. However, it has decreased the influence of Brussels, left many countries heavily indebted, and in the worst cases, has been tainted by bribery and corruption. A European response is required. The EU should expand its aid program, too, including lending for infrastructure. Beijing's attempt is to put China at the geo-economic center of the world; Europe should also be attempting to put itself at the center of this new world.

The European Parliament has called on the EU to "speak with one voice" to China on this and other matters. And Europe has a choice: let each country strive to get what advantages from relations with China they can or find a common policy framework based on European solidarity. Hopefully, Europe will take the latter course.

## UNDERSTANDING THE ROOTS OF THE CURRENT POLITICAL MOMENT

Europe must gird itself to deal with the pressing problems described above. However, even as it contends with the unpredictable array of surprises generated by Trump's erraticism, it must also understand the deeper economic causes behind the current political moment. After all, xenophobic nationalist populism is not unique to the United States. Washington is simply where such a political movement has reached its most startling heights. Many, if not all, countries in Europe are now threatened by figures and movements with similar underlying beliefs.

The root problem on both sides of the Atlantic is a failure to deal with the distributive consequences of the enormous changes of the last 30 to 40 years. Technological change, globalization, financialization, and so forth, may have increased the size of the pie, but they have left large numbers of people worse off. Intertwined with these changes were adjustments in the rules governing the economy, which this book has outlined. And rather than countering the underlying divisive forces, the new rules exacerbated them. Indeed, as we have repeatedly said, the underlying drivers of change, like globalization, have been shaped by these rules in ways that have contributed to the growing societal divide.

As we have explained, trade integration with developing countries and emerging markets, by itself, would have led to lower wages of unskilled workers. However, we could have had a globalization that was far less devastating to workers. We did not need to do so much to further weaken workers' bargaining power. We did not need to make financial markets so much more unstable. We could have provided more help to those hurt by globalization.

The failure to manage globalization well meant that globalization failed to deliver on its promises, or even, in some countries, to make most people better off. Globalization, as it has been managed and in conjunction with other factors, has helped cause inequality to rise precipitously in most advanced countries. The middle class has shrunk and insecurity has grown. Further, economic crises have increased in frequency, and a problem in one country can quickly spread around the world, as happened with the made-in-the-USA 2008 financial crisis. In this new world, multinational corporations have grown as powerful, in some ways, as nation-states. They have shaped laws, contributed to environmental destruction, and even undermined the sense of self-determination; part of the nationalist bent in so many movements today may in part be a reaction to this. International corporations have managed to push policies that boost their profits and market power, even at the expense of society's general interests—whether it is the right to privacy, data ownership, or the availability of non-GMO food. Further, the intellectual property rules of globalization have caused drug prices to increase, limited the spread of knowledge, and favored giant businesses over smaller outfits.[1]

Globalization was supposed to create jobs and to quicken and sustain economic growth. It has done neither reliably and has sometimes even done the opposite. It has also weakened workers' bargaining power and created regulatory races to the bottom between countries.

It was not inevitable that globalization would have all of these negative consequences—quite the contrary. The integration of global markets has the potential to create wealth and prosperity. Globalization was sold to the public as a commitment to an undistorted playing field, when it was really managed by and for large multinational corporate interests. The result has been a system with robust opportunities for tax avoidance and evasion, concentration of market power, and funneling of gains to the top. For large multinational corporations and the world's thin layer of the ultra-wealthy, globalization has worked just fine. European and American voters understand this, at varying levels. Their embrace of figures like Trump, misguided as it is, is a rejection of the status quo.

Globalization is not the sole force responsible for growing inequality and other adverse trends. Technological change also plays a role. But the mismanagement of globalization has amplified these other effects and has compounded already challenging problems.

The advanced countries, including those of the EU, fell prey to this version of globalization, in large part because of a belief that if the national pie were larger, everyone would be better off. It has long been known that trade liberalization carries the risk of creating distinct groups of winners and losers, and over the last few decades, economists have further developed theories and compiled evidence to fortify this view.

Markets for risk (insurance markets) are almost always imperfect, so individuals cannot buy insurance to guard against the most important risks they face, such as job loss. Moreover, trade liberalization often confronts firms with new risks, again against which they cannot buy insurance. Capital markets are also imperfect, so that new enterprises that seek to take advantage of new export opportunities that have opened up as a result of a trade agreement often cannot get the capital they need. As a result, job destruction often outpaces job creation. The presumption that free trade is welfare-enhancing is simply less true than had been realized. Examining the effects of trade liberalization in an economy that was based on the notion of perfect markets provided less insight into the world as it exists than advocates of globalization had assumed.

In short, a limited and well-structured agenda of trade liberalization can enhance societal well-being, but it will do so only if the government takes an active role in ensuring that the benefits of globalization are equitably shared. But many of the same advocates of trade liberalization sought to scale back government, limiting its ability to do what had to be done to make sure that globalization would benefit most of society.

Globalization's advocates liked to pick and choose their theories. They liked results that said trade liberalization could be of benefit to both countries. So they touted these findings while glossing over evidence that unskilled workers would be worse off and that without finance, small businesses could not avail themselves of globalization's new export opportunities. This selective reading of the evidence, made manifest in policy, led to exactly what we should expect: a loss of trust in politicians and other elites.

The case of the Nordic countries, with their strong welfare states, shows how good government policy can protect citizens against the risks of globalization. In contrast, the United States has provided paltry worker assistance and has weakened worker bargaining power, thus exacerbating the problems and risks of globalization.

If the state is to perform the tasks that it should with any degree of effectiveness, it will need the financial resources required to counter adverse trade impacts. If the state does not play this role, there is little hope that liberalization will generate anything different from what we have seen for the last third of a century. In this case, the situation could become even graver.

## AN AGENDA FOR MAKING GLOBALIZATION WORK FOR EUROPE

Globalization is a means to an end and not an end in itself. The aim is shared prosperity. Globalization should only be pursued as far as this end is furthered. For the past 30-odd years, Europe has pursued globalization in ways that have been deleterious for large segments of the population. Moreover, in many places within Europe, governments weakened the welfare state that should protect citizens from the worst consequences of globalization at precisely the time they should have strengthened it. If we make the changes suggested in the previous nine chapters, there is a much better chance of globalization working for more people. Furthermore, there will be an even better chance of success if we rewrite the rules of globalization itself. In the following ten sections, we describe briefly how that might be done.

## 1. Global Cooperation

An essential benefit of rules-based multilateral frameworks is predictability, acquired through vigorous consensus-building about the nature of the rules. Flawed as our rules and institutions may be, they are what stand between us and even more dystopian versions of globalization in which corporations are even more dismissive of their costs to society and in which events are far more unpredictable, even to the point of conflict. It is essential to preserve and improve our rules-based international system and the multilateral institutions through which the world cooperates, working together to advance common interests.

Global interdependence demands global cooperation. Cross-border externalities are increasingly common, whether they are obvious, like climate change, in which carbon dioxide pollution from the United States and China devastates tropical countries, or less visible, such as financial contagion, where toxic mortgages produced in the United States infected the international economy and brought on a global financial crisis. When what one country does affects others in significant ways, the world needs rules and referees to prevent countries from harming others, and to encourage actions that benefit all.

Governments should focus on those areas in which cross-border externalities are particularly significant. The problem is that too little attention has been paid to those areas, such as tax and regulatory competition, in which there are significant adverse externalities.* There has been far too much attention paid to regulatory harmonization in areas where cross-border externalities are simply not as significant.

Global public goods—things that benefit everyone in the world,

---

* The costs of short-term capital flows can be especially great for developing countries; and there are a variety of measures that they can take to stabilize those flows, such as preventing surges of short-term money into or out of a country. But even Europe can face problems when capital flows result in large changes in exchange rates in a short span of time.

such as global security, global health, and global knowledge, or problems that everybody suffers from, such as climate change and pandemics—present an especially important challenge. Carbon dioxide molecules do not apply for visas and passports, and neither do the viruses associated with bird flu or Zika. Climate change is the quintessential global public good because we all share the same atmosphere. Only through collective global action can climate change be addressed. Similarly, if we do not act in concert to contain contagious diseases, we risk facing global epidemics.*

## 2. Global Macroeconomics and Finance

Earlier chapters described the importance of keeping the economy at full employment and the challenges posed by a single currency in ensuring that all European countries succeed. Macroeconomics is one area with important cross-border spillovers. For example, if the United States stimulates its economy, the EU benefits because Americans will then buy more goods from Europe (and the reverse is also true). In the absence of coordination, each country will have less-than-optimal incentives for stimulus in a deep downturn. The world grasped this reality in 2008 and 2009. Under the influence of Gordon Brown, then Britain's prime minister, the G-20 agreed to coordinated expansionary policies to combat the contraction that the financial crisis kicked off. However, this spirit of cooperation evaporated, especially as austerity and pre-Keynesian doctrines of fiscal rectitude took hold in Germany and elsewhere. Had there been more coordination and cooperation, the global economy almost surely would have been able to recover more quickly. In fact, Europe would have been one of the big beneficiaries

---

* There are many other areas where cooperation is essential. For instance, excessive use of antibiotics risks creating drug-resistant strains of disease.

of this stronger recovery. Europe should promote stronger macroeconomic cooperation, based on the tenets that we outlined in Part I of this book.

In finance especially, more concerted action is crucial, and here, too, Europe must take the lead. In the absence of such coordination, there is a risk of what is known as *regulatory arbitrage*, when countries try to attract banks by offering a less regulated environment (often dressed up as "business friendly"). Given the high degree of interdependence among global financial institutions, reflected in the speed with which problems in American markets translated into problems elsewhere, cooperation in financial regulation is crucial.

However, the last ten years have shown how difficult it is to achieve such cooperation, and with Trump, matters will now be even more difficult. The question remains: How should Europe respond?

First, the competition to attract banks is a race that is not worth winning. Having a larger financial sector brings with it more volatility and a more distorted economy with more inequality.

Second, Europe has to protect itself against failures elsewhere. It failed to do that before the crisis, and it simply cannot allow underregulated American banks to operate in Europe on the assumption that the United States provides adequate oversight. Instead, Europe should ensure that any foreign bank operating within its borders is well-capitalized and remains so in the event of a crisis—that money can't be quickly drawn out of Europe to shore up banks elsewhere. These American (and other foreign) banks should be subject to all the regulations and rules that apply to any European bank, including those pertaining to capital and liquidity.

Third, Europe should continue to fight, in every forum in which these matters are discussed, for tougher bank regulation of the sort outlined in Chapter 5.

Finally, Europe should recognize that borders matter. Cross-border flows are different from flows within a country and need to be subject to more stringent regulations. Instability in these flows gives rise to exchange-rate instability, which in turn gives rise to macroeconomic instability.

## 3. Rule of Law

Economists have long noted the importance of the rule of law for growth and efficiency. The modern market economy could not exist without a modicum of the rule of law.[2] As the world globalized, the imperative for creating an international rule of law only grew, but so far, we have fallen short of what is needed. Our international trade agreements, flawed as they may be, are a step in the right direction, and are especially important for smaller countries. The United States, the EU, and China might be able to fight it out in mercantilist fashion, but the rest of the world—some 38 percent of global GDP—would suffer the collateral damage. And they would be in a disadvantageous position in bargaining against the great powers. With Trump announcing a US retreat from globalization and the global rule of law, China has stepped forward as its defender. It is understandable that it has done so: its remarkable growth would not have been possible without globalization.[3]

The creation of the World Trade Organization in 1995 was a critical step forward in creating a global rules-based system. The WTO rests on a set of ideas, which include the most-favored-nation principle and other rules to limit discrimination among members.* Most importantly, it also includes a system for adjudicating disputes. However, its enforcement mechanism is limited—if a country violates its obligations,

---

* The most-favored-nation principle prohibits countries from discriminating between their trading partners. All countries are treated *as if* they were the most-favored nation. The main exception is that one can give tariff-free access to a country that is part of a free-trade agreement, without granting it to others.

then the injured country can impose duties in an equivalent amount on the offending country. The offending country can, of course, choose to continue to impose the tariffs, but not without consequences. So far, this system has proven remarkably effective. It has, for instance, prevented trade wars, or at least limited them. There was considerable worry in the aftermath of the 2008 crisis that countries would attempt to reignite their economies by shifting demand away from imports to their own economies, as happened in the Great Depression.[4] It did not happen, and the WTO system deserves considerable credit.

Trump has announced that he intends to upend this system, and that he will not honor adverse rulings. He has also blocked the appointment of new judges, which means that if he does not relent, the system of adjudication may break down. Europe needs to make it clear that multilateralism is too important to be destroyed by one individual, especially one without any conception of how the world is supposed to work together in peace and harmony. Europe must resolve to save whatever it can. If the United States refuses to appoint judges, new judges should be appointed anyway. There is some disagreement among legal experts as to whether such a move would violate the WTO agreement, but these legalities may not be the critical issue; the United States is unlikely to obey any adverse WTO rulings in any case.

With new judges appointed without US consent, the international rule of law would still be preserved for the rest of the world, with the rest of the world agreeing to be bound by WTO decisions. Trump's damage will have been contained. That said, as long as Trump is around, the law of the jungle may very well prevail, which will imply that trading with the United States is riskier than trading with other countries. Countries and companies will have to take this into account. The United States will pay the price for walking away from the rule of law. Europe's objective should be to minimize the price that Europe will have to pay for America's unilateralism. The international community should welcome the United States back into the fold when the time comes, but the world will have learned the important lesson: that it is dangerous to give too much power to, or rely too much on, any single country.

## 4. Democratic Governance, Including Transparency

One of the major reasons that globalization has so far been badly mismanaged is that trade agreements and international rules were made without democratic transparency and in sometimes near-secrecy. And with corporations and big finance at the table, it is not a surprise that trade agreements reflect their interests and perspective. Indeed, trade agreements are often used as end-runs around domestic legislation—attempts to get through trade negotiations what could not be achieved through democratic processes.

For instance, every country has faced the challenge of balancing the big pharmaceutical companies—which do much of the work of developing new drugs, typically based on government-supported research, and bringing them to the market—with generics. When things work well, the former drives new products and the latter drives down prices and increases accessibility. Because the real driver of innovation is basic research, which comes from government-funded laboratories, the right balance entails a large role for generics, which governments have recognized. Pharmaceutical companies have sought to use the opaque process of negotiating trade agreements to obtain rules that give them more protection from generics, for instance by putting up impediments to the entry of generics. In these endeavors, the industry has been enormously successful—far more so than if there had been an open public debate.

Who makes the rules about globalization and how is vitally important. One of the reasons for the failures of globalization is who contributed to decision making and who did not. Good governance must be based on the few simple principles of representativeness, legitimacy, transparency, and accountability. If the rule of law is to have any legitimacy, it cannot be written by and for corporations, and politicians and governments cannot be held accountable in the absence of transparency.

Government and civil society will both have to be part of the system regulating and tempering globalization. There has been excessive faith in markets and the private sector. The private sector, on its own, created many of the central problems that national economies and the global society are facing, namely inequality, environmental degradation, and instability. The private sector, on its own, will not solve these problems.

Europe's approach to external trade has sometimes shown a lack of transparency during treaty negotiation processes that too often gave privileged corporate access. The 2009 Lisbon Treaty, which placed external trade under the exclusive competence of the EU, aimed to make the policymaking process more democratic. Under the pre-Lisbon regime, the EU's external trade agreements were largely crafted by a European Commission that was at liberty to steer negotiations with a third-country partner (though following loose guidelines set by the member states), and the European Council would enter at the end of negotiations to approve the final deal.

Under Lisbon, the European Parliament enjoys a more formal and influential role in this process, since it is now elevated to coequal status with the council. This arrangement means that any trade agreement that falls under the exclusive competence of the EU must win approval from both the council and parliament. The point of this new arrangement was to give a clearer and louder democratic voice to the shaping of EU-level trade deals, which had largely been controlled by career politicians in the European Commission and national economy ministries—in a process in which corporate voices were clearly listened to, but not the voices of civil society.

Unfortunately, the reality of Lisbon falls short of this lofty goal. For one, the post-Lisbon regime fails to give the European Parliament a strong role during negotiations, which essentially remains the exclusive domain of the commission, with the parliament playing its most decisive role only after the negotiated text is finalized. The parliament then often seemingly faces a take-it-or-leave-it choice. In the negotiation process, corporate lobbies often seem to play an important role, and by expanding the number of trade policy areas that fall under the EU's exclusive authority, Lisbon actually creates new opportunities for powerful business lobbies in Brussels to influence Europe's trade agenda.

These limitations are fully visible in the crafting of recently proposed trade agreements. The opaqueness of trade talks was a rallying point for opponents of the Transatlantic Trade and Investment Partnership (T-TIP)—and rightly so, since that agreement appeared greatly beholden to business interests. For example, during preparations for the agreement's negotiations, between January 2012 and April 2013, at least 119 of the commission's 130 stakeholder meetings took place with large corporations and their lobbying groups.[5] Similar concerns arose over negotiations for a trade agreement with Canada and an agreement on services in the WTO.

In short, corporations have enjoyed privileged access to these trade talks, with the European Commission, in effect, seemingly negotiating on their behalf, while other key stakeholders (including labor unions, consumer protection groups, NGOs, including environmental groups, and even the EU and national parliaments) lacked similar access and influence. The concern is that these powerful agreements will work to promote and protect business interests, even when they compromise fundamental rights, protective standards, and the common good—as they often can and do.

Rebalancing the EU's trade policy will require an opening up of the negotiation and drafting procedures. The European Commission should increase its communication with the public and lawmakers, clarify its negotiating positions where strategically feasible, and offer updates on the process of trade talks. It should give all stakeholders an equal opportunity to help shape these agreements. Finally, the commission should give these consultations consideration equal to that of business groups, since listening to a diverse set of perspectives means nothing unless those views can directly affect the negotiation process.

Trump, though his critique is laced with a horrifying xenophobia, has forcefully raised the question of whether recent trade agreements are fair. With American and European corporations playing such a large role in negotiations, it is not a surprise that they are unfair to workers in both developed and developing countries.

Agreements that are unfair to Europe's neighbors to the south (to Africa) have significant long-run effects on Europe. When these countries are hurt, and their citizens do not do well, they look elsewhere for economic opportunity. The failure to negotiate agreements with Africa that would help their economies grow contributes to migration pressures.

## 5. Trade

To many, globalization is synonymous with trade agreements. Hopefully, this chapter will have made clear that this premise is not correct. Yes, trade agreements have been particularly controversial because of job losses and downward pressure on wages in the advanced economies. On the other side, advocates of trade agreements argue that exports create jobs. The truth is that most agreements between the EU and developing countries probably result in a net job loss, and even when jobs are created, the job creation is typically slower than the job destruction.* But all of this misses the central point: trade agreements are not about jobs. Fiscal and monetary policy are supposed to keep the economy at full employment, as we have argued repeatedly here. Trade is about increasing standards of living, by allowing countries to specialize in their areas of strength, in those activities in which they have a comparative advantage.

Trade agreements always come with compromises. For example, countries cannot impose tariffs at will. However, the benefits of this slight loss of sovereignty, through reciprocity, can be large relative to the cost. So, when there are disputes about one party or the other in honoring the agreement, there has to be a mechanism for resolving such disputes, and both sides have to agree to respect the outcome of the dispute resolution mechanism. The world is far short of an international government, but these are small steps toward creating an international rule of law.

Trade agreements can have further benefits, such as achieving worthy foreign policy goals. The free-trade agreement between the United States and Jordan, which entered into force in 2001, was not about economic policy; it was a helping hand to an ally. NAFTA was intended to increase incomes in both Mexico and the United States, with an ancillary benefit being that higher incomes in Mexico would reduce immigration pressure. That has in fact happened, though NAFTA may have played only a minor role.

However, the economic benefits of additional trade agreements are, at the very least, debatable. Tariffs are generally low around the world. More agreements are thus likely to have only marginal value on that account, as the Trans-Pacific Partnership illustrates. Despite being

---

* The reason is that increased imports destroy jobs as exports increase them, and the imports destroyed are more labor-intensive than the exports created; if Europe maintains (roughly) trade balance, then net, jobs are destroyed.

touted as a trade deal—the largest trade deal ever, by some accounts, embracing 44 percent of global trade—even the US government calculated that its impact on GDP was negligible, some 0.15 percent of GDP after 15 years, and that may have been a gross exaggeration.

Since tariffs are now almost universally very low, the new trade agreements focus on other matters, including regulations, intellectual property, and investment. Producers in both countries can easily agree that they could make higher profits if the government only got rid of some regulation, for instance, on emissions of pollutants or safety. Trade ministers may quickly agree to get rid of the regulations in both countries—trade ministries are typically influenced by producer interests. But while consumers in both countries gain when tariffs (and prices) are lowered, citizens in both countries lose from the weakening of important protective regulations—while the corporations gain.

International trade becomes their ally in arguing for the kind of world that they, the corporations, had sought but could not get because domestically, within each country's parliament, society balances the cost and benefits of these regulations. Provisions in recent trade agreements, going back to NAFTA, are designed to make it difficult, if not impossible, for new regulations to be imposed that adversely affect foreign investors, no matter what the social benefit.

Corporations offer weak justification for their demands. They have said it is important to *harmonize* regulations and that different regulations act as *non-tariff barriers to trade.* They pleaded that all they are asking for is a reduction in these non-tariff barriers. However, when the corporations ask for harmonization, they typically mean doing so at the bottom, and not harmonizing *up* to the most stringent standards. The agenda of regulatory harmonization is actually an agenda for weakening regulations. But in most sectors and on most topics, we simply do not need to have full harmonization of regulations. Instead, we should be asking for the minimal level of harmonization required to make the global system work. Europe's principle of subsidiarity—that there should be as much delegation of responsibility to national (or subnational) authorities as possible—may apply as much to regulations as it does to other areas of governmental activity. In the name of harmonization, Europe should not give up its values and principles, whether it pertains to privacy or to the health and safety of its people or the protection of the environment.

Though recent trade agreements have been designed to reduce prospects of future increases in regulations and, where possible, to engineer regulatory rollbacks under the guise of harmonization, the broader and more invidious agenda involved seeking a system of rules under which countries competed in every way possible to attract business. This competition entailed lower wages, weaker regulations, and reduced taxation. But corporations do not exist in a vacuum. They have shareholders and executives, who, try as they might, cannot insulate themselves from what is going on outside their buildings. If the environment is polluted, if climate change accelerates, they too will suffer—though perhaps not as much as will the rest of society.

The most important issue on the global and European agenda should thus not be the creation of new trade agreements but the preservation and improvement of existing ones, chief among them the WTO.

## 6. Taxation

Managing globalization requires that we eliminate tax havens and create a fair system of multinational taxation. In no area is the corporate agenda more in evidence. Large multinationals worked hard to pass double taxation agreements (to make sure that profits were never taxed twice) but did nothing to make sure that profits would be taxed at least once. As we noted in Chapter 6, firms like Apple have been as ingenious in tax avoidance as they have been in providing products that people like. As we explained there, globalization has made it possible for corporations and individuals to avoid and evade the taxes that they should pay, and corporations have induced competition among jurisdictions around the world to lower taxes. Corporations enjoy the benefit of a trained labor force, good infrastructure, and a rule of law that a country provides, but seek a free ride on other taxpayers, many of whom are far less able to support these public goods.

"Fiscal paradises"—places where individuals and corporations can avoid or evade taxes—have cropped up around the world, from Macau and Singapore to Panama, the Cayman Islands, Luxembourg, Ireland, and the Channel Islands.* Tax avoidance is a particularly grave issue because now more than ever governments need resources to provide social protection or assistance in retraining to workers who need help—often as a result of globalization itself.

Eliminating tax havens and destructive tax competition will not be politically easy, but the principles are simple and clear. First, an ultimatum to all fiscal paradises: if they do not conform to the transparency and regulatory standards of Europe (including those against money laundering), it will be illegal for any European to engage in business with them. These jurisdictions should be cut off from all European banks. Sufficient penalties imposed on European citizens who violate the law would act as a strong deterrent. Second, a global minimum tax: any firm doing business in Europe would have to report its global income, including that of all subsidiaries, and there would be a minimum tax on this global income (say, 20 or 25 percent). If the jurisdictions that the company claimed to be the source of this income did not tax it, Europe should do so. This minimum tax would stop the race

---

* As we noted in Chapter 6, though we often think of these as "offshore financial centers," some jurisdictions in the United States (Nevada, Delaware) and the City of London have also profited from these nefarious activities.

to the bottom—countries would no longer have an incentive to try to recruit European firms by promising tax benefits. It would start a race to the top: it would be foolish for any country not to impose a tax at the rate of Europe's minimum tax.

## 7. Investment Agreements

Investment agreements, supposedly to protect Europe's investments abroad from expropriation and discrimination, are particularly problematic. Europe should work with other countries to revise them and to reject any further deals until there is a broader consensus on what they should contain.

These provisions give foreign companies a privileged position by allowing them to sue a European country in which they have located whenever a newly passed regulation compromises profitability, something domestic companies can't do. Similarly, it strengthens the property rights of European firms when they invest abroad, creating an incentive to move oversees, at the expense of jobs in Europe. It also weakens European workers' bargaining power, as the threat of moving out becomes more credible.

Making these provisions even worse is the way such claims by corporations are adjudicated. The investor-state dispute settlement procedure (ISDS) entails disputes being heard by special tribunals, with the adjudicators appointed by the contestants. These erstwhile judges are usually lawyers, many of whom have multiple conflicts of interest, and are typically beholden to corporate interests. The costly proceedings favor large multinationals.* Because tribunal members are paid by the

---

* According to a 2015 report by the United Nations Conference on Trade and Development, around 60 percent of completed ISDS cases favored investors while only 40 percent favored governments.

day, they have perverse incentives to draw out proceedings, which can be prohibitively expensive for small businesses and developing countries. The EU has embraced these procedures in recent agreements with Singapore and Vietnam and discussed doing so in the now-suspended talks with the United States.*

The historic significance of introducing ISDS (and its equivalents) in these agreements cannot be underplayed, particularly because they generate enormous and unevenly distributed risks for workers, consumers, small businesses, taxpayers, and the rule of law, at the EU and country levels. Suits can be brought for any regulation or law that decreases the firm's bottom line. And the compensation is not just the value of the lost investment; the firm can sue for the loss of expected profits—a highly speculative number that can easily become bloated.

ISDS creates a parallel legal system that works to the advantage of foreign corporations. This is attributable to the scheme's following core characteristics: (1) that only foreign investors can seek protection under ISDS proceedings, while domestic investors, citizens, and governments cannot; (2) that foreign investors have broad remit to attack protective regulations, including in critical areas ranging from agriculture, to the environment, to public health; and (3) if the country loses, it faces the burden of paying large amounts, based on an illusory notion of "loss of potential profits," rather than a more concrete "recovery of investment expenditures." Moreover, the proceedings occur in secret with no appeal, little transparency, and no way of resolving differences

---

* While similar provisions existed in some 1,400 bilateral investment treaties, the new agreements mark the first time these provisions fall under an EU-level trade deal with application to all economic sectors. The Comprehensive Economic and Trade Agreement with Canada, which was signed in 2017, embraces ISDS, but with judges chosen from a permanent 15-member tribunal. It has made other improvements, for instance in adopting UNCITRAL (UN Commission on International Trade Law) rules on transparency, but in other ways, the standard criticisms of investment agreements still apply. See the discussion below.

in outcomes in seemingly similar cases. In short, ISDS falls far short of what a twenty-first-century judicial procedure should look like.

The modified ISDS schemes under the EU-Canada agreement and Europe's agreement with Vietnam are only modest improvements. While their use of an independent tribunal structure does respond to many of the conflict-of-interest issues in ISDS, they still give foreign investors wide latitude to sue host countries and attack domestic regulations (with almost limitless compensatory claims).

The problems just described are not just hypothetical, theoretical possibilities. Under NAFTA, Canada has paid some €135 million to American corporations under just seven ISDS cases, with foreign investors seeking an additional €4 billion in ongoing proceedings. These formidable sums do not even take into account the €45 million that the Canadian government has spent defending itself in just these cases. The threat of large compensation payouts can also have the effect of discouraging policymakers from pursuing new regulations to protect the environment, health, safety, or even the economy itself.

Perhaps the most tragic aspect of ISDS is that it is generally unnecessary in the context of the EU's agreements with developed countries. Historically, ISDS has been used in cases where investors from rich countries require additional protection for their projects in developing economies, due to inadequacies in the latter's courts. Certainly, such a need would not exist in any EU agreement with a developed economy, such as Canada, since the judicial systems of the partners would be more than adequate to handle the cases.

In short, these provisions have created imbalanced and unjustified advantages for large foreign corporations, while undermining the fundamental role of the EU and member states to protect European citizens. ISDS creates a vast and wholly unnecessary deficit of democracy in countries that submit to this dispute resolution process. In some countries, it arguably runs counter to basic constitutional principles. It is quite simply hard to imagine a process for redress of grievances that runs more counter to European values than this one.

The European Union should not include these investor-protection procedures in the EU's trade agreements with any country with good protections for property rights. If they are included, new agreements should substantially narrow the scope of the process. Corporations should only be allowed to sue in cases in which a rule, regulation, or other public action clearly discriminates against the foreign investor.* The amount recovered should be limited to the amount invested and not to some speculative notion of the profits the investment would otherwise have generated. The system should require claimants to first seek remedy in the domestic courts, or to explain why the case could not be adequately handled in such a way.

Where a parallel arbitration system is necessary, the EU should insist on the creation of a permanent, independent, and transparent dispute resolution system with publicly paid judges that allows all relevant actors—including host countries and affected third parties (such as workers and environmental groups)—to seek the exact same legal recourse that is enjoyed by foreign investors. To ensure greater balance, NGOs and others should also have the reciprocal right to sue the government or businesses when they fail to live up to their obligations under, for instance, environmental or labor laws. If business finds ISDS good for enforcing rules it likes, it should accept the same for other rules. With rights come responsibilities, and corporate investors have sought the first without the second.

---

* This would mean, in particular, that a foreign firm could not sue simply because, say, an environmental law reduced profits. It could only sue if it could establish that the law was only being enforced against foreign firms.

## 8. Intellectual Property Rights

The governance of global knowledge is an important part of the governance of international economic relations in our modern, knowledge-based economy. But here again, the rules of the game have largely been written by and for large corporations. Even as the architects of globalization have pushed for the free movement of capital, they have used trade agreements to limit the free movement of ideas.

As we discussed in Chapter 4, intellectual property rights are a social construct designed to promote societal well-being by carefully balancing the benefits of increased innovation and the costs resulting from impediments in the efficient use of knowledge. In many respects, though, the current system is based only on one objective: maximizing corporate profits. As we have noted, poorly designed rules not only impede the use of information, but they may also even discourage innovation.

As we think about the appropriate global regime for intellectual property, several general precepts are worth considering. First, it is simply not true that stronger protections for rights holders are better; good regimes represent a balancing of concerns. Second, the outcome of this balancing may differ from time to time and from country to country. This observation has, in turn, several implications. There is no globally optimal system, and systems may need to change over time. Third, in a democracy, balancing requires the voices of all affected parties to be at the table. For instance, health advocates must be at the table when patents for pharmaceuticals are under discussion.

There is no compelling reason for intellectual property to fall under trade deals, which are crafted by trade ministers who know very little about research and innovation. There is already an international body concerned with innovation—the World Intellectual Property Organization, which was established in 1967 and is headquartered in Geneva. The only reason that patents, copyrights, and trademarks are in trade agreements is because it gave the governments of the advanced countries a sledgehammer with which to strengthen and enforce the rights of powerful domestic lobbies.

The reason for not including intellectual property in trade agreements is not only because it is an arena in which trade ministers have no real competence, but it is also that trade ministries traditionally ally closely with producer interests and give short shrift to other societal concerns. In our discussion of non-tariff barriers, for example, we noted the increased risk that this alliance with producer interests across countries leads to a skewed regulatory regime. There is an even greater risk in the case of intellectual property. Two sectors for which intellectual property protection are particularly important, pharmaceuticals and entertainment (copyrights), are not representative of the economy as a whole. A regime designed for maximizing corporate profits in these sectors can hardly maximize societal welfare.

Within Europe, within the rules that govern generics, there is a balancing of concerns of innovation with access to drugs. In trade agreements, the voice of the large pharmaceutical companies is almost always dominant. The result is that trade agreements lead to higher drug prices, less access, poorer health, and greater government expenditures. In Europe, where there is a commitment by most governments to provide access to medicines, this creates a direct fiscal cost; in effect, ordinary citizens pay through drug prices or taxes. But ordinary citizens are not at the table for these negotiations, neither as taxpayers nor as consumers.

The intellectual property rules included in most recent trade agreements entail provisions even more pro-corporate than before; for example, by making entry of generics even more difficult in spite of the wide consensus that the opposite is needed.[6]

Advocates of including such rules in trade agreements argue that doing so presents an opportunity to "raise" standards. But even this language reflects a bias. Any efforts to use trade agreements to force Europe and the rest of the world to have the same intellectual property regime may not be good for Europe. Europe, for instance, has procedures designed to prevent issuing "bad patents," rules that the United States does not have. It would be a mistake for Europe to give up these provisions in the name of harmonization.

In short, there should be a presumption against including these provisions within a trade agreement. If an intellectual property provision is included, it should state broad principles, with great latitude for each country to design a regime appropriate for its own circumstances. The European Commission should be particularly mindful of preserving Europe's ability to design a regime that works for all of society. This also entails shielding intellectual property protections from investment dispute settlement proceedings.

Global cooperation, in which Europe could take the lead, should focus on making better and cheaper drugs. Knowledge is a global public good and it is important that everyone contributes to funding its advancement. A global health research fund, with contributions from all the advanced countries (say at 0.5 percent of GDP), with the medicines discovered being made available to all producers at a small license fee, would employ competition where most effective—namely, in driving down production costs and prices and enhancing distribution.

## 9. Competition Policy

With globe-straddling corporations (particularly American firms in the information technology sector) threatening to stifle competition worldwide, and with US antitrust enforcement in decline for the better part of two decades, the EU must assume leadership in this arena.

In his new study of American competition policy, Columbia University law professor Tim Wu gives the right amount of credit to the

EU. Progress is apparent but more needs to happen. "European anti-trust is far from perfect," Wu writes, "but its leadership and willingness to bring big cases when competition is clearly under threat should serve as a model for American enforcers and for the rest of the world."[7]

As we discussed in Chapter 4, the EU has tackled some important cases, such as by putting companies like Microsoft, Google, and Facebook on notice that their practices will not go unchallenged by competition authorities, and by challenging mergers that would substantially reduce competition, such as that of Honeywell and General Electric in 2001 (even though it had gained approval by American authorities). These efforts should continue, and European authorities should not shy away from decisive measures like major divestitures or breakups if they conclude that the behemoths inhibit competition.

The new technology companies have presented the double threat of both the loss of privacy and the stunting of competition. Artificial intelligence, as well, can give a company with more data an insurmountable advantage over competitors. This data can be used to engage in discriminatory pricing, thereby enriching the corporation at the expense of consumers. The EU took an important step forward in this respect with the issuance of its General Data Protection Regulation in May 2018, a step that looks out for the privacy of ordinary European citizens and regulates what can be done with the data a firm collects. This move is essential for any modern democracy but is not enough and should be viewed as just a beginning.

Hopefully, Europe's efforts will inspire better competition policy in the United States in the coming years. California has already passed a law (the California Consumer Privacy Act of 2018) that in some respects protects privacy better than rules in Europe. One also hopes that Europe and the United States will eventually provide a mutual check on each other by bringing cases in which politics on either side of the Atlantic discourages strong action.

## 10. Climate Change

Addressing climate change is an existential issue for the world. It is a global problem that can only be solved by global reductions in carbon emissions. Climate change is a global public good (or more accurately, a public *bad*) because everybody is affected by it. Hence, there is the classic free-rider problem: everyone would like others to bear the burden of reducing emissions while they themselves enjoy the benefits. The Paris agreement represented a global consensus on the need to limit emissions, with voluntary reductions on the part of each country. The hope was that if everyone saw that there was a global commitment to reduce carbon emissions, everyone would want to join in, and those slow to adopt green technologies would fall behind.

The use of this voluntary approach was not a matter of choice, since it was clear that the US Congress would not approve any agreement compelling reductions. The magnitude of the voluntary reductions was impressive, but even then, the goal of limiting the effects of climate change to a rise of 1.5 to 2 degrees Celsius would not be met on the basis of these reductions alone. Also, there was no enforcement mechanism. The Trump administration has announced it will leave the agreement in 2020, but its departure will have no direct consequences for the United States, though it may eventually give American firms an unfair advantage in carbon-intensive industries. Worryingly, it may also unravel the agreement.*

The fight against climate change and its failures perfectly encapsulate many of the central problems we have reviewed in this chapter. No issue could be more fundamental to our shared well-being, since the consequences of accelerating climate change go beyond the realm of

---

* Fortunately, many states, cities, and corporations within the United States have continued with or even strengthened their commitment to reduce carbon emissions.

economics and will be borne by all human beings (though disproportionately by the most disadvantaged). Here again, Europe must take the lead, not only out of responsibility to the world but also, pressingly, out of its own self-interest.

Again, cooperation is important and should be pursued with any country that is ready to do so on the issue, even in cases such as China, where other interests may not align. But punishments for countries unwilling to take necessary steps to mitigate climate change must also be part of the response. Such punishment mechanisms must apply to anyone who is not playing their part, including Europe's traditional allies, such as the United States. There can be no free riders. Europe should lead the way in imposing a border tax on any goods coming from a country that has not imposed, either through taxes or regulations, an adequate price on carbon. If Europe takes a tough approach, it can eliminate the incentive for the United States to gain a competitive advantage on others by polluting the world. It might even change the political economy of carbon in the United States.

## CONCLUSION

Protectionist sentiments growing around the world provide evidence that globalization has not been managed well. Mismanaged globalization has contributed to lower wages and incomes of workers, and higher unemployment, especially among unskilled workers. When globalization's advocates argue that to compete, one has to cut wages still more and that government has to cut benefits, it is understandable that citizens will question the value of globalization. An honest appraisal would concede that governments managed globalization in a way that predominately helped corporations and wealthier individuals. For example, financial globalization helped the bankers but led to a global financial cataclysm in which ordinary people paid the price. Furthermore, it has enabled tax avoidance and evasion, with an increasing share of the tax burden being imposed on ordinary citizens.

Many of the ideas behind the flawed globalization we have inherited are the same that created the problems in the construction of the Eurozone: neoliberal ideas that said unfettered markets are more efficient and would benefit everyone by promoting growth. The global architecture that resulted from this belief often worked to the detriment of the poorest countries. But it also worked to the detriment of a large fraction of Europeans. It did benefit some Europeans, but only the few at the top. This chapter has outlined what kind of international architecture would be better for Europe—all of Europe and not just those at the top. Such a system would require a far different set of agreements and arrangements than those in place today.

But even with the right global rules, globalization will create winners and losers within Europe. Europe needed a stronger welfare system to protect those hurt by globalization (as well as by other changes to our economy), but the advocates of globalization did everything they could to weaken the systems of social protection and the policies that facilitate economic restructuring. What we outlined in this chapter, and in the previous ones, is all of a piece. Only with good macroeconomic and monetary policies, a financial system that serves Europe's citizens, vibrant and competitive markets, and a twenty-first-century welfare state that provides real security will globalization generate the benefits for ordinary citizens that its advocates have long claimed.

# NOTES

## FOREWORD

1. Joseph E. Stiglitz, with Nell Abernathy, Adam Hersh, Susan Holmberg, and Mike Konczal, *Rewriting the Rules of the American Economy: An Agenda for Growth and Shared Prosperity* (New York: W. W. Norton, 2015). Also available at http://www.rewritetherules.org.
2. Won-Soon Park et al., *Rewriting the Rules of the Korean Economy* (Seoul Institute, 2018).

## CHAPTER 1: EMPLOYMENT, NOT AUSTERITY

1. As this book goes to press, for instance, the United States, under President Trump, is causing another global shock through its protectionist policies and attacks on the global rules-based system. We do not yet know how disturbing these actions will be to the global economy. There is also worry about a shock arising from climate change—including what will happen when markets finally realize the world will need to impose a carbon tax of as much as €100 per ton to achieve the Paris–Copenhagen goals of limiting the increase in temperature to 1.5 to 2 degrees Celsius. See Lord Nicholas Stern and Joseph E. Stiglitz, *Report of the High-Level Commission on Carbon Prices*, World Bank Group, May 29, 2017, https://static1.squarespace.com/static/54ff9c5ce4b0a53decccfb4c/t/59b7f2409f8dce5316811916/1505227332748/CarbonPricing_FullReport.pdf.

2. Eurostat, "Unemployment by Sex and Age," European Commission, Feb. 14, 2019, https://ec.europa.eu/eurostat/web/products-datasets/-/une_rt_a.

3. Eurostat, "Part-Time Employment as Percentage of the Total Employment," European Commission, Feb. 2, 2019, http://appsso.eurostat.ec.europa.eu/nui/show.do?dataset=lfsa_eppgan&lang=en.

4. European leaders have always had to fend off popular opposition to the EU, as evidenced by referenda in France and the Netherlands over the EU Constitution in 2005. That said, opinion surveys have consistently shown broad approval for the euro, despite the post-crisis travails. See Europa, Documents and Publications, "Statistics and Opinion Polls," November 2018, https://ec.europa.eu/commfrontoffice/publicopinion/index.cfm/Survey/getSurveyDetail/yearFrom/1974/yearTo/2019/surveyKy/2211.

5. Robert A. Mundell, "A Theory of Optimum Currency Areas," *The American Economic Review* 51, no. 4 (1961): 657–65.

6. Banque de France, "The Cost of Deficiencies in Euro Area Economic Policy Coordination," *Quarterly Selection of Articles*, Banque de France, no. 46 (2019): 19–30.

7. Jaime Guajardo, Daniel Leigh, and Andrea Pescatori, "Expansionary Austerity? International Evidence," *Journal of the European Economic Association* 12, no. 4 (2014): 949–68, https://doi.org/10.1111/jeea.12083.

8. The Gini coefficient is a common measurement of inequality; the higher the number, the greater the inequality. Typically, Gini coefficients change little from year to year, so these large changes in a span of eight years are unusual. See Eurostat, "Gini Coefficient of Advertised Disposable Income," European Commission, Feb. 15, 2019, http://appsso.eurostat.ec.europa.eu/nui/show.do?dataset=ilc_di12b&lang=en.

9. Eurostat, "Gini Coefficient of Equivalized Disposable Income," European Commission, Aug. 17, 2018, https://ec.europa.eu/eurostat/tgm/table.do?tab=table&init=1&language=en&pcode=tessi190&plugin=1.

10. Organisation for Economic Co-operation and Development, "Labour Productivity Levels in the Total Economy," OECD.Stat, Nov. 2013, https://stats.oecd.org/Index.aspx?DatasetCode=LEVEL#.

11. Paul J. Zak and Stephen Knack, "Trust and Growth," *The Economic Journal* 111, no. 470 (2001): 295–321.

12. Joseph E. Stiglitz, "Beyond GDP," Project Syndicate, Dec. 3, 2018, https://www.project-syndicate.org/commentary/new-metrics-of-wellbeing-not-just-gdp-by-joseph-e-stiglitz-2018-12.

13. Jan Strupczewski, "German Position Paper Urges Wider Role for Euro Zone Bailout Fund," *Reuters*, Oct. 9, 2017, https://www.reuters.com/article/ eurozone-eurogroup-esm-germany/update-1-german-position-paper-urges -wider-role-for-euro-zone-bailout-fund-idUSL8N1MK5B9.

## CHAPTER 2: MONETARY POLICY

1. European Central Bank, "Monetary Policy," 2019, https://www.ecb.europa .eu/mopo/html/index.en.html.

2. "ECB Chief Calls for Stability as Ireland Joins the Wave of Bail-Outs," *Guardian*, Dec. 15, 2008, https://www.theguardian.com/business/2008/dec/15/euro peanbanks-banking.

3. Nikolaus Blome, "So Deutsch Ist der Neue EZB-Chef," *Bild*, Apr. 29, 2011, https://www.bild.de/geld/wirtschaft/mario-draghi/ist-neuer-ezb-chef-17630794 .bild.html.

4. Arthur Beesley, "Berlin in Constant Fear ECB Will Be Lender of Last Resort," *Irish Times*, Jan. 16, 2015, https://www.irishtimes.com/business/economy/ berlin-in-constant-fear-ecb-will-be-lender-of-last-resort-1.2067701.

5. The difference between the lending rate to SMEs and to governments is also referred to as the lending "spread." It can change markedly. Thus, a key mistake of the ECB was to focus on the rate at which government could borrow, not the rate at which ordinary businesses could. And models based on perfect markets with perfect information led to a focus on interest rates, not on credit availability. Especially in economic downturns, there may be widespread credit rationing. Central banks then need to focus more on credit availability. See Joseph E. Stiglitz and Bruce Greenwald, *Towards a New Paradigm for Monetary Policy* (Cambridge: Cambridge University Press, 2003).

6. Philippe Andrade, Johannes Breckenfelder, Fiorella De Fiore, Peter Karadi, and Oreste Tristani, *The ECB's Asset Purchase Programme: An Early Assessment* (European Central Bank Working Paper 1956, Sept. 2016), https://www.ecb .europa.eu/pub/pdf/scpwps/ecbwp1956.en.pdf.

7. For instance, when Japan instituted negative interest rates, it was careful to apply them only at the margin. Japan sought to minimize the adverse balance-sheet effect but maintain the incentive effect.

8. Joseph E. Stiglitz, *The Euro: How a Common Currency Threatens the Future of Europe* (New York: W. W. Norton, 2016).

CHAPTER 3: INVESTING FOR AN EQUITABLE FUTURE

1. Marcin Szczepański, "Public Investment to Support Long-Term Economic Growth in the EU," European Parliamentary Research Service, July 2016, http://www.europarl.europa.eu/RegData/etudes/BRIE/2016/583831/EPRS_BRI(2016)583831_EN.pdf.

2. Eurostat, "How Much Does Your Country Invest?," European Commission, May 14, 2018, https://ec.europa.eu/eurostat/web/products-eurostat-news/-/DDN-20180514-1.

3. "Gross Fixed Capital Formation," The World Bank Data, 2019, https://data.worldbank.org/indicator/NE.GDI.FTOT.ZS?end=2017&locations=GR&start=2000.

4. European Commission, "Commission Issues Guidance to Encourage Structural Reforms and Investment," European Commission Press Release Database, Jan. 13, 2015, http://europa.eu/rapid/press-release_MEMO-15-3221_en.htm.

5. Data are from the European Investment Bank and represent the allocations as of March 2018. See *Evaluation of the Functioning of the European Fund for Strategic Investments*, European Investment Bank, Sept. 2016, http://www.eib.org/attachments/ev/ev_evaluation_efsi_en.pdf.

6. Eulalia Rubio, David Rinaldi, and Thomas Pellerin-Carlin, *Investment in Europe: Making the Best of the Juncker Plan with Case Studies on Digital Infrastructure and Energy Efficiency* (Studies & Reports no. 108, Paris: Jacques Delors Institute, 2016).

7. As of September 2016, Bulgaria and Hungary had zero projects approved and/or signed within the EFSI. Neighboring Romania and Croatia had only one project each. In comparison, countries including Denmark and the Netherlands managed to get 10 and 17 projects, respectively. This divide proves that there is still some way to go in achieving an equitable geographical distribution of funds, especially if convergence in development levels is an objective. See "EFSI Project List," European Investment Bank, Mar. 2018, http://www.eib.org/efsi/efsi-projects/index.htm.

CHAPTER 4: PROMOTING COMPETITIVE MARKETS

1. Mariana Mazzucato, *The Entrepreneurial State: Debunking Public vs. Private Sector Myths* (London: Anthem Press, 2011).

2. This is the major message of the Organisation for Economic Co-operation and

Development Better Living Index and the Report of the International Commission on the Measurement of Economic Performance and Social Progress. See Joseph E. Stiglitz, Jean-Paul Fitoussi, and Amartya Sen, *Mismeasuring Our Lives: Why GDP Doesn't Add Up* (New York: The New Press, 2010); and the subsequent report of the High-Level Expert Group at the OECD, *Measuring What Counts: Moving beyond GDP* (New York: The New Press, 2019).

3. "Human Development Indices and Indicators," UNDP, 2018 Statistical Update (New York: United Nations Development Programme, 2018).

4. As a result of multiple market imperfections, including imperfect information and incomplete risk markets. Stiglitz first established this result in 1972. See Joseph E. Stiglitz, "On the Optimality of the Stock Market Allocation of Investment," *Quarterly Journal of Economics* 86, no. 1, Feb. 1972, 25–60. More general proofs were provided in Sanford J. Grossman and Joseph E. Stiglitz, "On Value Maximization and Alternative Objectives of the Firm," *Journal of Finance* 32, no. 2 (May 1977): 389–402.

5. Bloomberg Global CEO Pay Index, Dec. 2017.

6. See Patrick Bolton and Frédéric Samama, "Loyalty-Shares: Rewarding Long-Term Investors," *Journal of Applied Corporate Finance* 25, no. 3 (2013): 86–97.

7. Alissa Pelatan and Roberto Randazzo, "The First European Benefit Corporation," Esela—The Legal Network for Social Impact, https://www.bwbllp .com/file/benefit-corporation-article-june-16-pdf, and "B Corp Movement in BeNeLux," B Lab Europe, 2019, https://bcorporation.eu/about-b-lab/country -partner/benelux.

8. Keith Collins, "A Patent that Helped Amazon Take Over Online Commerce Is about to Expire," *Quartz*, Aug. 19, 2017, https://qz.com/1057490/a-patent -that-helped-amazon-take-over-online-commerce-is-about-to-expire/.

9. George A. Akerlof and Robert J. Shiller, *Phishing for Phools: The Economics of Manipulation and Deception* (Princeton, NJ: Princeton University Press, 2015).

## CHAPTER 5: TOWARD A FINANCIAL SYSTEM THAT SERVES SOCIETY

1. Tori and Onaran (2017) use panel data on the balance sheets of publicly listed nonfinancial companies (from Worldscope) for the period 1995–2015. See Daniele Tori and Özlem Onaran, "The Effects of Financialisation and Financial Development on Investment: Evidence from Firm-Level Data in Europe," *Greenwich Papers in Political Economy*, no. 44 (2017). See also Marshall Steinbaum, Eric Harris Bernstein, and John Sturm, *Powerless: How Lax*

*Antitrust and Concentrated Market Power Rig the Economy against American Workers, Consumers, and Communities* (New York: Roosevelt Institute, 2018); and J. W. Mason, *Disgorge the Cash: The Disconnect between Corporate Borrowing and Investment* (New York: Roosevelt Institute, 2015).

2. See Joan Robinson, "The Generalization of the General Theory," in *The Rate of Interest, and Other Essays* (London: Macmillan, 1952), 67–142.

3. Maria Gerhardt and Rudi Vander Vennet, "Bank Bailouts in Europe and Bank Performance," *Finance Research Letters* 22, Aug. 2017, 74–80, https://doi .org/10.1016/j.frl.2016.12.028.

4. Thomas Hale, "ECB's Long-Term, Cheap Funding Proves Lifeline for Banks," *Financial Times*, June 18, 2017, https://www.ft.com/content/3bfc55da -477b-11e7-8519-9f94ee97d996.

5. See, for instance, Joseph E. Stiglitz, "The Measurement of Wealth: Recessions, Sustainability and Inequality," in *Contemporary Issues in Macroeconomics: Lessons from the Crisis and Beyond*, ed. Joseph E. Stiglitz and Martin Guzman, IEA Conference Vol. No. 155-II (Houndmills, UK, and New York: Palgrave Macmillan, 2015). (Paper presented at a special session of the International Economic Association World Congress, Dead Sea, Jordan, June 2014, sponsored by the Organisation for Economic Co-operation and Development, available at http://www.nber.org/papers/w21327.pdf.)

6. "High-level Expert Group on Reforming the Structure of the EU Banking Sector," European Parliament, Oct. 2, 2012, https://ec.europa.eu/info/ system/files/liikanen-report-02102012_en.pdf.

7. See Joseph E. Stiglitz and Bruce Greenwald, *Towards a New Paradigm for Monetary Policy* (Cambridge: Cambridge University Press, 2003).

8. "Too-Big-to-Regulate: The EU's Bank Structural Reform Proposal Failed," *Finance Watch*, Oct. 25, 2017, https://www.finance-watch.org/press-release/ too-big-to-regulate-the-eus-bank-structural-reform-proposal-failed/.

9. Vanessa Le Lesle, *Bank Debt in Europe: Are Funding Models Broken?* (International Monetary Fund Working Paper no. 12/229, 2012).

10. Julian Chow and Jay Surti, *Making Banks Safer: Can Volcker and Vickers Do It?* (International Monetary Fund Working Paper no. 11/236, 2011).

11. Daniela Gabor and Cornel Ban, "Banking on Bonds: The New Links between States and Markets," *Journal of Common Market Studies* 54, no. 3 (2016): 617–35.

12. "Regulation on Transparency of Securities Financing Transactions and of Reuse," European Commission Press Release Database, Oct. 29, 2015, http:// europa.eu/rapid/press-release_MEMO-15-5931_en.htm.

13. See Gabor and Ban, "Banking on Bonds."

14. "The Performance of German Credit Institutions in 2017," Bundesbank, Sept. 2018, https://www.bundesbank.de/resource/blob/760004/6d8b3367ff98c77e 715eac6c7c12bfc7/mL/2018-09-ertragslage-data.pdf.

## CHAPTER 6: TAXATION TO PROMOTE
## JUSTICE AND GROWTH

1. For 2016, the net pension replacement rate (how pension benefits compare to working-age income) for the United States and the EU was 49 percent and 70 percent, respectively. See "Net Pension Replacement Rates," Organisation for Economic Co-operation and Development, 2018, doi: 10.1787/4b03f028-en.

2. See Bert Brys, Sarah Perret, Alastair Thomas, and Pierce O'Reilly, *Tax Design for Inclusive Economic Growth* (Organisation for Economic Co-operation and Development Taxation Working Papers no. 26, Paris: OECD Publishing, July 2016), https://doi.org/10.1787/5jlv74ggk0g7-en; Facundo Alvaredo, Lucas Chancel, Thomas Piketty, Emmanuel Saez, and Gabriel Zucman, *World Inequality Report 2018* (Paris: Paris School of Economics, 2017).

3. Brian Sloan, Günther Ebling, Martin Becker, Luis Peragon Lorenzo, and Antonella Caiumi, eds., *Taxation Trends in the European Union* (Luxembourg: Publications Office of the European Union, 2018), https://ec.europa.eu/taxation_ customs/sites/taxation/files/taxation_trends_report_2018.pdf.

4. Organisation for Economic Co-operation and Development, *The Role and Design of Net Wealth Taxes in the OECD* (OECD Tax Policy Study, no. 26, Paris: OECD Publishing, 2018), https://read.oecd-ilibrary.org/taxation/the-role-and -design-of-net-wealth-taxes-in-the-oecd_9789264290303-en#page25.

5. For a detailed discussion of the reform needs and options for European tax systems from a gender perspective, see Åsa Gunnarsson, Ulrike Spangenberg, and Margit Schratzenstaller, *Gender Equality and Taxation in the European Union*, Study for the FEMM Committee (Brussels: Policy Department for Citizens' Rights and Constitutional Affairs, Apr. 2017), http:// www.europarl.europa.eu/RegData/etudes/STUD/2017/583138/IPOL_ STU(2017)583138_EN.pdf.

6. Thomas Piketty, Emmanuel Saez, and Stefanie Stantcheva, "Optimal Taxation of Top Labor Incomes: A Tale of Three Elasticities," *American Economic Journal: Economic Policy* 6, no. 1 (2014): 230–71; and Thomas Piketty, Emmanuel Saez, and Stefanie Stantcheva, "Taxing the 1%: Why the Top Tax Rate Could Be Over 80%," VoxEU, Dec. 2011, https://voxeu.org/article/ taxing-1-why-top-tax-rate-could-be-over-80; Danny Yagan, *Tax Progressiv-*

*ity and Top Incomes: Evidence from Tax Reforms* (CEPR Discussion Paper no. 11936, Washington, DC: Center for Economic and Policy Research, 2015).

7. See also Joseph E. Stiglitz, "Wealth and Income Inequality in the Twenty-First Century," paper presented at the 18th World Congress of the International Economic Association, Mexico City, June 19–23, 2017, available at http://bit.ly/2DVMdHz.

8. Wojciech Kopczuk, "Taxation of Intergenerational Transfers and Wealth," in Alan Auerbach, Raj Chetty, Martin Feldstein, and Emmanuel Saez, eds., *Handbook of Public Economics 5* (Amsterdam: Elsevier B.V., 2013), 329–90.

9. Sloan, Ebling, Becker, Lorenzo, and Caiumi, *Taxation Trends in the European Union*.

10. European Commission, *Tax Policies in the European Union* (Luxembourg: Publications Office of the European Union, 2018), https://ec.europa.eu/taxation_customs/sites/taxation/files/tax_policies_survey_2018.pdf.

11. Because the cost of capital for equity financing is not tax deductible in most EU countries (Italy, Belgium, Cyprus, and Portugal grant an allowance for corporate equity), in these countries, there is a debt-equity bias favoring debt financing over equity financing. But even apart from these tax considerations, imperfections of information give rise to a preference for debt. See European Commission, *Tax Policies in the European Union*.

12. Joseph E. Stiglitz, "Taxation, Corporate Financial Policy and the Cost of Capital," *Journal of Public Economics*, no. 2 (Feb. 1973): 1–34.

13. European Commission, *A Fair and Efficient Tax System in the European Union for the Digital Single Market* (no. 547 final, Brussels: European Commission, Sept. 2017), https://ec.europa.eu/taxation_customs/sites/taxation/files/communication_taxation_digital_single_market_en.pdf.

14. Thomas Tørsløv, Ludvig Wier, and Gabriel Zucman, *The Missing Profits of Nations* (NBER Working Paper 24701, Cambridge, MA: National Bureau of Economic Research, 2018).

15. Organisation for Economic Co-operation and Development, *Measuring and Monitoring BEPS*, (Action 11–2015 Final Report, OECD/G20 Base Erosion and Profit Shifting Project, Paris: OECD Publishing, 2015), https://dx.doi.org/10.1787/9789264241343-en.

16. María Álvarez-Martinez, Salvador Barrios, Diego d'Andria, Maria Gesualdo, Gaëtan Nicodème, and Jonathan Pycroft, *How Large is the Corporate Tax Base Erosion and Profit Shifting? A General Equilibrium Approach* (CEPR Discussion Paper no. DP12637, London: Centre for Economic Policy Research, 2018). For a larger group of emerging and less-developed countries, the num-

ber is about 5 percent, according to IMF estimates. See Michael Keen, Victoria Perry, Ruud de Mooij, Thornton Matheson, Roberto Schatan, Peter Mullins, and Ernesto Crivelli, *Spillovers in International Corporate Taxation* (Washington, DC: International Monetary Fund, 2014).

17. In 2016, the European Commission put forward a proposal for the introduction of a common consolidated corporate tax base in the EU. According to this proposal, a common corporate tax base would be implemented in a first step. In a second step, profits and losses incurred by the affiliates of multinational enterprises active in the EU would be consolidated and allocated, based on a formula that captures value creation in the individual EU countries in which multinationals are active, to the countries involved, where they would be taxed at national corporate income tax rates. This proposal is currently being debated among EU member states. For a brief summary of the current state of the debate, see the European Commission, *Tax Policies in the European Union: 2018 Survey* (Luxembourg: Publications Office of the European Union), https://ec.europa.eu/taxation_customs/sites/taxation/files/tax_policies_survey_2018.pdf.

18. See most recently Alan J. Auerbach, "Measuring the Effects of Corporate Tax Cuts," *Journal of Economic Perspectives* 32, no. 4 (2018): 97–120.

19. The most famous instance occurred in 2014, when France was forced to abolish its super income tax rate of 75 percent on very wealthy individuals, after its richest citizen Bernard Arnault, head of luxury goods group LVMH, threatened to shift his residency to Belgium. See Anne Penketh, "France Drops 75 Percent Supertax after Meagre Returns," *The Guardian*, Dec. 2014, https://www.theguardian.com/world/2014/dec/31/france-drops-75percent-supertax.

20. Long before the creation of the single European market, economic theory had pointed to the limitations that free mobility of labor imposes on the imposition of progressive taxes. See, for instance, Joseph E. Stiglitz, "Theory of Local Public Goods," in *The Economics of Public Services*, ed. M. S. Feldstein and R. P. Inman (London: Macmillan Press, 1977): 274–333.

21. Alexander Krenek and Margit Schratzenstaller, *A European Net Wealth Tax* (WIFO Working Papers no. 561, Vienna: Austrian Institute of Economic Research, 2018), https://www.wifo.ac.at/jart/prj3/wifo/resources/person_dokument/person_dokument.jart?publikationsid=61040&mime_type=application/pdf.

22. For the potential of alcohol taxes to decrease harmful alcohol use, see the Organisation for Economic Co-operation and Development, *Tackling Harmful Alcohol Use: Economics and Public Health Policy* (Paris: OECD Publishing,

2015); for a review of a large number of empirical studies showing that tobacco taxes can be an effective tool to curb tobacco consumption, see Frank J. Chaloupka, "How Effective Are Taxes in Reducing Tobacco Consumption?," in *Valuing the Cost of Smoking. Assessment. Methods, Risk Perception and Policy Options*, ed. Claude Jeanrenaud and Nils Soguel (Boston: Kluwer, 1999), 205–18; or Frank J. Chaloupka, Ayda Yurekli, and Geoffrey T. Fong, "Tobacco Taxes as a Tobacco Control Strategy," *Tobacco Control* 21, no. 2 (2011): 172–80; see also the World Health Organization, *WHO Report on the Global Tobacco Epidemic, 2015: Raising Taxes on Tobacco* (Geneva: World Health Organization, 2015).

23. Annerie Bouw, *Tobacco Taxation in the European Union: An Overview* (Brussels: European Commission, 2017), http://documents.worldbank.org/curated/en/493581492415549898/pdf/114324-REPLACEMENT-PUBLIC-25-4-2017-19-59-40-TTEUR.pdf.

24. Organisation for Economic Co-operation and Development, *Consumption Tax Trends: VAT/GST and Excise Rates, Trends and Policy Issues* (Paris: OECD Publishing, 2018), https://read.oecd-ilibrary.org/taxation/consumption-tax-trends-2018_ctt-2018-en#page1.

25. World Health Organization Regional Office for Europe, *Using Price Policies to Promote Healthier Diets* (Copenhagen: WHO Regional Office for Europe, 2015), http://www.euro.who.int/__data/assets/pdf_file/0008/273662/Using-price-policies-to-promote-healthier-diets.pdf?ua=1.

26. Sloan, Ebling, Becker, Lorenzo, and Caiumi, *Taxation Trends in the European Union*.

27. Lord Nicholas Stern and Joseph E. Stiglitz, *Report on the High-Level Commission on Carbon Prices* (Washington, DC: World Bank, 2017).

28. Alexander Krenek and Margit Schratzenstaller, "Sustainability-Oriented EU Taxes: A Carbon-Based Flight Ticket Tax," *Journal for a Progressive Economy*, no. 8 (2016): 44–49.

29. The yellow-vests movement in France has shown that in designing carbon taxes, governments will need to be sensitive to distributional concerns even if overall a carbon tax is progressive, for instance because transportation constitutes a much higher proportion of consumption for poor people compared to the rich. The high prices levied on gasoline imply that the carbon tax already levied is high; focusing on increasing the carbon tax in other areas might not have had the same political backlash. See Corbett Grainger and Charles Kolstad, "Who Pays a Price on Carbon?," *Environmental and Resource Economics* 46, no. 3 (2010): 359–76.

30. Alexander Krenek, Mark Sommer, and Margit Schratzenstaller, *Sustainability-Oriented Future EU Funding: A European Border Carbon Adjustment* (Fair-Tax Working Paper no. 15, 2018), http://umu.diva-portal.org/smash/get/diva2:1178081/FULLTEXT01.pdf.

31. There is a long literature arguing that such short-term transactions are counterproductive and explaining how a financial transactions tax would discourage them. See John Maynard Keynes, *General Theory* (London: Palgrave, 1936), 160; and Joseph E. Stiglitz, "Using Tax Policy to Curb Speculative Short-Term Trading," *Journal of Financial Services Research* 3 no. 2–3, (Dec. 1989): 101–15. Reprinted in *The Selected Works of Joseph E. Stiglitz, Volume II: Information and Economic Analysis: Applications to Capital, Labor, and Product Markets* (Oxford: Oxford University Press, 2013), 85–98.

32. High-frequency trading has taken short-termism to an extreme, and actually worsens the overall performance of financial markets. See Joseph E. Stiglitz, "Tapping the Brakes: Are Less Active Markets Safer and Better for the Economy?," paper presented at the Federal Reserve Bank of Atlanta 2014 Financial Markets Conference: Tuning Financial Regulation for Stability and Efficiency, Atlanta, GA, Apr. 15, 2014, available at http://www.frbatlanta.org/documents/news/conferences/14fmc/Stiglitz.pdf.

33. "The Financial Transactions Tax (FTT)–the Time Is Now," ETUC.org, May 17, 2016, https://www.etuc.org/en/document/financial-transactions-tax-ftt-time-now.

34. James Tobin, *The New Economics—One Decade Older* (Princeton, NJ: Princeton University Press, 1974).

35. "Financial Transaction Tax: How Severe?," Goldman Sachs Global Investment Research, May 1, 2013.

36. For a popular account, see Michael Lewis, *Flash Boys: A Wall Street Revolt* (New York: W. W. Norton & Company, 2014). For a more technical discussion, see Stiglitz, "Using Tax Policy," and Stiglitz, "Tapping the Brakes."

## CHAPTER 7: POVERTY, INEQUALITY, AND THE WELFARE STATE

1. For a review of the evidence on the link between inequality and growth in Europe, see Catherine Mathieu and Henri Sterdyniak, "Growth and Inequality in the European Union," OFCE le Blog, Sept. 12, 2017, https://www.ofce.sciences-po.fr/blog/growth-and-inequality-in-the-european-union/; and Jonathan Ostry, Andrew Berg, and Charalambos Tsangarides, *Redistribution,*

*Inequality, and Growth* (IMF Staff Discussion Note, SDN/14/02, International Monetary Fund, Feb. 2014), https://www.imf.org/external/pubs/ft/sdn/2014/ sdn1402.pdf; for a discussion of the link between inequality and political stability, see Joseph E. Stiglitz, *The Price of Inequality: How Today's Divided Society Endangers Our Future* (New York: W. W. Norton, 2012); Joseph E. Stiglitz, *The Great Divide: Unequal Societies and What We Can Do about Them* (New York: W. W. Norton, 2016); Thomas Piketty, *Capital in the Twenty-First Century* (Cambridge, MA: Harvard University Press, 2014).

2. Brian Blackstone, Matthew Karnitschnig, and Robert Thomson, "Europe's Banker Talks Tough," *Wall Street Journal*, Feb. 24, 2012, https://www.wsj .com/articles/SB10001424052970203960804577241221244896782.

3. *Report by the Commission on the Measurement of Economic Performance and Social Progress*, chaired by Joseph E. Stiglitz, Amartya Sen, and Jean-Paul Fitoussi, https://ec.europa.eu/eurostat/documents/118025/118123/Fitoussi+Commission+ report.

4. World Inequality Database (https://wid.world), extracted on Jan. 23, 2019.

5. Joseph E. Stiglitz, *Making Globalization Work* (New York: W. W. Norton, 2007); and Joseph E. Stiglitz, *Globalization and Its Discontents Revisited: Anti-Globalization in the Era of Trump* (New York: W. W. Norton, 2017).

6. Recent data from Eurosat (2018) show a concentration of the European Union's scientists and engineers in the UK and Germany. The brain drain is most acute in countries with high unemployment in southern and eastern Europe, to the point that this brain drain is threatening the countries' recoveries. See, for instance, "Spain's Brain Drain Is a Eurozone Problem: Spain's Best Workers Are Leaving, Undermining the Euro and Spain's Economic Chances," *Bloomberg*, Sept. 28, 2015; or "Greece Brain Drain Hampers Recovery from Economic Crisis," *Financial Times*, Aug. 16, 2018.

7. Organisation for Economic Co-operation and Development, *Key Indicators on Early Childhood Education and Care* (Paris: OECD Publishing, 2017).

8. At the moment, this idea exists as a youth guarantee, focusing on opportunity for young people as they make the transition from school to work, a discussion that continues later in the chapter. See "The Youth Guarantee Country by Country," European Commission, Directorate for Employment, Social Affairs, and Inclusion, 2019, accessed Dec. 27, 2018, https://ec.europa.eu/ social/main.jsp?catId=1161&langId=en.

9. See "S&Ds Call for Establishing the European Child Guarantee to End Child Poverty in the EU," Group of the Progressive Alliance of Socialists and Democrats of the European Parliament, Sept. 26, 2018, https://www

.socialistsanddemocrats.eu/newsroom/sds-call-establishing-european-child
-guarantee-end-child-poverty-eu; and "Child Guarantee for Vulnerable Children," European Commission, Directorate for Employment, Social Affairs,
and Inclusion, 2018, accessed Aug. 31, 2018, https://ec.europa.eu/social/main
.jsp?catId=1428&langId=en.

10. See "The Best Universities in Europe 2019," *The Times Higher Education*, Nov.
21, 2018, https://www.timeshighereducation.com/student/best-universities/
best-universities-europe.

11. Center on Education Policy, *Are Private High Schools Better Academically than Public
High Schools?* (Washington, DC: CEP, 2007); Henry Braun, Frank Jenkins, and
Wendy Grigg, *Comparing Private Schools and Public Schools Using Hierarchical Lin-
ear Modeling* (Washington, DC: National Center for Education Statistics, 2006),
https://files.eric.ed.gov/fulltext/ED492570.pdf; Kevin Lang and Russell Wein-
stein, "Evaluating Student Outcomes at For-Profit Colleges" (NBER, Working
Paper no. 18201, Cambridge, MA: National Bureau of Economic Research, June
2012), http://www.nber.org/papers/w18201. For a review of charter schools in the
United States, see Gary Miron, William Mathis, and Kevin Welner, review of
"Separating Fact and Fiction: What You Need to Know about Charter Schools,"
*National Education Policy Center* (Boulder: University of Colorado, 2015).

12. For more information, see the European Commission website, "The Youth
Guarantee," https://ec.europa.eu/social/main.jsp?catId=1079.

13. Susanne Soederberg, "Evictions: A Global and Capitalist Phenomenon,"
*Development and Change* 49, no. 2, Feb. 2018, 10.1111/dech.12383.

14. Michela Scatigna, Robert Szemere, and Kostas Tsatsaronis, "Residential
Property Price Statistics across the Globe," *BIS Quarterly Review*, Sept. 2014;
Katharina Knoll, Moritz Schularick, and Thomas Steger, *No Price Like Home:
Global House Prices, 1870–2012* (Working Paper no. 208, Federal Reserve
Bank of Dallas Globalization and Monetary Policy Institute, Oct. 2014),
https://www.dallasfed.org/~/media/documents/institute/wpapers/2014/0208
.pdf; Organisation for Economic Co-operation and Development, *Housing
Costs over Income* (OECD, Feb. 13, 2017), https://www.oecd.org/els/family/
HC1-2-Housing-costs-over-income.pdf; André Christophe, *Household Debt
in OECD Countries: Stylised Facts and Policy Issues* (Economics Department
Working Papers no. 1277, Organisation for Economic Co-operation and
Development, 2017); Eurofound, *Inadequate Housing in Europe: Costs and Con-
sequences* (Luxembourg: Publications Office of the European Union, 2016).

15. Given the penalties for tax evasion and the direct information the government receives from employers about their workers, underreporting should be

limited. Joseph E. Stiglitz, *Rewriting the Rules of the American Economy: An Agenda for Growth and Shared Prosperity* (New York: W. W. Norton, 2015), 87.

## CHAPTER 8: A EUROPEAN SOCIAL SECURITY SYSTEM FOR THE TWENTY-FIRST CENTURY

1. Nelly Papalambros, "The Public Health Crisis in Greece," *Public Health Review* 4, no. 1 (2017).

2. Sarah Thomson et al., *Economic Crisis, Health Systems and Health in Europe: Impact and Implications for Policy* (Copenhagen: World Health Organization Regional Office for Europe, 2014); International Labour Organization, *World Social Protection Report 2014–15: Building Economic Recovery, Inclusive Development and Social Justice* (Geneva: International Labour Organization, 2014).

3. Marina Karanikolos et al., "Financial Crisis, Austerity, and Health in Europe," *The Lancet* 381, no. 9874 (2013): 1323–31.

4. See Sarah Thomson et al., *Economic Crisis, Health Systems and Health in Europe*.

5. See Peter Orszag and Joseph E. Stiglitz in *New Ideas about Old Age Security: Toward Sustainable Pension Systems in the 21st Century*, ed. Robert Holzmann and Joseph E. Stiglitz (Washington, DC: The World Bank, 2001): 17–56. The failures of privatization described in Box 8.1 are matched elsewhere in the world; see Isabel Ortiz et al., *Reversing Pension Privatizations: Rebuilding Public Pension Systems in Eastern Europe and Latin America* (Geneva: International Labour Organization, 2018). Perhaps the most famous failure was in Chile, the system originally hailed as the "model" of privatization. The Chilean government had to come to the rescue of the system in the aftermath of the 2008 crisis and the state (the taxpayer) had to pay twice—first, the very high cost of the transition to privatization, and second, by pension top-ups during the crisis. See Joseph E. Stiglitz presentation, "Rethinking Old Age Security in the Aftermath of the Global Financial Crisis" (presented June 16, 2015), available at https://www.previsionsocial.gob.cl/sps/download/estudios -previsionales/comisionpensiones/seminario_sistema_de_pensiones:_ experiencias_y_tendencias_internacionales/presentaciones_seminario/joseph -stiglitz_rethinking-old-age-security.pdf.

6. Office of the UN High Commissioner for Human Rights (OHCHR), *Report on Austerity Measures and Economic, Social and Cultural Rights*, presented to United Nations Economic and Social Council, Substantive Session of 2013, Geneva, July 1–26, E/2013/82.

7. International Labour Organization, *World Social Protection Report 2017–*

*19* (Geneva: International Labour Organization, 2017), https://www.ilo
.org/wcmsp5/groups/public/---dgreports/---dcomm/---publ/documents/
publication/wcms_604882.pdf.

8. *Access to Social Protection for People Working on Non-Standard Contracts and as Self-Employed in Europe: A Study of National Policies* (European Commission, 2017); *Promoting Adequate Social Protection and Social Security Coverage for All Workers, Including Those in Non-Standard Forms of Employment* (International Labour Organization and Organisation for Economic Co-operation and Development, Paper for the G20 Employment Working Group, 2018); *Non-Standard Employment around the World: Understanding Challenges, Shaping Prospects* (International Labour Organization, 2016).

9. Given that the prevalence of disabilities increases with age, it is no surprise that the global proportion of people with disabilities aged 55 and over was 46 percent in 2004, compared to 15 percent for all ages. *World Report on Disability* (World Health Organization and World Bank, 2011), https://www.who .int/disabilities/world_report/2011/report.pdf.

10. The UN reports that women devote one to three hours more a day to housework than men, and two to ten times the amount of time that men spend caring for children, the elderly, and the sick. In the European Union, 25 percent of women report care and other family and personal responsibilities as the reason for not being in the labor force, versus only 3 percent of men. See UN Women, "Transforming Work For Women's Rights," chapter 2 in *Progress of the World's Women 2015–2016: Transforming Economies, Realizing Rights* (New York: UN Women, 2015), http://progress.unwomen.org/en/2015/pdf/ UNW_progressreport.pdf.

11. *Help Wanted?: Providing and Paying for Long-Term Care* (Organization for Economic Co-operation and Development, 2011), https://www.oecd.org/els/ health-systems/47903344.pdf.

12. Xenia Scheil-Adlung, *Long-Term Care Protection for Older Persons: A Review of Coverage Deficits in 46 Countries* (ESS—Working Paper no. 50, Geneva: International Labour Organization, 2015), https://www.ilo.org/wcmsp5/groups/ public/---ed_protect/---soc_sec/documents/publication/wcms_407620.pdf.

13. Guy Standing, *Basic Income: And How We Can Make It Happen* (London: Pelican, 2017); Philippe Van Parijs and Yannick Vanderborght, *Basic Income: A Radical Proposal for a Free Society and a Sane Economy* (Cambridge, MA: Harvard University Press, 2017); Andy Stern and Lee Kravitz, *Raising the Floor: How a Universal Basic Income Can Renew Our Economy and Rebuild the American Dream* (New York: Public Affairs, 2016).

14. By 5 points on average across countries in the standard measure of inequality. See *IMF Fiscal Monitor: Tackling Inequality* (International Monetary Fund, Oct. 2017), https://www.imf.org/en/Publications/FM/Issues/2017/10/05/fiscal-monitor-october-2017.

15. See Sarath Davala, Renana Jhabvala, Soumya Kapoor Mehta, and Guy Standing, *Basic Income: A Transformative Policy for India* (London: Bloomsbury Academic, 2015); see Isabel Ortiz, Christina Behrendt, Andrés Acuña-Ulate, and Quynh Anh Nguyen, *Universal Basic Income Proposals in Light of ILO Standards* (ESS—Working Paper no. 62, Geneva: International Labour Organization, 2018), https://www.ilo.org/wcmsp5/groups/public/---ed_protect/---soc_sec/documents/publication/wcms_648602.pdf.

16. Karl Widerquist, "What (If Anything) Can We Learn from the Negative Income Tax Experiments?" in Karl Widerquist, José A. Noguera, and Yannick Vanderborght, eds., *Basic Income: An Anthology of Contemporary Research* (Oxford: Wiley-Blackwell, 2013), 216–29.

## CHAPTER 9: LABOR MARKETS, GOOD WAGES, AND WORKING CONDITIONS

1. According to the ILO's *Global Wage Report 2018/19: What Lies behind Gender Pay Gaps* (Geneva: International Labour Organization, 2018), the median increase of real wages in northern, southern, and western Europe in the decade 2008–2017 has been 0.7 percent: https://www.ilo.org/global/research/global-reports/global-wage-report/2018/lang--en/index.htm.

2. One of the key reasons for the decline in income (instead of the growth, which was predicted by the Troika) was that lower wages decreased demand for non-traded goods, and the contraction in that part of the economy more than offset any expansion in exports. These effects interacted with and compounded the weakening of the financial sector, as money fled from the banking systems of the crisis countries to safer havens, as we have described in earlier chapters. See also Joseph E. Stiglitz, *The Euro: How a Common Currency Threatens the Future of Europe* (New York: W. W. Norton, 2017).

3. "National Industrial Relations across Europe: Collective Bargaining," European Trade Union Institute, 2015, accessed Dec. 29, 2018, https://www.worker-participation.eu/National-Industrial-Relations/Across-Europe/Collective-Bargaining2.

4. Trends have differed markedly across Europe. For example, the number of

agreements has increased in Germany, France, the Netherlands, and Belgium. But in most countries, measures indicate that the process of collective bargaining is weaker.

5. David Card and Alan Krueger, "Minimum Wages and Employment: A Case Study of the Fast-Food Industry in New Jersey and Pennsylvania," *The American Economic Review* 84, no. 4 (Sept. 1994): 772–93.

6. See the metastudies (quantitative studies of studies) on the United States: Hristos Doucouliagos and T. D. Stanley, "Publication Selection Bias in Minimum-Wage Research? A Meta-Regression Analysis," *British Journal of Industrial Relations* (June 2009) and *The Effects of a Minimum Wage Increase on Employment and Family Income* (Washington, DC: Congressional Budget Office, Feb. 2014). For the UK: Megan de Linde Leonard, T. D. Stanley, and Hristos Doucouliagos, "Does the UK Minimum Wage Reduce Employment? A Meta-Regression Analysis," *British Journal of Industrial Relations* (Sept. 2014). For developed countries: Dale Belman and Paul Wolfson, *What Does the Minimum Wage Do?* (Kalamazoo, MI: Upjohn Press, 2014). These conclusions are also reflected in World Bank publications: see Arvo Kuddo, David Robalino, and Michael Weber, *Balancing Regulations to Promote Jobs—from Employment Contracts to Unemployment Benefits* (Working Paper no. 10156, World Bank, 2015).

7. A telling debate on this matter took place recently in South Africa, a country with economic inequalities that dwarf those internal to the EU. After considering all economic projections, stakeholders judged that the benefits from the adoption of a national minimum wage would outweigh any short-term costs in terms of reduced competitiveness. See Ilan Strauss and Gilad Isaacs, *Labour Compensation Growth in the South African Economy* (Working Paper Series no. 4, WITS University, 2016).

8. For a nontechnical critique of the arguments against minimum wages, see James Kwak, "The Curse of Economics 101," *The Atlantic*, Jan. 14, 2017. He argues that these arguments are based on a simplistic and ideological application of economics.

9. *A Mapping Report on Labour Inspection Services in 15 European Countries* (Brussels: European Federation of Public Service Unions, 2012), https://www .epsu.org/sites/default/files/article/files/EPSU_Final_report_on_Labour_ Inspection_Services.pdf.

10. *Matching Skills and Jobs in Europe* (Thessaloniki, Greece: European Centre for the Development of Vocational Training, 2015), http://www.cedefop .europa.eu/files/8088_en.pdf; also in "Europe 2020 Indicators: Employment,"

Eurostat, 2016, https://ec.europa.eu/eurostat/statistics-explained/index.php/Europe_2020_indicators_-_employment.

11. See Regulation (EU) No. 1296/2013 of The European Parliament and of the Council on a European Union Programme for Employment and Social Innovation (EaSI) and amending Decision No. 283/2010/EU establishing a European Progress Microfinance Facility for employment and social inclusion, Dec. 11, 2013, https://eur-lex.europa.eu/LexUriServ/LexUriServ.do?uri=OJ:L:2013:347:0238:0252:EN:PDF.

12. For a discussion of these effects, see Servaas Storm and Jeronim Capaldo, *Labor Institutions and Development under Globalization* (Working Papers no. 76, New York: Institute for New Economic Thinking, 2018), https://www.ineteconomics.org/uploads/papers/WP_76-Storm-and-Capaldo-Final.pdf.

13. See *Benefit Sanctions* (London: UK National Audit Office, 2016), https://www.nao.org.uk/wp-content/uploads/2016/11/Benefit-sanctions.pdf. This important evaluation, ordered by the UK House of Commons, revealed that there was limited understanding of the impact of sanctions. Researchers studied 3.5 million people in the UK who rely on out-of-work benefits, and the conditions they have to comply with. About 11.4 percent (400,000 people) were sanctioned for noncompliance, with a decrease or loss of benefit payments. The administration of social security sanctions and conditions for the 11.4 percent of beneficiaries in the period studied cost £244 million; sanctions saved £132 million.

## CHAPTER 10: THE FUTURE OF EUROPE IN A GLOBALIZED WORLD

1. Explained in much greater detail in Joseph E. Stiglitz, *Globalization and Its Discontents Revisited: Anti-Globalization in the Era of Trump* (New York: W. W. Norton, 2018), from which this passage and others in the section draw heavily.

2. For a popular account, see Daron Acemoglu and James A. Robinson, *Why Nations Fail: The Origins of Power, Prosperity, and Poverty* (New York: Crown Business, 2013).

3. See President Xi's speech in Davos. Xi Jingping, "President Xi's Speech to Davos in Full" (speech, Jan. 17, 2017), available at https://www.weforum.org/agenda/2017/01/full-text-of-xi-jinping-keynote-at-the-world-economic-forum.

4. See, for instance, *The Stiglitz Report: Reforming the International Monetary and Financial Systems in the Wake of the Global Crisis*, with Members of the Commission of Experts on Reforms of the International Monetary and Financial System appointed by the president of the United Nations General Assembly (New York: The New Press, 2010).

5. "European Commission Preparing for EU-US Trade Talks: 119 Meetings with Industry Lobbyists," Corporate Observatory Europe, Sept. 4, 2013, https://corporateeurope.org/trade/2013/09/european-commission-preparing -eu-us-trade-talks-119-meetings-industry-lobbyists.

6. See, for instance, the 2004 report of the ILO World Commission on the Social Dimensions of Globalization: *A Fair Globalization: Creating Opportunities for All* (Geneva: International Labour Organization, Feb. 2004), https:// www.ilo.org/public/english/wcsdg/docs/report.pdf.

7. Tim Wu, *The Curse of Bigness: Antitrust in the New Gilded Age* (New York: Columbia Global Reports, 2018).

# INDEX

Page numbers in *italics* refer to charts.